Prosocial Development in Children
Caring, Helping, and Cooperating

REFERENCE BOOKS ON
FAMILY ISSUES
(VOL. 19)

GARLAND REFERENCE LIBRARY
OF SOCIAL SCIENCE
(VOL. 538)

PROSOCIAL DEVELOPMENT IN CHILDREN
CARING, HELPING, AND COOPERATING
A Bibliographic Resource Guide

Alice Sterling Honig
Donna Sasse Wittmer

GARLAND PUBLISHING, INC. • NEW YORK & LONDON
1992

Library of Congress Cataloging-in-Publication Data

Honig, Alice S.
   Prosocial development in children : caring, helping, and
cooperating ; a resource guide / Alice Sterling Honig, Donna
Sasse Wittmer.
        p.   cm. — (Reference books on family issues ; vol. 19)
(Garland reference library of social science ; vol. 538)
   Includes index.
   ISBN 0–8240–7846–2 (acid-free)
   1. Child development—Bibliography.   2. Social interaction in
children—Bibliography.   3. Caring—Bibliography.   4. Helping
behavior in children—Bibliography.   5. Cooperation—Bibliography.
I. Wittmer, Donna Sasse.   II. Title.   III. Series. Reference books
on family issues ; vol. 19.   IV. Series: Garland reference library of
social science ; v. 538.
   Z7164.C5H66   1992
   [HQ767.9]. H66 1992
   016.305.23'1—dc20   91–36676
                                                            CIP

Printed on acid-free, 250-year-life paper
Manufactured in the United States of America

Contents

Preface

The ideals which have lighted my way, and time after time have given me new courage to face life cheerfully, have been kindness, beauty, and truth.

Albert Einstein

This volume contains annotated references to two types of materials on prosocial or altruistic interactions. The first section references researches on the development of, practice of, assessment of, and inter-relationships among various kinds of prosocial behaviors. Among the wide variety of such behaviors which researchers have studied are: sharing, helping, generosity, empathy, fairness, loyalty, donations, cooperation, honesty under stress, kindness, nurturing, and expressing caring concern.

In the first section can also be found *theoretical* articles which illuminate the intrapersonal, interpersonal, and situational factors that influence children's prosocial reasoning skills and behavioral responses. Cross-cultural researches are included where English language references are available. References focus on beliefs and ideas as well as behaviors in the prosocial domain, and they include populations of normal as well as special needs children.

The second section provides *applied resources.* These references reflect materials that have been effective in helping teachers, parents, caregivers, counselors, and school administrators increase children's ability to mediate disputes or resolve conflicts in positive ways. This section, in addition, presents ways in which caregivers can *promote* the development of positive techniques in social interactions among children or in adult-child interactions.

The references in this collection reflect predominantly the past 20 years (1970–1991) of research and application in the field of prosocial behaviors. Only *published* references are included, that is, books, journals, articles, book chapters, newsletters, monographs, dissertation abstracts and magazines. ERIC system materials are referenced by their ED numbers as these resources are easy to order from Urbana, Illinois. Audiovisual resources such as films, audiotapes and videotapes which are published are also referenced. Edited books, some of whose chapters may be annotated, may be listed but not annotated.

Annotated resources on prosocial development and interactions included in this compilation are focused specifically on *children.* Thus, articles on increasing tactfulness in adults or reducing international war tensions between nations are not included. Materials on late adolescence and adults are only included if they increase knowledge of important variables, such as sex differences or effects of parental child-rearing styles.

A wide variety of **research methods** have been used by those whose work is annotated in Section I of this volume. Listed below are a bakers' dozen of techniques, strategies, and domains of inquiry that researchers in this volume have utilized in trying to tease out the ways in which prosocial behaviors develop, with what social or environmental variables prosocial behaviors are correlated, and how prosocial actions are or are not interrelated with one another:

1. Naturalistic Observation

Children are observed in natural settings, such as free play with a friend at home, in order to assess the naturally occurring rates of a variety of prosocial interactions and behaviors. These ecologically valid measures may include specialized settings such as summer day camps, or a day care setting specifically set up to facilitate naturalistic observations over a period of time during which children, peers, and adults become more intimately acquainted. In some more standardized situations, children are brought in pairs into a playroom, and their sharing or cooperating is observed through a one-way mirror after the experimenter leaves the room on a pretext.

2. Models of Different Kinds

Nurturant (warm, concerned, interested) adults interact with children under specific conditions and the rates of prosocial behaviors of these children are contrasted with the rates of children exposed to cold or non-nurturant adult models. In some modeling researches, the effects of *model attributes* are varied to find out whether models with more power, prestige, or control over resources will have differential effects on subsequent prosocial behaviors emitted by or requested of children. Sometimes sex of model is also varied to see whether model gender influences imitation.

3. Donation Opportunities

In some experimental studies, children are given opportunities, or are encouraged, to donate to a "Save the Children Fund" or to a "Hospital for Sick Children", after they have won tokens or toys in a game set up to allow them to win an experimentally determined number of times or prizes.

4. Open-ended Interviews

Clinical open-ended questions are administered in order to determine the reasoning processes children use in their responses to moral dilemmas. Piaget, Kohlberg and Eisenberg have used moral and prosocial dilemmas in order to understand the cognitive thinking and reasoning processes children use in their responses to stories about other children who, for example, have transgressed or who have to decide whether or not to help a peer, e.g. by climbing a tree to rescue a kitten, after being told by a parent that they are not to climb a tree ever again.

5. Sociometric Questionnaires

Sociometric questionnaires are given to each child in a given classroom in order that peers nominate children who most strongly exhibit specified altruistic traits. Typically, children are asked to nominate three peers who most strongly exhibit the described behaviors. For example, children may be asked to "Name three classmates who stick up for a kid who is being teased".

6. Parenting Styles and Values

Parental child-rearing practices, communication styles, discipline techniques and verbal attributions are studied through observations, interviews, rankings, checklists, or forced choice questionnaires in order to elucidate the role that parental child-rearing techniques play in the development and maintenance of altruistic dispositions and behaviors. Parental values may be elicited and their relative rankings then correlated with the degree of children's nurturance. For example, the higher the value that a parent places on altruism, the more likely the child will be peer-nominated by classmates as a particularly prosocial child. Parental use of reasoning and inductive methods to help their children understand how others feel if hurt and to understand the importance of reparation and apology, may be contrasted with parental preference for power-assertive methods of changing children's behavior. Parental styles are then related to the degree of altruism that the children exhibit.

7. Structural Variables

Potentially relevant demographic variables are correlated with children's observed frequency or rate or type of prosocial behavior. Such variables include level of parental education, socioeconomic class, child sex, and age. Socioeconomic variables, such as entrepreneurial or bureaucratic family background, are examined in relation to children's induced or emitted prosocial interactions.

8. Intrapersonal Child Variables

Effects of personal/dispositional child variables have been related to degree of altruism. These variables include child mood, values, attitudes, beliefs, IQ, or cognitive level of reasoning, role-taking ability, degree of empathic responsiveness, anxiety level, temperament, and skill levels in providing effective helping actions.

9. Situational Variables

Many researchers manipulate situational variables to see their effect on prosocial behaviors. Two-dimensional pictorial materials are provided as props to elicit children's positive prosocial responses. For example, cards are shown where all children except for one pictured youngster have an ice cream cone. The study child is then asked how the left-out child can be helped to feel better or to be provided with resources or treats also. Three-dimensional materials, such as dioramas, have been used both to model prosocial responses to the pictured scenes and to allow the child to have a turn at acting out a prosocial offer with the diorama figures. Some situational manipulations in the laboratory involve the playing of tapes as if a child in a nearby room were in severe distress. The child in the study clearly hears the distress. Through a one-way screen, researchers observe the child's emotional and behavioral responses to the staged distress. Sometimes the size of groups is manipulated to see the effect of a crowd of children on their propensity for helpfulness when a peer or a stranger is in distress. Cross-age tutoring of younger children by older children has been used as a situational technique to enhance the self-esteem as well as the helpfulness of the tutoring child.

10. Television Research

The effect of regular viewing of prosocial films or TV programs, such as Mr. Rogers' Neighborhood, is studied for frequency and kind of prosocial peer interactions occurring subsequent to the viewing. Sometimes television program viewing is combined with other types of interventions, such as teacher-led sessions about prosocial responsiveness, and the differential effects of TV presentations alone vs. TV plus teacher interventions are analyzed.

11. Reinforcements and Rewards

Direct social or material reinforcements or personal attributions are manipulated to learn about their possible effects on child prosocial behaviors. Many researches are concerned with the possible differential effectiveness of varieties of and amounts of reinforcers for prosocial actions. Some studies contrast positive personal attributions (whereby the child's altruistic actions are specifically labeled and approved of) with social reinforcements, where the general class of prosocial acts may be labeled as good or nice to do. Behaviorist researchers study the possible effectiveness of material reinforcers such as tokens or toys in increasing children's prosocial actions.

12. Staged Distress

Live distress situations are enacted in some researches. Adults "stage" a fall or pretend to have an accident (such as hurting fingers in a drawer) or spill a bag of groceries or a box of pencils or wince as if spraining an ankle. Sometimes the staging involves a live animal, as when a kitten becomes entangled in a ball of yarn or a gerbil in a cage cannot reach the water supply because the water tube has been placed too high. Children's responses are assessed in terms of empathic understanding and reactions to the events staged as well as the degree of help that they may or may not offer.

13. Role-playing Researches

Role-taking and empathy skill measures have been widely researched as a component of prosocial actions. Some researches emphasize the cognitive and some the affective component of role-taking. Some researches specifically train children to take roles in stories and to switch roles, so that the children can learn to take the viewpoint or position of a variety of characters in prosocial or moral dilemma stories. Children may be asked to choose faces that are appropriate to various distress or altruism situations. Sometimes children are asked to tell how they feel, or they may rate on a smiling-face scale how they feel having seen a set of slides or videos representing emotionally-toned (sad, happy, angry, fearful) interpersonal situations.

Strategies for Caregivers

In the second section of this book, many strategies for helping children become more prosocial are identified in annotated research and practical articles, chapters, and books. While many ideas are explicitly stated, others are implied from the researches that correlate certain characteristics of children and of their environments with increases in prosocial behavior. The development of child characteristics such as a positive self-esteem, assertiveness, and the ability to take the role of others as well as teacher/parent interaction styles and classroom climate: all are important in helping children become more prosocial.

Thirty techniques for teachers and parents to promote young children's prosocial development or for researchers to utilize in further applied research studies are identified. With each strategy, at least one author whose work has been annotated in this book is cited. There may be many other authors whose work also relates to a specific strategy. However, in keeping with our attempt to identify many strategies and keep the description of each short, only a few authors will be cited under each technique.

1. **Help children become assertive and less timid concerning prosocial matters.**

Barrett & Yarrow (1977) have noted that if a child has high perspective-taking skills and is assertive, then the child is more likely to be prosocial. In contrast, if a child has high perspective-taking skills and is timid then the child is less likely to be prosocial.

2. Emphasize empathy: Help children become empathic.

Children who are low in empathy, but high in perspective-taking have been found to demonstrate Machiavellianism (a tendency to take advantage, in a negative way, of their knowledge concerning another person's feelings and thoughts) (Barnett, M., & Thompson, S., 1985). College students who scored high on an empathy scale remembered their parents as having been more empathic and affectionate when the students were children (Barnett, M., Howard, J., King, L., & Dino, G., 1980). Two training techniques for promoting empathy in children are role-playing and maximizing the perceived similarity between the observer and the stimulus person (Feshbach, N., 1975).

3. Use positive discipline strategies.

Positive discipline techniques such as reasoning, use of positive reinforcement, empathic listening, and authoritative techniques (Baumrind, D., 1977) are associated with children's prosocial behavior. An interaction has been found between parents' positive discipline techniques and the effects of prosocial and antisocial television programs. Abelman, R. (1986) reports that parents who are most inductive (use reasoning) and who very rarely use love withdrawal and power-assertion, have children who are *most* affected by prosocial television and *least* affected by antisocial fare. The reverse is also true. Positive discipline, then, is a powerful buffer that contributes to children not being as negatively affected by antisocial media materials as are children who are exposed to negative discipline techniques. Children's level of reasoning is related to *non-authoritarian, non-punitive* maternal practices (Eisenberg, N., Lennon, R., & Roth, K., 1983). The more non-authoritarian and non-punitive, the higher the levels of reasoning. Discipline that is *emotionally intense*, but not punitive is effective with toddlers (Yarrow, M., & Waxler, C., 1976).

4. Facilitate perspective and role-taking skills.

Both a child's ability to identify accurately the emotional state of another as well as the empathic ability to experience the feelings of another contribute to prosocial behavior (Barnett, M., & Thompson, S., 1985). Altruistic children have been found to display more empathy and perspective-taking skills (a cognitive measure). When 16 girls (ages 10 to 16) were trained through role-playing to enhance their perspective-taking skills, referential communication and empathy scores increased for the group of girls in the training program, but not for a control group of girls who had been in a fitness training program (Chalmers, J., & Townsend, M., 1990). Iannotti, R. (1985) involved six- and nine-year-old boys in role-playing and role-switching experiences. Six-year-olds with role-taking training donated more candy to the poor than controls and the most sharing was seen for the six-year-old boys who had switched roles.

5. Point out the consequences of the child's behavior.

Edwards (1986) advises pointing out the results of the child's actions upon another person. Yarrow, M., & Waxler, C. (1976) report that parents of toddlers who were most prosocial emphasized the negative consequences of their toddlers' aggressive acts on other children.

6. **Respond and provide alternatives to aggressive behaviors.**

Caldwell (1977) advises caregivers not to ignore aggression or permit aggression to be expressed and assume that this will "discharge the tension". Bullying that is ignored does not disappear, and, in order to control aggression, we must strengthen altruism by teaching children what they can do to help others feel good.

7. **Videotape children acting out prosocial roles in order to facilitate sharing.**

The role-taking abilities of boys (ages 11-13) showed significant improvement after an experimental training program videotaping themselves and others. Delinquencies among the boys were reduced by one-half (Chandler, 1973). Third-grade children were involved in viewing videotapes of themselves and models in situations involving sharing. This technique was effective in increasing sharing immediately following training and one week later (Devoe, M., & Sherman, T., 1978).

8. **Provide specific training in social skills.**

Cartledge, G., & Milburn, J. (1980) recommend defining skills to be taught in behavioral terms, assessing children's level of competence, teaching the skills lacking, evaluating the results of teaching, and providing opportunities for practice and generalization of transfer of new social skills to new situations. Goldstein (1989) uses structured learning therapy to teach prosocial skills such as *negotiation, self-relaxation*, and *anger control* with adolescents. Preschool children who were given training and encouraged to (1) use politeness words, (2) listen to who is talking, (3) participate with a peer in an activity, (4) share, (5) take turns, and (6) help another person have fun were more sociable in a specific training classroom and at follow-up (Factor, D., & Schilmoeller, G., 1983).

9. Model prosocial behaviors.

Adults who model prosocial behaviors influence children's willingness to behave prosocially (Bandura, 1986). Bryan, J. (1977) stresses that children will imitate the helping activities of models whether those models are alive and present or televised and absent. Modeling has proved more powerful than preaching.

10. Label and identify prosocial and antisocial behaviors.

When adults label behaviors, as, for example, "inconsiderate to others", "aggravating others", "considerate toward peers", and "positive leadership," then children's dialogues and role-taking abilities are increased (Vorrath, H., 1985). Attributing positive intentions, "You shared because you like to help others" or "You're the kind of person who likes to help others whenever you can" results in children donating more (Grusec, J., Kuczynski, J., Rushton, P., & Simultis, Z., 1978; Grusec, J., & Redler, E., 1980).

11. Arrange regular viewing of prosocial media and video games.

Prosocial videos and television programs increase children's social contacts, smiling, praising, and hugging (Coates, B., Pusser, H., & Goodman, I. 1976), children's sharing, cooperating, turn-taking, and positive verbal/physical contact (Forge, K., & Phemister,

S., 1987), and children's willingness to help puppies (Poulds, R., Rubenstein, E., & Leibert, R., 1975). Prosocial television, particularly Mr. Rogers' neighborhood, has resulted in higher levels of task persistence, rule obedience, and tolerance of delay of gratification. Children from low SES families showed increased cooperative play, nurturance, and verbalization of feelings (Friedrich, L., & Stein, A., 1973). Children who were exposed to aggressive video games donated less than children who played prosocial video games by themselves (Chambers, J. 1987).

12. **Use Socratic questions to elicit prosocial planfulness and recognition of responsibility.**

When a child is misbehaving in such a way as to disturb his own or class progress, quietly ask, "How does that help you?" This technique, recommended by Fugitt, E. (1983), can be expanded to encourage group awareness by asking the child, "How is that helping the group?" or "How is that helping your neighbor?" This strategy is designed to help children recognize and take responsibility for their own behavior.

13. **Value and emphasize consideration for others' needs.**

When parents value their child having concern for others and press for consideration of others, toddlers (Yarrow, M., & Waxler, C., 1976) and learning disabled boys (Elardo, R., & Freund, J., 1981) behave more prosocially. Moral exhortation, emphasizing the importance of children helping others whenever possible, resulted in children helping sick children more frequently (Grusec, J., Saas-Kortsaak, P., & Simultis, Z., 1978) Parents who esteem altruism highly have children who are peer nominated as highly prosocial (Rutherford, E., & Mussen, P.

(1968).

14. Use cooperative and conflict-resolution games.

New games and variations of traditional children's games that encourage cooperation rather than competition facilitate prosocial interactions (Orlick, T., 1982, 1985; Prutzman, P., Sgern, L., Berger, H., & Boderhamer, G., 1988). Conflict resolution games help keep peace in the classroom (Kreidler, W., 1984).

15. Facilitate classroom cooperation in lesson preparation rather than competition.

A competitive classroom can result in a child fearing failure. In a cooperative interaction classroom the emphasis is on children working together to accomplish mutual goals (Aronson, E., Bridgeman, D., & Geffner, R., 1978). In cooperative classrooms children learn that each child has an essential and unique contribution to make. One technique has been called the "jigsaw technique" because each child is provided with one piece of information about a lesson and all children must work cooperatively in groups to learn all the materials necessary for a complete presentation (Aronson, E., Stephan, C., Sikes, J., Blaney, N., & Snapp, M., 1978).

16. Encourage child-initiation in classrooms.

Children in adult-directed preschool classrooms engage in less prosocial behavior than children in classrooms that encourage more child-initiated learnings and interactions (Huston-Stein, A., Friedrich-Cofer, & Susman, E., 1977; Schweinhart, L. J., Weikart, D. P., & Larner, M. B., 1986). Social-cognitive competence was higher among children in a constructivist classroom as compared to a Montessori classroom (Devries, R., & Goncu, A.,

1990). Four-year-olds in the constructivist classroom were given many opportunities for autonomous construction of attitudes, principles, and social problem-solving strategies.

17. Create a quality preschool and kindergarten classroom environment.

The arrangement of space and the types of toys and learning materials teachers provide affect prosocial behavior. More prosocial responses were given by young children attending day care or nursery school programs when (1) a variety of age appropriate materials were available and (2) space was arranged to accommodate groups of varying sizes (Holloway, S., & Reichhart-Erickson, M., 1988). Rogers, D. (1987) has found that children learn more positive social problem-solving skills in the block areas.

18. Pair "social isolates" with younger sociable children.

Placing a child who is experiencing social problems with a friendly younger playmate increased the "social isolate's" sociability (Furman, W., Rahe, D., & Hartup, H. 1978).

19. Identify children's personal strengths and interests.

Adcock, D., & Segal, M. (1983) describe a child who was having difficulty in social relations. When an activity that he loved, such as water play, was found, then he behaved more prosocially in order to continue participating in the activity.

20. Puppets can facilitate children learning prosocial behaviors.

Travato, C. (1987) created the puppets,

"Hattie Helper", "Carl Defender", "Robert Rescuer", "Debra Defender", "Kevin Comforter", and "Sharon Sharer" for adults to use to help young children learn prosocial behaviors with other children.

21. **Acknowledge children's feelings; use activities that encourage understanding and expression of own and others' feelings.**

Empathy with a peer who is experiencing sadness, anger, or distress may depend on a child having a prior personal similar experience with those feelings (Barnett, M., 1984). Children from ages three to eight are becoming aware of happy feelings (3 1/2 years), fear (3 1/2 to four years) and anger and sadness (least consistent age trends (Borke, H., 1971). Caregivers can help children put feelings into words, and to encourage children to understand the feelings of themselves and others (Adcock, D., & Segal, M., 1983). One way teachers and parents can do this is to acknowledge and reflect the feelings of children by making comments such as, "It seems as if you are feeling so sad". Meadow, K., & Larabee, G. (1982) use a feeling wheel with eight to nine-year-old children with hearing impairment. The wheel, divided into 16 feeling segments, helps children discuss how and why they are feeling a certain way, and also helps them understand other peoples' emotions.

22. **Incorporate children's literature and bibliotherapy into daily reading activities.**

Many book publishers (such as the Albert Whitman Company) have published excellent books for adults to read to young children in order to help children cope with disturbing concerns such as a yelling parent, divorce, or scared feelings. Teachers and parents can choose children's literature for prosocial themes and characters to provide models (such as Horton the Elephant) for young children to behave prosocially. McMath, J. (1989) gives ideas for using open-ended questions to help children think about and understand the motives and actions of story-book characters.

23. **Give reasons and explanations to help children understand why prosocial behavior is important.**

When preschool children were given explanations as to why sharing was important and how to share, sharing increased (Barton, E. &, Osborne, J., 1978). When teachers set aside classroom time to discuss how children were being helpful/kind with one another, prosocial interactions increased among peers (Honig, A., & Pollack, B. 1990).

24. **Encourage children to care for young siblings and children.**

Anthropologists, studying six different cultures, found that when children helped care for younger siblings and interacted with a cross-age variety of children in social groups in non-school settings, they felt more responsible for the welfare of the group, and they gained more skills in nurturing (Whiting, B., & Whiting, J., 1975).

25. **Provide stability as well as prosocial interactions in child care settings.**

Finkelstein (1982) reported that children who had attended a high quality research child care program that emphasized cognitive development were more aggressive when they entered kindergarten than a control group of children who had not been in child care or who had attended community child care. When a prosocial curriculum was instituted in the child care program, this difference disappeared. Howes, C., & Stewart, P. (1987) reported that families who are most stressed chose the lowest quality child care arrangements for their children and were the most likely to change arrangements. These children had the lowest levels of competence during social play with peers. Children who had experienced high quality child care and supportive parents had acquired the ability to decode and regulate emotional signals in peer play. Children who stayed in the *same* child care center with the same peer group increased their proportion of complementary and reciprocal peer play more than did children who stayed in the same child care center but changed peer groups (Howes, C., 1987). Continuity of child care center and continuity of peer groups is important in the development of a child's social competence. Park, K., & Honig, A. (1991) found that the more highly trained and stable the preschool staff the lower were preschool aggression scores.

26. **Notice and positively reinforce prosocial behaviors, but do not overuse external reward.**

Social reinforcement for sharing has increased sharing among young children even when the experimenter was no longer present (Rushton, J., & Teachman, G., 1978). Goffin, S. (1987) recommends that teachers notice when children share mutual goals, ideas, and materials, as well as when they negotiate and bargain in decision-making and accomplishing goals. When teachers and parents use external reinforcement too much however, prosocial behaviors may decrease. Fabes, R., Fultz, J., Eisenberg, N., May-Plumlee, T., & Christopher, F. (1989) reported that mothers who have positive feelings about using rewards can undermine their children's internalized desire to behave prosocially by increasing the salience of external rather than internal rewards.

27. Become familiar with structured curriculum packages designed to promote prosocial development.

Complete programs provide materials and ideas for enhancing prosocial behaviors in the classroom. *Communicating to make friends* (Fox, L., 1980), for example, provides 18 weeks of planned activities to promote peer acceptance. Dinkmeyer, D., & Dinkmeyer, D. (1982) created a program *Developing Understanding of Self and Others (Rev. DUSO-R)* that provides puppets, activity cards, charts, and audio cassettes to promote children's awareness of others' feelings and social skills. *My friends and me*, instituted by the Abededarian program, succeeded in eliminating differences in aggressive acts of the program graduates compared to their controls.

28. Use strategies to encourage social interaction of children with special needs with typical children in integrated settings.

Teachers must use social skills training strategies to facilitate the social integration of children who have disabilities with typical children because prosocial interactions usually do not occur naturally (Honig, A., & McCarron, P., 1990; Gresham, F., 1981).

29. Implement a comprehensive school-based program.

Brown, D., & Solomon, D. (1983) have applied research to create a *comprehensive* program that promotes prosocial attitudes and behavior among elementary school children and their families in communities.

30. Cherish the children.

Children who are well loved learn best. Many of the attachment researchers, such as

Ainsworth and Sroufe, have shown clearly that the more sensitive to distress and responsively attuned that a parent is, the more affectionate, cooperative, compliant, and easy-to-raise are the children. Baumrind (1977) found such positive outcomes with authoritative parenting, and Pines' (1979) review of researches by Yarrow and Zahn-Waxler also confirms that modeling of tender, responsive care, and loving attentiveness to comforting an infant in distress is most likely to result in baby altruists, and later childhood altruism.

Section 1

Theoretical Perspectives, Research, and Assessment

1. Abelman, R. (1985).   Styles of parental disciplinary practices as mediators of children's learning from prosocial television portrayals. *Child Study Journal, 15* (2), 131–146.

    The effects of two main types of parental disciplinary practices on what children learned from prosocial and aggressive television shows were studied. *Induction* was defined as communication-oriented and *sensitization* was described as power-based and merely sensitizing the child to the anticipation of punishment. The children of parents who use inductive techniques were the most affected by pro-social television content and least affected by antisocial programs. In contrast, the children of those parents who were high in sensitizing techniques were the ones whose children appeared to be least affected by prosocial television and most affected by the antisocial shows. The overriding discipline strategy used in the home seems to affect what behaviors children find attractive on TV.

2. Abelman, R. (1986). Children's awareness of television's prosocial fare: Parental discipline as an antecedent. *Journal of Family Issues,* 7, 51–66.

    Those parents who were mostly inductive (gave reasons) and who only occasionally resorted to techniques such as power assertion and love withdrawal were the ones whose children seemed to be the most affected by prosocial television content and least affected by antisocial fare.

Note: Cross-references are to works in both Section 1 and Section 2.

3.   Abraham, K., Kuehl, R., & Christopherson, V. (1983). Age specific influence of parental behaviors on the development of empathy in preschool children. *Child Study Journal, 13,* 175–185.

Families (N=122) of preschool children from six day care centers filled out questionnaires on environmental history and the Iowa Parent Behavior Inventory, in a study to determine the relationship between parental behaviors and children's development of empathy as a function of child age. The six parent subscales of the Iowa are: (a) parental involvement; (b) limit setting; (c) responsiveness; (d) reasoning guidance; (e) free expression; and (f) intimacy. The Borke Interpersonal Awareness Test was individually administered to each child and child empathy scores were correlated with parental behaviors. Limit setting by fathers was negatively associated with Borke empathy scores for 3-year-olds but positively associated for the 5-year-olds. Reasoning guidance for fathers was positively correlated with Borke scores for threes and not for older preschoolers. Limit setting by mothers was negatively associated with Borke scores for fives, but not for 3's and 4's. Mother intimacy and free expression of emotion were negatively associated with Borke scores for threes only. Different aspects of parental interactions seem to support child empathy development at different preschool ages.

4.   Ahammar, I. M., & Murray, J. P. (1979). Kindness in the kindergarten: The relative influence of role playing and prosocial television in facilitating altruism. *The Journal of Behavioral Development, 2,* 133–157.

Four training programs, designed to foster altruism, were carried out with 97 4-5-year olds. Programs (lasting for 4 weeks, 1/2 hour daily) centered on cognitive perceptual and affective role-taking (empathy) skills were compared with programs in which altruistic behavior was either watched on TV or role-played by the children. Control children watched neutral TV or were in a regular preschool program. Altruism was significantly enhanced in the three role-playing programs, while prosocial TV viewing was less effective than the role-play conditions and barely superior to neutral TV viewing. A variety of altruistic behaviors such as sharing and helping were strengthened by a child's ability to take the role of the other, although there was lack of relationship between role-taking and cooperation.

5. Archer, R., Diaz-Loving, R., Gollwitzer, P., Davis, M., & Foushee, H. C. (1981). The role of dispositional empathy and social evaluation in the empathic mediation of helping. *Journal of Personality and Social Psychology, 40,* 786-796.

A dispositional tendency to experience emotional empathy was related to students' reactions of both empathic concern and personal distress. Individual variation in empathic tendencies was an important factor in influencing students' emotional reactions and helping behavior.

6. Aronfreed, J. (1970). The socialization of altruistic and sympathetic behavior: Some theoretical and experimental analyses. In J. Macaulay & L. Berkowitz (Eds.), *Altruism and helping behavior.* New York: Academic Press.

Empathy is proposed as the essential and underlying mechanism for motivating the occurrence of helping behavior. Aronfreed suggests that perceiving another's emotional state through an affective response reflects an *empathic* relationship; perceiving the emotionally arousing situation and affect refers to a *vicarious* relationship, and involves taking situational cues into account.

7. Aronson, E., Bridgeman, D., & Geffner, R. (1978). Interdependent interactions and prosocial behavior. *Journal of Research and Development in Education, 12* (1), 16–27.

A competitive classroom can result in a child who fears failure. In a cooperative interaction classroom, the emphasis is on children working together to accomplish mutual goals. Students are placed in small groups of five or six in the *jigsaw model*. One segment of the day's lesson is given to each child in each group. Every child is responsible for teaching his or her segment to the other children. The children learn to teach and to listen to each other. They learn that none can do well without the help of the other and that each child has an essential and unique contribution to make. Self-esteem and students' perceptions of ethnic minorities improves. Self-defeating attributions decrease most for poorly performing students in the jigsaw model. Children increase in role-taking ability when they engage in a cooperative rather than a competitive classroom. In a role-play situation, for example, when a mailman delivered a toy airplane to a little boy whose father had left town on an airplane, students in the jigsaw group were more successful at realizing that the mailman could not possibly know or predict that the boy would cry. Empathic role-taking may be a key ability which mediates other prosocial behaviors. The aim of the jigsaw technique is to teach cooperation as a skill so that children can use that skill under appropriate conditions as a more reasonable strategy.

8. Asher, S. R., & Gottman, J. R. (Eds.)(1981). *The development of children's friendships.* New York: Cambridge University Press.

    Contains: Selman, R. (1981)

9. Asher, S. R., Hymel, S., & Renshaw, P. D. (1984). Loneliness in children. *Child Development, 55,* 1456–1464.

    A 16-item self-report measure of loneliness and social dissatisfaction examined whether children (from grades 3 to 6) least accepted by their classmates were indeed more lonely. A 24-item questionnaire on a 5-point scale (ranging from always true to not true at all) was used along with sociometric measures. Of the 500 children (half boys and half girls) 100% reported feelings of loneliness and social dissatisfaction. Children whose status was the lowest reported more loneliness and social dissatisfaction (e.g., I feel alone or I have nobody to talk to).

10. Asher, S. R., Renshaw, P. D., & Hymel, S. (1982). Peer relations and the development of social skills. In S. G. Moore & C. R. Cooper (Eds.), *The young child: Reviews of research,* Vol. 3 (pp. 157–158). Washington D.C.: NAEYC.

Teachers need to adopt a social-skills perspective on peer relations to help children initiate positive peer interactions, maintain ongoing positive relations, and resolve interpersonal conflicts. Research on popular children suggests they use more sophisticated strategies to join a game. They may wait for a natural break in the others' play, offer a greeting, give and request information, extend inclusion themselves ("Wanna come over to my house sometime?"). Peer acceptance has been positively related to friendly social behaviors – e.g. giving approval, personal acceptance, and affection. Social skills training programs and researches are reviewed and critiqued.

11. Badcock, C. R. (1986). *The problem of altruism: Freudian-Darwinian solutions*. London: Basil Blackwell.

In this theoretical volume, the author examines the ideas of Darwin and Freud as they bear on altruism. In a Darwinian framework kin altruism is found as well as reciprocal altruism, in which one organism performs a service or sacrifice for another who is, correspondingly, a provider of services. Considering Freudian theory, the author discusses masochistic self-sacrificing altruism, altruism-through-identification, superego internalization of cultural mores, "narcissistic identifications underlying kin altruism", and competitive induced altruism that the ego undertakes. With more reliable internal insights into itself, the ego could better free itself from "exorbitant and irrational compulsions of the superego and from impulsive and uncomprehending enslavement to the peremptory demands of the id" (p. 196). Then there could be a natural basis for reciprocity.

12. Baldwin, C. P., & Baldwin, A. L. (1970). Children's judgments of kindness. *Child Development, 41,* 29–47.

Undergraduates (N=110) and children from grades 2, 4, 6, and 8 were presented with pairs of kindness-picture stories and asked to select the picture in which they thought the child was kinder and to provide explanations as to why they thought so. Adults demonstrated a consensus on judgments of kindness. Children acquired an understanding of different aspects of kindness at different ages. Children gave consistent, clearly articulated reasons for cases where they judged a situation differently compared with adults.

13. Balk, D. (1989). Arousing empathy and promoting prosocial behavior toward bereaved peers: Using guided fantasy with elementary school children. *Death Studies, 13* (5), 425–442.

Research into empathy and prosocial behavior of children indicates that elementary school children possess the cognitive and emotional capacity to imagine how someone else would react to a loss as complete as the death of a family member or close friend. These empathic capabilities provide an opportunity to teach children about means of coping with the stresses presented by the death of a loved one and to learn means to help others who are experiencing such distress. Ninety-five fourth and fifth graders, listened to two presentations concerning grief, making final goodbyes, and helping people distressed over a death. A guided fantasy technique making use of common relaxation and imagery procedures was used. The children were encouraged to write a letter to a classmate troubled over the death of a sibling. Eight of the children participating in the study had lost a sibling. Written remarks from the children at the end of each session indicated sensitivity to other children's experiences of grief.

14. Bandura, A. (1986). *The social foundation of thought and action: A social cognitive theory.* Englewood Cliffs, NJ: Prentice-Hall.

Bandura stresses the importance of *modeling* for children's learning positive social interactions in this theoretical treatment of how social learning theory accounts for positive social behaviors. Cognitive mediators of social behaviors are important. But learning occurs through children's observations of appropriate social transactions within particular settings and situations. Social behavior is controlled at first mainly by external consequences of the child's behaviors; but in time it comes to be regulated by covert self-reinforcing operations which depend on symbolically generated consequences in the form of reactions by which the child enhances his or her own self-esteem by behaving in positive social ways.

15. Barnett, M. (1984). Similarity of experience and empathy in preschoolers. *The Journal of Genetic Psychology, 145,* 241–250.

The 42 preschoolers (mean age 52 months) who participated in this experiment were assigned to one of several groups. Some preschoolers played one of two games (Puzzle Board or Ping Pong Balls in Buckets) and were informed that they had either succeeded or failed. For failure, children's names were removed from a superstar display board. Next, each child saw a staged videotape of a peer failing on the Puzzle game and looking very sad, while the observed child's facial reaction was unobtrusively videotaped and later coded. Immediately after, each child rated how he or she felt on a 7-point smiley-face rating scale. All the children had been given prior experience in rating from *very happy* to *very sad* on this scale. Children who had failed the Puzzle game (through deliberate manipulations of the experimenter in each case) had significantly sadder faces while watching the videotape and also rated sadder feelings on the smiley scale. Empathy with a peer may depend on prior personal similar sad or distressful experience.

16. Barnett, M., & Bryan, J. (1974). Effects of competition with outcome feedback on children's helping behavior. *Developmental Psychology, 10,* 838–842.

Eighty second- and fifth-grade boys played an individual bowling game in either a competitive or non-competitive situation involving an absent boy (depicted on videotape). In the competitive situation, outcomes of "win", "tie", or "lose" to the other were randomly assigned and were communicated to the participant at the end of the game. Each child then received 30 tokens. Competitors were told that tokens were given for a win, tie, or loss; non-competitors were told that tokens were given for playing. Children were then left alone and given the chance to donate tokens to "less fortunate" children. Competition with feedback did not affect the donation behavior of second-grade boys. For fifth-graders, competition depressed donations, particularly in the "lose" and "tie" situations.

17. Barnett, M., Howard, J., King, L., & Dino, G. (1980a). Antecedents of empathy: Retrospective accounts of early socialization. *Personality and Social Psychology Bulletin, 6* (3), 361-365.

Scores from the Mehrabian & Epstein empathy scale completed by college students were related to their retrospective memories estimating the level of parental empathic and affectionate relationships with them when they were 10 years old. Those rated high (in contrast to low) on empathy reported more parental time spent, more affection, more parental empathy and emphasis on feelings during their childhood.

18. Barnett, M., Howard, J., King, L., & Dino, G. (1980b). Empathy in young children: Relation to parents' empathy, affection, and emphasis on the feelings of others. *Developmental Psychology, 16,* 243-244.

Fifty-four boys and girls enrolled in preschool and kindergarten classes in Kansas were tested on the Feshbach & Roe measures of empathy, while their parents were interviewed individually about their approach to discipline, affectionate interactions with their child and the degree to which they focused on feelings of others in non-discipline situations. For girls only, heightened empathy correlated with high mother-empathy and low father-empathy.

19. Barnett, M., & Thompson, S. (1985). The role of perspective-taking and empathy in children's Machiavellianism, prosocial behavior, and motive for helping. *The Journal of Genetic Psychology, 146,* 295-305.

Both a child's ability to identify accurately the emotional state of another as well as the empathic ability to experience the feelings of another contribute to prosocial behavior. A child's knowledge of another's affect may sometimes be used to hurt, manipulate or deceive another (Machiavellianism). Fourth- and fifth-grade children (N=117) were assessed with the Bryant Empathy scale and the Ryan (APT) (Affective-Perspective Taking) Scale. Those in the low-empathy/ high APT group had significantly higher Machiavellianism scores. Highly empathic children are more helpful. These children cited other-oriented reasons for their own helping behaviors more frequently than did less empathic children.

20. Barrett, D. E., & Yarrow, M. R. (1977). Prosocial behavior, social inferential ability, and assertiveness in young children. *Child Development, 48,* 475-481.

Observations on forty children (5-8 years) in naturalistic play activities during a six-week summer camp were coded for assertions, aggressive behaviors, prosocial behaviors and bids for opportunities to act prosocially. Children viewed interactions depicting an abrupt change in behavior by the main character in response to an affective experience (overhearing parents arguing). Then they drew inferences as to why the character's behavior had changed. Inferential ability was positively related to prosocial behavior among highly assertive children, but negatively related among timid children. A high level of cognitive ability *and* assertiveness, together, best predicted altruism.

21. Bar-Tal, D. (1976). *Prosocial behavior: Theory and research*. New York: Wiley.

Researches are described on types of prosocial behavior and how they vary with age, sex, degree of dependency, modeling by others, race, personality traits, emergency situation, and other helper variables, such as cost-benefit ratios. Two types of prosocial behavior are posited: *Altruism* is defined as benefiting another purely voluntarily without external threat or enforcement, without expectation of a reward, as an end in itself, and perceived by others as doing good. *Restitution* is prosocial behavior that reciprocates previously received help or benefit or is compensating for harm done earlier.

22. Bar-Tal, D., Raviv, A., & Leiser, T. (1980). The development of altruistic behavior. Empirical evidence. *Developmental Psychology*, *16*, 516-524.

Children (61 boys and 63 girls) from middle SES families were put in situations in which they were provided with an opportunity to share. Five situations were constructed and ordered according to the sequences of stages of helping behavior suggested by the authors. Children who did not share in the advanced experimental situation were provided with an opportunity to share in progressively lower level experimental situations. Results indicate that older children shared more in the advanced level and also expressed advanced levels of motivations when queried about their motive for sharing. A high level of motivation would be "personal empathic willingness to share without expectation of any rewards" and a low level would be "sharing because of approval or rewards."

23. Bar-Tal, D., Raviv, A., & Shavit, N. (1981). Motives for helping behavior: Kibbutz and city children in kindergarten and school. *Developmental Psychology, 16,* 516-524.

Children 4/5 and 7/8 years old were interviewed concerning whether they would help and why in hypothetical helping, sharing, and comforting situations. Responses were coded into 8 categories reflecting 6 developmental stages of motives for helping:

1. external initiation with tangible reward
2. external initiation with no reward
3. self-initiation with tangible reward
4. self-initiation with social reward
5. self-initiation with expectation of some future reciprocity from the child in need
6. self-initiation with generalized reciprocity
7. self-initiation with an internal reward
8. self-initiation with no reward

Most of the older children said they would give help because the other child would help them someday. The majority of younger children said that help is given when an external reward is promised. Perhaps children think about hedonistic rewards more if there isn't much pain or urgency for the recipient child in the distress story. Also, the children were asked what they *would* do, and such answers may be different from what one *should* do.

24. Bar-tal, D., Sharabany, R., & Raviv, A. (1982). Cognitive basis of the development of altruistic behavior. In V. Derlega, & J. Grzelak (Eds.), *Cooperation and helping behavior: Theories and research.* New York: Academic Press.

Bar-tal reviews definitions of altruism and concludes that altruistic behavior is *self-*

initiated and *aimed at benefiting another person without expectation of external rewards.* All helping acts, then, are not considered altruistic if they do not meet the three parts of this definition. The authors summarize research to demonstrate that helping behavior increases with age and is related to cognitive and moral development. Six developmental stages of helping behavior are identified:

Stage 1: Compliance and concretely defined reinforcement. The person carries out a helping act because it is requested or commanded and there is promise of a reward or threat of punishment.

Stage 2: Compliance. The person complies with authority.

Stage 3: Internal initiative and concrete reward. The person initiates the helping behavior; however, the behavior is contingent on receiving a reward.

Stage 4: Normative behavior. The person helps in order to comply with societal demands. Individuals help because they are expected to do so and they want to be good people in others' eyes.

Stage 5: Specific and generalized reciprocity. People help, believing that one day when they need help, they will be helped in return.

Stage 6: Altruistic behavior. In this stage an individual initiates the helping act voluntarily, for its own end, and to benefit another, and does so not expecting external rewards.

Only in the sixth stage, then, are children capable of performing an altruistic act. In the authors' study of kindergarten and grade school

children, the answers of the kindergarten
children corresponded to Stages 3 and 4 while
the answers of grade school children corresponded to stages 4 and 5. The findings can be
very helpful for parents and teachers.

25. Barton, E. J., & Ascione, F. R. (1979).
Sharing in preschool children: Facilitation,
stimulus generalization, response
generalization, and maintenance. *Journal of
Applied Behavior Analysis, 12,* 417-430.

The experimenter explained to preschool
children how to share appropriately and why
sharing was desirable. The children had to
rehearse the behavior with the experimenter
and were prompted and praised during the
rehearsal. Sharing increased from verbal and
physical practice and the behavior was both
lasting and generalized to other situations.

26. Barton, E., & Osborne, J. (1978). The
development of classroom sharing by a
teacher using positive practice. *Behavior
Modification, 2,* 231-251.

"Positive practice" worked in inducing five
children with moderate to severe hearing loss
and poor speech communication to share. The
positive practice procedure required that the
children practice verbal sharing when it did not
occur. The teacher modeled and also taught the
children how to initiate verbal sharing when it
didn't happen and to accept such sharing.
Physical sharing increased after the procedure
whereby children practiced these roles.

27. Batson, C. D. (1988). Prosocial motivation: Is it ever truly altruistic? In L. Berkowitz (Ed.), *Advances in experimental social psychology* (Vol. 20, pp. 65-117). New York: Academic Press.

Altruism is considered as egoistic, as prosocial behavior to reduce aversive arousal, or as prosocial behavior seeking internal rewards. This review considers the theories of Hoffman, Krebs, Rosenhan, and others, while developing a theory (through factor-analyzed data collected with college students) that empathic emotion *leads* to altruistic helping.

28. Batson, C. D. (1990). How social an animal? The human capacity for caring. *American Psychologist, 45,* 336-346.

The author opts for the inclusion of altruism as a basic characteristic of humans. Very young children, of course, begin life helpless and dependent on others. But as they grow, they can learn to choose to give assistance to others.

29. Batson, C. D., Dyck, J., Brandt, R., Baton, J., Powell, A., McMaster, M. R., & Griffitt, C. (1988). Five studies testing two new egoistic alternatives to the empathy-altruism hypothesis. *Journal of Personality and Social Psychology, 55* (1), 52-77.

These authors have suggested, in previous research, that empathy evokes motivation directed toward the ultimate goal of benefitting the person for whom empathy is felt, not toward some subtle form of self-benefit. This assumption contradicts the general assumption of psychologists that all motivation is ultimately egoistic. Two new egoistic alternatives to the empathy-altruism hypothesis were explored. Study 1 tested the empathy-specific reward hypothesis, proposing that the prosocial motivation associated with empathy has the goal of social or self-rewards.

Studies 2-4 tested the empathy-specific punishment hypothesis that prosocial motivation is directed toward the goal of avoiding social or self-punishments (censure, guilt, shame). Study 5 assessed the role of reward-relevant, punishment-relevant, and victim-relevant cognition in mediating the empathy-helping relationship. The empathy-altruism hypothesis was supported and the authors affirm that "evidence that empathic emotion evokes altruistic motivation continues to mount".

30. Batson, C. D. (1991). *The altruism question: Toward a social-psychological answer.* Hillsdale, NJ: Lawrence Erlbaum.

The question of whether altruistic motivation is some form of egoism because self-benefit is involved, is illuminated by an empirically-testable theory of altruistic motivation plus reports on a series of experiments to test that theory. Specifically, the author introduces a three-path model of egoistic and altruistic motivation *to* help, including aversive-arousal reduction, empathy-specific punishment, and empathy-specific reward. Limitations of the empathy-altruism hypothesis are discussed.

31. Baumrind, D. (1980). New directions in socialization research. *American Psychologist 35*, 639-652.

Baumrind proposes that we can best understand children's responsiveness to parents and teachers if we remember that adults and children have *reciprocal* rights and obligations. There is unfairness and a scarcity of resources in life. Parents need to cherish and care for children unconditionally. But, *reciprocally*, children need to learn to cooperate with and comply with their caregivers.

32. Bell, D. (Ed.) (1989). *Children's social networks and social supports*. New York: Wiley.

   Contains: Parke, R., & Bhavnagri, N. (1989)

33. Bengtsson, H., & Johnson, L. (1987). Cognitions related to empathy in five- to eleven-year-old children. *Child Development, 58*, 1001–1012.

   Swedish kindergarten, first- and fourth-grade students (N=48) responded to four stories involving two story characters: a *"target"* child who reacts to specific events happening to the *"other character"*. Stories differed regarding the sex of story characters and the nature of their feelings for each other (e.g., like or dislike). Using a seven-point scale of emotions (ranging from very happy to neutral to very sad) students predicted how the target child would react to the other character's experience. Students then listened to two additional stories involving detailed descriptions of very sad circumstances. For one story, they were instructed to attempt to avoid feeling sad themselves, while for the other, students were to try to feel as sad as possible. Students described what they did to evoke or avoid feeling sad.

First- and fourth-graders predicted that the main story character would respond significantly with stronger emotional responses to liked than disliked peers, while kindergartners expected strong responses regardless of the feelings of liking or disliking the peer. In minimizing and maximizing feelings of sadness, older students imagined themselves in the role of the character or involved in similar incidents, while younger students evoked sadness by thinking about sad things unrelated to the story. Empathy was stronger in response to sad events than to happy events.

34. Berkowitz, L. (Ed.) (1974). *Advances in experimental social psychology, Vol. 7.* New York: Academic Press.

Contains: Staub, E. (1974)

35. Berkowitz, L. (Ed.) (1987). *Advances in experimental social psychology,* Vol. 20. New York: Academic Press.

Contains: Batson, C. (1987)

36. Berkowitz, M., & Oser, F. (Eds.) (1985). *Moral Education.* Hillsdale, NJ: Erlbaum Associates.

This volume contains a variety of chapters by different authors who address different aspects of moral education.

Contains: Kohlberg, L. (1985)
Lickona, T. (1985)

37. Berndt (1981). Effects of friendship on prosocial intentions and behavior. *Child Development, 52,* 636-643.

Male and female kindergartners (N=44), second-graders (N=40) and fourth-graders (N=32) were interviewed and paired with a close friend or acquaintance based on a sociometric measure. The children were asked questions designed to assess three components regarded as determinants of behavioral intentions, i.e., (a) how long they thought they should share or help the partner (personal norms), (b) how long the partner would expect them to share or help (social norms), and (c) how long they really wanted to share or help (attitudes towards the behavior).

Behavioral intentions towards friends and acquaintances were significantly different only for girls. Girls said they would share and help a friend more than an acquaintance; boys said they would treat friends and acquaintances similarly. What children said they would do was highly correlated with what they said they should do and wanted to do, but uncorrelated with what they believed their partner expected them to do. Sex differences were also found for a task which involved sharing a crayon. Boys behaved less prosocially towards friends than towards acquaintances.

38. Blackmon, A., & Dembo, M. (1984). Prosocial behavior in mainstreamed preschoolers. *Child Study Journal, 14,* 205-214.

Prosocial interactions were investigated as a measure of friendship towards handicapped children in a mainstreamed preschool (N=32 non-handicapped 4-5 year-olds and 13 developmentally disabled 3-5 year-old children) from middle class families. Each non-handicapped preschooler was observed in the classroom for empathic, helping, and altruistic behaviors directed towards both handicapped and non-handicapped peers.

Handicapped children were significantly under-represented as recipients of prosocial behaviors. Empathic responses were the least frequently exhibited followed by helping behaviors and altruistic behaviors.

39. Blaney, N., Stephan, C., Rosenfield, D. & Sikes, J. (1977). Interdependence in the classroom: A field study. *Journal of Educational Psychology, 69,* 139-146.

In a recently desegregated Texas school, fifth-graders were introduced to the jigsaw technique. Each jigsaw group consisted of approximately three Anglos, one Black, and one Mexican-American student. They met for 45 minutes per day, three days per week for six weeks. Measures of attitudes toward school, themselves, and classroom cooperation with peers were taken prior to and after the research, using traditional classrooms as controls in seven elementary schools. Anglo students in jigsaw classes increased their liking for school while those in the control classes decreased. Black jigsaw classroom students decreased their liking for school, but control Blacks decreased their liking even more. Mexican-American controls liked school much more after than did the jigsaw experimentals. Experimental subjects significantly increased in self-esteem compared with controls, and decreased in schoolwork competitiveness while control students increased in competitiveness over time. The Mexican-American children in the jigsaw classes may have been under more stress since they were *compelled* to participate. Cooperative jigsaw classrooms may not help children enjoy learning more if the children feel coerced to participate without understanding the purpose of the new method.

40. Blasi, A. (1987). Autonomy in obedience: The development of distance in socialized action. In W. Edelstein (Ed.), *Contemporary approaches to social cognition.* Frankfurt: Suhrkamp.

In this research, authority's dictates and rules are pitted against the alternative of helping another. Moral dilemmas were posed to first, sixth, and tenth/eleventh graders. Examples are: helping a child who has fallen in the yard when parent's order is to stay in the house; bringing food (to a boy being punished in camp) against the order of the camp director. For the older children one dilemma involved a city official who could help a business man avoid bankruptcy but only by violating a city law. Children were asked what the story protagonist should do and why as well as questioned about obligations, non-compliance, and personal responsibility.

Dramatic age changes in reasoning were found. First-graders were much more attuned to another's needs than to the rules of an authority, and they were more concrete in their concerns. They referred to objective consideration of the other child's need and to circumstances, such as nobody else being around to help. Sixth-graders tended to mention more general concerns, such as duty, loyalty, law, or authority. Of the high-school students, 27% justified their decisions mostly with references to persons' rights and universal or societal values.

41. Boehnke, K., Silbereisen, R., Eisenberg, N., Reykowski, J., & Palmonari, A. (1989). Developmental pattern of prosocial motivation: A cross national study. *Journal of Cross-Cultural Psychology, 20* (3), 219-243.

The authors examined changes in patterns of prosocial motivation in five samples of children between the grades of 2 and 12 from four countries: West Germany, Poland, Italy, and the United States. Participants took the Prosocial Motivation Questionnaire (PSMQ). The PSMQ consists of 24 scenarios, each describing situations in which there is an opportunity for prosocial action. The decision to assist or not is already made in the scenarios. After each scenario, five possible motives are presented, each corresponding to a level of development: hedonism, self-interest, conformity, task orientation, and other-orientation. Intrinsic motives (task and other-orientation) were most highly valued, and conformity was always in-between. Age-related increases were found only for task orientation. Gender differences emerged at age 12, confirming prior findings that girls prefer intrinsic motives more than boys do.

42. Borke, H. (1971). Interpersonal perception of young children: Egocentrism or empathy? *Developmental Psychology, 5,* 263-269.

Empathic responses were assessed for 200 children (from 3 to 8 years of age) to a series of short stories. Children pointed to the picture of the face (happy, sad, afraid, or angry) that matched how the children in the story felt about their situation. Despite an increase in social sensitivity with age, empathic responses varied greatly depending on the emotion being identified. Awareness of happy feelings emerged by three to three-and-a half, fear by three-and-a-half to four. Anger and sadness showed the least consistent trends with age. No sex differences in emotional sensitivity were identified.

43. Borke, H. (1973). The development of empathy in Chinese and American children between three and six years of age: A cross-culture study. *Developmental Psychology, 9,* 102-108.

Borke's earlier work showing the ability of three-year-old American children to perceive others' emotions is extended to these Chinese youngsters. Borke suggests that this cross-cultural finding may indicate that empathy is a universal human characteristic. Happy versus unhappy was easy, fear was more difficult, and sadness and anger were confused, with boys having more difficulty than girls. Social learning may be crucial for perceiving other's emotions. Adults need to teach children to understand *how* to read cues from another person in order to understand how that person is feeling.

44. Bridgeman, D. L. (Ed.) (1983). *The nature of prosocial development: Interdisciplinary theories and strategies.* New York: Academic Press.

This excellent text provides articles on a wide variety of theoretical issues and experimental investigations relating to prosocial development. Chapters include work on sociobiological approaches to prosocial development; a study of the value of considerateness to children; children's perspective-taking and the effects of exhortations on their prosocial behaviors; altruism and moral development; the genesis of prosocial behavior, including gender and age differences in children's interactions with infants and toddlers; cross-cultural approaches to prosocial development including a specific look at prosocial behaviors on a Polynesian island and a field study of in-school curricula to enhance prosocial development.

> Contains: Brown, D., & Solomon, D. (1983)
> Graves, N., & Graves, T. (1983)
> Puka, B. (1983)
> Smith, C. L., Leinbach, M. D., Stewart, B. J., & Blackwell, J. M. (1983)
> Whiting, B. (1983)

45. Bryan, J. H. (1977). Prosocial behavior. In H. L. Hom, Jr., & P. A. Robinson (Eds.), *Psychological processes in early education.* New York: Academic Press.

The author stresses that children will imitate the helping activities of models whether those models are alive and present, or televised and absent. Helping actions can be learned by observing caregiver models.

46. Bryan, J. H., & London, P. (1970). Altruistic behavior by children. *Psychological Bulletin, 73* (3), 200–211.

This review of 1960's studies of self-sacrificing activities by children stresses the role of *modeling* and of *reinforcement.* For example, in one study, four-year-olds tended to share marbles with another (unknown) child if their sharing was rewarded by bubble gum. Altruistic models elicit more altruistic behavior from children. Generosity increases with age. Social class makes a difference: reciprocity was strongest in one study of working class subjects, particularly when recipients were previously unfamiliar. Also, children have been found to assume that a stranger was in greater need than a friend in experiments on sharing toys among 8-year-olds. Children do appear to learn norms which determine whether or not and how they will aid others.

47. Bryan, J. H., & Walbek, N. H. (1970). The impact of words and deeds concerning altruism upon children. *Child Development, 41*, 747-757.

A model's *practices* influenced children's prosocial behavior (that is, collecting tokens for themselves and then being presented with an actual opportunity to donate to other children) while the model's *preaching* did not. However, both preaching and practices did influence the child's judgment of the model's attractiveness. Possibly, exposure to a model simply produces conformity to the demands of the immediate situation.

48. Bryant, B. K. (1982). An index of empathy for children and adolescents. *Child Development, 53*, 413-425.

A new measure of children's empathy is based on extending downward the Mehrabian and Epstein (1972) scale for adults. Empathy is defined as a *vicarious emotional response to the perceived affect of others*, in contrast with other definitions that highlight *cognitive social insight or social/affective role-taking*. Students in first-, fourth- and seventh-grade (N=404) answered individual, oral, and pencil and paper measures. These included: Bryant's adapted measure of emotional empathy; an adult measure of empathy; an early childhood measure of empathy; acceptance of individual differences measure; social desirability questionnaire; measure of aggressiveness; and a reading achievement score. The new index of empathy met the minimum standards for construct validity, and, when compared to other measures of empathy, convergent validity. Discriminant validity was documented with regard to social desirability and reading achievement scores. Scores on this empathy index correlated positively with acceptance of individual differences and negatively with measures of aggressiveness.

49. Bryant, B. K., & Crockenberg, S. B. (1980). Correlates and dimensions of prosocial behavior: A study of female siblings with their mothers. *Child Development, 51,* 429–544.

Fifty mothers were videotaped with their first born and later born daughters in a semi-naturalistic game-playing setting. The mean age of the older daughter was 10-15 years and the younger 7-11 years. These games ranged from a block-building task to a marble-pull task to determine cooperative and competitive behavior between sisters. The more a mother responded sensitively to her older daughter's emotional needs, the more frequent was the prosocial interaction between the children. Siblings influenced the antisocial and prosocial behaviors of the younger child.

50. Buckley, N., Siegel, L., & Ness, S. (1979). Egocentrism, empathy, and altruistic behavior in young children. *Developmental Psychology, 15,* 329-330.

A significant cognitive component was found in altruistic behavior of 41 children (3 to 8 year olds). Researchers compared children's scores on perspective-taking (the cognitive measure) with scores of empathy and altruism (sharing and helping) measures. No significant relationship between age and altruistic behavior was found. However, altruistic children displayed more empathy and perspective-taking ability. They identified better the emotion of a character in a story compared with children who were not altruistic.

51. Bukowski, W. (1990). Age differences in children's memory of information about aggressive, socially withdrawn, and prosociable boys and girls. *Child Development, 61,* (5), 1326-1334.

In grades 2 and 6, 22 boys and 22 girls were tested for memory about aggression, social withdrawal, and prosociable (kind, sharing and cooperative) helpfulness in stories read about hypothetical peers. Young children's recall of information was better for aggressive male peers rather than female peers, and recognition memory about an aggressive peer was better if the peer was a boy (for the older children). Marginally significant increases in memory were found for the prosocial peer story. Children's memory about aggression and prosociability varied as a function of sex of target peer. The researchers note that this could cause more difficulties in social reputation for males.

52. Burleson, B. (1982). The development of comforting communication skills in childhood and adolescence. *Child Development, 53,* 1578-88.

Students in grades one through 12 (N=37) described what they would say to help a same-sex friend feel better in four hypothetical situations. Responses were coded for the number of different message strategies used, and for the qualitative level of the message (e.g., the extent to which it explicitly acknowledged, elaborated on, and legitimized the friend's feelings). The number, variety, and quality of comfort-intended messages increased with age, with females consistently outperforming their male peers. Situational effects were evident, as students at all ages gave fewer and lower-level comforting responses to a story involving the friend and known/liked teacher. Significant individual consistency existed over the four situations.

53. Carlo, G., Knight, G., & Eisenberg, N. (1991). Cognitive processes and prosocial behaviors among children: The role of affective attributions and reconciliations. *Developmental Psychology, 27* (3), 456-461.

Preschool through second-grade children (N=89) carried out an affective attribution and reasoning task. After each of a set of stories with congruent or incongruent pictures, the children chose a matching emotion from a pair of photos, and indicated how they felt, how the character in the story felt, and how they knew the character felt that way. In the cognitive perspective-taking task, the children heard a story about a dog who chased a boy, who then climbed a tree to escape, and lastly ate an apple from the tree. The children repeated the story and were given 4 of 7 story pictures (but not the apple eating picture) to show an imaginary friend. They were asked what story the friend would tell. Scores depended on whether the children realized that unless they mentioned it, a friend would not know about the apple eating from the pictures. Next, children had a chance to help a peer (with a plaster cast on the hand) to get more toys by helping turn a stiff crank faster. In the incongruent condition, the confederate (seen on TV from another room) looked smiling, even though his crank was hard to turn. In the congruent condition, the peer with cast looked frustrated and remarked how hard it was to turn the crank, especially with the casted hand.

Sad attributions in the congruent stories were positively related to the children's helping in the congruent condition. Reconciliations, where a child explained away an incongruent cue ("He's looking sad at a birthday party because he did not get the present he wanted"; or "She is sad even though she's smiling") were positively related to helping in the incongruent condition. Thus, aside from perspective taking, children need another cognitive ability – to reconcile conflicting affective cues.

54. Cauley, K., & Tyler, B. (1989). The relationship of self-concept to prosocial behavior in children. *Early Childhood Research Quarterly, 4* (1), 51-60.

The influence of the personality variable, self-concept, on prosocial behavior was studied with 52 four- and five-year-old children attending child care. The children were observed during free play and were administered the Purdue Self-Concept scale for preschool children. A forced-order multiple regression analysis examined the relationship between self-concept and prosocial behavior, controlling for the effects of sex, age, family size, and number of years in day care. The data clearly indicate that the way 4- and 5-year-old children feel about themselves is related to the frequency of their prosocial behavior when it is confined to cooperating. The findings support the theoretical position that a child with a positive self-concept has less need to engage in competitive interactions with other children and is more willing to engage in cooperative behavior.

55. Chalmers, J., & Townsend, M. (1990). The effects of training in social perspective taking on socially maladjusted girls. *Child Development, 61,* 178–190.

Sixteen low SES girls from unstable families, aged 10 years to 16 years, in a New Zealand institution for delinquents were trained through role-play to enhance their perspective-taking. Girls in the control group participated in a fitness program. The program involved 15 l-hour sessions spaced over 6 weeks. The skills taught covered interpreting non-verbal behavior, expressions, gestures, mood and emotional reactions; making inferences from non-verbal and verbal behavior; and recognizing how our words and actions affect others. Class discussions were led on how these skills might be important in their interpersonal relations. The girls were encouraged to present real-life situations where they had interpersonal difficulties, and to role-play characters in scenarios. Social Perspective-taking tasks and an Interpersonal Problem Analysis task, plus Bryant's Index of Empathy showed that referential communication and empathy scores increased for the trained group but not for the fitness group. Observed prosocial classroom behaviors also increased only for the trained group. Counselors in juvenile detention programs may find a role-play skill training program effective.

56. Chambers, J. (1987). The effects of prosocial and aggressive video games on children's donating and helping. *The Journal of Genetic Psychology, 148,* 499-505.

Third-, fourth-, seventh-, and eighth-grade boys and girls (N=160) participated in a study to determine if prosocial or aggressive video games affected the children's helping and donating behaviors. Older children donated significantly more than did younger students. Children who played aggressive video games donated significantly less than did those who played prosocial games by themselves.

57. Chandler, M. (1973). Egocentrism and antisocial behavior: The assessment and training of social perspective-taking skills. *Developmental Psychology, 9,* 326-332.

The role-taking ability of boys (ages 11-13) showed significant improvement after an experimental training program videotaping themselves and each other. The 18 month follow-up data showed a reduction by one-half in the number of delinquencies in the experimental group, as compared to only slight decreases in the control and placebo groups.

58. Chapman, M., Zahn-Waxler, C., Cooperman, G., & Iannotti, R. (1987). Empathy and responsibility in the motivation of children's helping. *Developmental Psychology, 23,* 140-145.

Children between the ages of four and eleven (N=60) were videotaped in laboratory situations where they were given opportunities to respond to staged distressing events involving a hungry kitten, an injured adult, and a crying infant. Children's reactions were scored for level of assistance offered, and compared with expressions of affect during the taped event. In addition, the participants were asked to describe the motives and feelings of fictional characters in stories depicting a variety of distress situations, and to assess the contribution of individual dispositional factors to the motivation for helping. Children's helping correlated positively with their story attributions of empathy, altruism and, very highly, with guilt. In addition, children's observed positive affect was interpreted as pleasure in helping rather than a reaction to others' distress.

59. Cialdini, R. B., Baumann, D. J., & Kendrick, D. T. (1981). Insights from sadness: A three-step model of the development of altruism as hedonism. *Developmental Review, 1,* 207-223.

Research on the effects of sad moods on helping is reviewed from a social learning theory perspective. The theory suggests, that, while helping does not start out as rewarding to the helper (at young ages), it becomes rewarding through the process of socialization. A three-step model for the socialization of altruism as a self-reinforcer is proposed. At stage one, the "presocialization" stage, altruism functions principally as a punishing event, involving the loss of resources without corresponding personal gain. Stage two, the "awareness of norms", occurs when children become aware of, and act to receive, adult approval/social rewards for helping. During stage three, the "internalization" level, altruism is experienced as internally self-gratifying, through its association with approval and reward (i.e., it has become a conditioned reinforcer). Young children typically show a decreased level of prosocial behaviors when sad, *except* in the presence of adults. When adults are present, saddened children are reliably found to be more helpful than control group members with neutral mood. Sad children who act altruistically may be striving to receive the approval/reward of adult attention.

60. Clary, E. G., & Miller, J. (1986). Socialization and situational influences on sustained altruism. *Child Development, 57,* 1358-1369.

Adult volunteers in a crisis-counseling center (N=55) completed a survey targeting the following categories of information: biographical, past and present relationship with parents; extent to which their own parents had preached and/or modeled altruism; empathy; and motivation for volunteering. Surveys were scored and categorized as reflecting either "autonomous altruism" (help that is internally directed by concern for others) or "normative altruism" (help that is motivated by concern for the self in terms of rewards/avoidance of punishment). Volunteers who completed the standard agency training were rated on a group cohesiveness scale. Volunteers' completion or non-completion of a six-month commitment to the agency served as a measure of sustained altruism. "Normative altruists" in highly cohesive groups helped longer than those in low cohesive groups. "Autonomous altruists" reported more warm, nurturant relationships with their own parents who had modeled altruism than did "normative altruists".

61. Coates, B., Pusser, H., & Goodman, I. (1976). The influence of "Sesame Street" and "Mr. Rogers' Neighborhood" on children's social behavior in the preschool. *Child Development, 47*, 138-144.

Thirty-two children in two preschool classrooms (3 to 5 years) watched selected "Sesame Street" or "Mister Rogers' Neighborhood" television programs for 15 minutes on four consecutive days. Children's interactions in school with peers and adults were observed during play time one week before (baseline), during the treatment week, and for one week after watching the television program. Children's behavior during all phases was coded for frequency of (1) social contact (verbal or physical) with another child or adult; (2) positive reinforcement (smiling, praising, hugging); and (3) punishment (criticizing, hitting, taking toys). "Sesame Street" viewing increased children's social contacts, positive reinforcement and punishment for children who scored in the lowest group during baseline. The viewing had no effect for children with high scores. "Mister Rogers" increased all children's social contacts and positive reinforcement, while increasing punishment for children with low baseline scores.

62. Cohen, S., & Comiskey, T. J. (Eds.) (1977). *Child development: Contemporary perspectives.* Itasca, IL: Peacock.

Contains: Hoffman, M. L. (1977)

63. Colby, A., & Kohlberg, L. (1987). *The Measurement of moral judgement: Vol. 1. Theoretical foundations and research.* New York: Cambridge University Press.
Colby, A., & Kohlberg, L. (1987). *The*

*Measurement of moral judgement: Vol. 2.
Standard issue scoring manual.* New York:
Cambridge University Press.

Here is the definitive presentation of the
system of classifying moral judgement created
by Lawrence Kohlberg. Volume 1 reviews
Kohlberg's stage theory of moral development,
including the large body of research on the
significance of his moral stages. Volume 2
presents the scoring system for the moral
judgment interview.

64. Coles, R. (1986). *The moral life of children.*
New York: Macmillan.

Impressions and experiences of this Harvard
psychiatrist attest to the strong moral sense
of some children who exhibit nobility and moral
principles in the face of life adversity.

65. Damon, W. (1977). *The social world of the
child.* San Francisco: Jossey-Bass.

Damon describes his positive justice levels
in terms of the kind of justice conflicts and
struggles toward fair distribution and sharing
that a child encounters and recognizes, the
techniques and ways by which the child resolves
such conflicts, the identification of relevant
others in the resolution, and the nature of the
child's justifications for the fairness of
decisions taken. Generally, the technique used
to discover children's reasoning is to get them
to respond to probes about *story-dilemmas.*
Some stories focus on child-adult authority
relations, as when a mother wants a child to
clean up his room just when a peer wants the
child to leave right away for a picnic. Another
is when the child cleans his room really well,

but the mother woke up cranky and decides the child still cannot go on the picnic. Does a kid have to do whatever his mother tells him to do? What if she tells you to steal a pretty necklace for her from the store? Does she have a right to do that? What should the kid do? Is it worse for a kid to break his promise to a mother or for a mother to break her promise to a kid?

Other vignettes focus on child–child authority relations. For example, six kids are on a team together. What gives one kid the right to tell another where to play? Can a team member ask the captain to run down and get him a Coke? Can a captain tell a kid to run down to the corner to get him a Coke? Does he have a right to do that? What will happen then? What's the difference?

In research on rules, manners, and sex-role conventions, Damon extends Turiel's categories to younger children. His stories pit one kind of disobedience against another to probe for children's ideas about table manners, rights, stealing, etc. For example: "Is it right or wrong to steal? What is the difference between stealing and eating with your fingers? Is one worse than the other? Are they equally as bad? Why/why not?" (p. 243). The findings, much in agreement with Turiel's, describe four levels of social-conventional and social rule knowledge expressed by the children.

Children move gradually through stages until they come to distinguish others' rules and social conventions as man-made (such as rules for what to wear on different occasions) and moral – as helping an injured peer, rather than further hurting the person.

66. Damon, W., & Killen, M. (1982). Peer interaction and the process of change in children's moral reasoning. *Merrill-Palmer Quarterly, 28* (3), 347-367.

Kindergarten to third-grade children (N=147) were given Damon's positive-justice interview, which poses a hypothetical problem in distributive justice, and requires children to reason about fairness. A typical item is:

"All these boys and girls are in the same class together. One day their teacher lets them spend the whole afternoon making paintings and crayon drawings. The teacher thought that these pictures were so good that the class could sell them at the fair. They sold the pictures to their parents, and together the class made a whole lot of money. Now all the children gathered the next day and tried to decide how to split up the money." (p. 352)

The children are given choices and asked probing questions. The choices sometimes involve giving poor kids more, or boys or girls more, or kids who did more of the work more. Two months after this pretest, experimental group children, in triads, participated in a positive-justice peer debate, in order to reach a consensus about a fair way to divide 10 candy bars among themselves and a fourth, younger child not present.

The children who participated in these discussions (usually about 10 minutes long) were more likely to advance in their moral reasoning about fairness than children just tested or who simply discussed such a problem with an adult or peer. Piaget's view that social interactions between equals are important for advancing children's concepts of morality is supported. Children who initially reasoned at lower levels, and changed to higher levels, worked with their peers in a reciprocal manner, clarified and

59

compromised, exhibiting "co-construction and conciliation" with their peers.

67. Davis, M. H. (1983). Measuring individual differences in empathy: Evidence for a multidimensional approach. *Journal of Personality and Social Psychology, 44,* 113-126.

The IRI (Interpersonal Reactivity Index) is a 28-item self-report questionnaire. This measure treats empathy as multidimensional with four subscales: perspective-taking (cognitive); empathic concern; personal distress (in stress or crisis); and fantasy (ability to imagine oneself as a character in a story or film).

The discriminant validity of the IRI scale subscales was established by comparing the relations between each of the subscales and measures of social competence, self-esteem, emotionality, and sensitivity to others. Perspective-taking was consistently associated with better social functioning and higher self-esteem.

68. Denham, S. (1986). Social cognition, prosocial behavior, and emotion in preschoolers: Contextual validation. *Child Development, 57,* 194-201.

Twenty-seven preschoolers (two to three years of age) were observed in free play settings. They participated in structured activities measuring their abilities to label emotions and to take another's perspective. For labeling of emotions, children identified four felt board faces portraying happy, sad, angry, and afraid expressions. For perspective-taking, children matched the proper face to puppets enacting 14 vignettes. In eight of the 14, the puppets portrayed *expected* emotions to common experiences (e.g., sadness at being hurt). In the other six, the puppet portrayed the *opposite* of the expected emotion (e.g., anger at receiving a gift). Children's reactions to spontaneous and planned displays of emotion were rated, from active ignoring to active assisting. The children recognized and labeled feelings displayed in the face and puppet activities. Specifically, children matched happy displays, showed concern when another was hurt, ignored sadness and moved away from anger. Level of overall knowledge of emotions positively correlated with children's frequency of prosocial responding.

69. Denham, S. A., McKinley, M., Couchoud, E. A., & Holt, R. (1990). Emotional and behavioral predictors of preschool peer ratings. *Child Development, 61,* 1145–1152.

Measures of likability, prosocial and aggressive behavior, peer competence, emotional knowledge, and expressed emotions were obtained for 65 preschool children (*M*=44 months). The children's standard score on the Preschool Behavior Questionnaire, which provides an aggression factor, was subtracted from the BPBQ teacher ratings, to create a prosocial behavior score. Items on the BPBQ (Baumrind Preschool Behavior Q-Sort) friendliness scale characterize a child as: understanding of other kids' position, sympathetic, helpful, not insulting or a bully, nurturant, and likely to share. Correlational analyses showed that emotional knowledge and prosocial behavior were direct predictors of likability. Helping a peer who is frustrated over a toppling block tower was an example of likable behavior. Children's prosocial behavior was a mediator, and significantly related to likability, even with effects of age and gender partialed out. Girls were better liked because they were more likely to behave prosocially.

70. Denham, S. A., Renwick, S. M., & Holt, R. W. (1991). Working and playing together: Prediction of preschool social-emotional competence from mother-child interaction. *Child Development, 62,* 242-249.

The researchers evaluated the impact of mother-child interaction (as measured by: preschoolers' compliance with directions, affection, dyadic interaction skills, and lack of dependence or avoidance) on peer interactions in preschool. Mothers and children (N=48; M=44 months) were videotaped in four challenging play teaching tasks, including Etch-a-Sketch tracing, shape/color form board, matching, and wheeled object naming. Mothers' ability to support the child pleasantly with structure, limits, and confidence in the child's success buffered the children from sadness and predicted children's socioemotional competence with peers. Maternal allowance of autonomy was a significant predictor for girls; maternal positive emotion with boys was a significant predictor for boys' scores on the teacher-rated Behar Problem Behavior Questionnaire and the Baumrind Preschool Behavior Q-Sort friendliness and assertiveness scales.

71. DePalma, D. J., & Foley, J. M. (Eds.) (1975). *Moral development: Current theory and research.* Hillsdale, New Jersey: Erlbaum.

This book examines critical issues pertinent in moral development such as the relationship between cognitive development and attainment of higher states of moral development, attempts at developing an objective measure of moral judgment, moral behavior in the life situation, developmental issues in moral development and personality, and the development of social concepts.

Contains: Staub (1975b)
Turiel (1975)

72. Derlega, V., & Grzelak, J. (Eds.) (1982). *Cooperation and helping behavior: Theories and research.* New York: Academic Press.

The important differences between cooperation and helping behavior are explored in the introduction. Both behaviors fall under the general category of positive social behavior. However, there are important differences in the two concepts. The authors explore the differences between exocentric motivation and endocentric motivation. Exocentric motivation is the basis for a person's helping because of actual or expected rewards. Endocentric motivation is the basis for a person's acting for others' benefit without any visible external reinforcement. The book is divided into chapters on the topics of cooperation and helping behavior.

Contains: Bar—Tal, D., Sharabany, R., Raviv, A. (1982),
Reykowski, J. (1982)

73. Deutsch, F. (1975). Effects of sex of subject and story character on preschoolers' perceptions of affective responses and intrapersonal behavior in story sequences. *Developmental Psychology, 11,* 112–113.

In a day care center for low-income children, 32 three- and four-year-olds were individually shown six three-card stories, half depicting main characters who were male, half female. The main character was alone in the first card, engaged in an incongruous negative interaction with characters in the second, and displayed positive affect in the third. Children's responses to the stories were scored for: accurate verbalization of character's affect and intrapersonal behavior and reasons for the final affective state that related to the interaction between the characters (card 2). Children performed better on same-sex than cross-sex stories. Those children with higher mental age scores scored significantly higher than their peers with lower scores on all stories.

74. Deutsch, F., & Madle, R. (1975). Empathy: Historic and current conceptualizations, measurement, and a cognitive theoretical perspective. *Human Development, 18,* 267–287.

This theoretical paper examines concepts of empathy: whether an empathic response is an understanding or sharing of affect, or a response to an object or another's affect. Also discussed are mechanisms to explain empathy. For example, empathy may involve a Freudian projection, when the internal becomes confused with the external. Or the empathic response may be considered cognitive and require clear self-other differentiation. Flavell has explained empathy via role-taking, an activity that tries to discriminate role attributes. Situational measures of empathy used in the 1960's are described together with psychometric characteristics.

75. Devoe, M., & Sherman, T. (1978). A microtechnology for teaching prosocial behavior to children. *Child Study Journal, 8,* (2), 83-92.

Third-grade children were taught to share by viewing videotapes of themselves and models in a situation involving sharing. The specific sharing behavior of the model was pointed out to the child and sharing was discussed. Results showed that the procedure was effective in increasing sharing immediately following the training and one week later.

76. DeVries, R., & Goncu, A. (1990). Interpersonal relations in four-year-old dyads from Constructivist and Montessori programs. In A. S. Honig (Ed.), *Optimizing early child care and education* (pp 11-28). London: Gordon & Breach.

Social-cognitive competence in playing a board game in pairs was assessed for forty 4-year-old children educated either in Montessori or in Constructivist classrooms. Analysis of interpersonal negotiation strategies showed that Constructivist program children were more advanced in their stage of social-cognitive competence. They used more valuing and coordination of thoughts, feelings, and wishes of self and other child. In the Constructivist classroom, teachers minimize exercise of authority and give children possibilities for autonomous construction of attitudes and principles to guide their interpersonal relations, which may account for their higher level of sociomoral development.

77. Dlugokinski, E. L., & Firestone, I. J. (1974). Other-centeredness and susceptibility to

charitable appeals: Effects of perceived discipline. *Developmental Psychology, 10,* 21–28.

Those 10- and 13-year-olds who reported that their mothers frequently used *inductive* discipline (other-oriented reasoning), were seen by their classmates as more considerate, and reported more other-centered values (e.g. "getting jobs that help others" rather than "having a life of comfort and pleasure"). They also donated more money to charity.

78. Dodge, K. A., Schlundt, D. C., Schocken, I., & Delugach, J. D. (1983). Social competence and children's sociometric status: The role of peer group entry strategies. *Merrill-Palmer Quarterly, 29* (3), 309–336.

The goal of this research was to uncover the patterns of social competence and success in children' peer group entry behavior. Popular, rejected, and neglected kindergarten boys and girls were asked to initiate play with two same-age peers in study 1, and were observed naturally interacting in free play in study 2. *Rejected* children engaged in 10 times as many disruptions of peer play as did the other groups, and were more likely to respond negatively to peer host remarks. *Neglected* children did more waiting and hovering. *Popular* children offered group-oriented statements or questions. They used tactics like imitating the others – in singing or ball-play. Popular children's Piagetian decentering – their empathic attunement to peer behaviors and desires – gained them group entry.

79. Dodge, M. K. (1984). Learning to care: Developing prosocial behavior among one-

and two-year-olds in group settings.
*Journal of Research and Development in
Education, 17* (2), 26-30.

The author expresses concern for the
development of positive social behavior
patterns among infants and toddlers in group
care. She notes that Chinese caregivers teach
1- and 2-year-olds to be gentle, helpful, and
caring. In Faigin's study of kibbutz babies 19
to 38 months, the children referred to all toys
as ours, and were encouraged to take turns and
share. Caregivers need to be warm, nurturant
persons who are directive, who value and
practice prosocial behaviors, yet who are
insistent and explicit in instructions to
children. In groups with familiar peers,
relationships may be more harmonious.

80. Doescher, S., & Sugawara, A. (1990). Sex
    role flexibility and prosocial behavior
    among preschool children. *Sex Roles, 22*
    (1/2), 111-123.

Research concerning sex differences in
children's prosocial behavior has shown no
definitive results, although when differences
are found, girls are more prosocial than boys.
The present study attempted to examine how the
variables of children's sex, age, IQ, and sex
role flexibility contributed to preschoolers' (16
boys and 18 girls ranging in age from 36-60
months) prosocial behavior. Sex role flexibility
referred to children's classification of sex-
typed traits as applicable to "both" boys and
girls. The Modified Prosocial Behavior
Questionnaire provided a measure of subject's
prosocial behavior according to teacher
ratings. Sex role flexibility and prosocial
behavior among boys were significantly and
positively related; among girls no significant
relationship was found.

81. Drabman, R., & Thomas, M. (1977). Children's imitation of aggressive and prosocial behavior when viewing alone and in pairs. *Journal of Communication, 27,* 199-205.

Forty black male preschoolers (age five years) watched one of two brief color films depicting the interactions of a clown named "Dodo" and an adult male. In the aggressive modeling film, Dodo is pictured in a room containing toys that "invite" aggressive action (e.g. a toy machine gun, a plastic mallet, a toy pistol, and a rubber knife). The adult joins Dodo, and begins to threaten and attack the clown with the toy weapons. In the prosocial modeling film, Dodo and the man play together with a different set of toys: a stuffed animal, a pretend service station and trucks, building logs, and an airplane. After viewing the film, each boy went, either individually or paired with a peer, to a nearby trailer. Dodo, with all toys from both films, waited inside. The experimenter introduced Dodo and told the boy(s) that he/they could play while the experimenter completed some paperwork. Boys' behaviors were recorded every ten seconds for instances of aggressive or prosocial interactions with Dodo, the materials, and (in the "pairs" condition) each other. Boys who watched the aggressive modeling film engaged in more aggression (e.g., assaulting the clown) than did those who viewed the prosocial film; while the second group demonstrated more constructive, friendly play. Boys who participated in pairs showed more aggression than those who played alone.

82. Dreman, S. B., & Greenbaum, C. W. (1976). Sharing behavior in Israeli school children: Cognitive and social learning factors. *Child Development, 47,* 186-194.

First-, fourth-, and seventh-grade Israeli boys (N=180) participated in a two-step experiment involving six different conditions. In part one, each boy drew a picture of a man and received a small bag of seven candies. The experimenter told the boy that if he wanted to he could share some of his candy with an absent classmate. Any donations would be made in private, by placing the candies in a separate bag. Experimental conditions that were manipulated were:

(1) whether or not the "donator" was identified
(2) whether or not the opportunity for reciprocity (receiving candies in return) existed and
(3) whether or not the intended recipient had made prior donations himself.

Older boys were more generous in their donations. Most first-graders did not donate any candies. They did so only in the condition where the "recipient" had previously donated candies (and reciprocity was expected).

83. Dunn, J. (1987). The beginnings of moral understanding. In J. Kagan & S. Lamb (Eds.), *The emergence of morality in young children.* Chicago: The University of Chicago Press.

Dunn explores the earliest stages of children's understanding of the "standards" of their social world and the feelings of those who share that world. During the second year of life, children make remarkable advances in their grasp of social rules and of the consequences of their actions for other people's feelings or needs. The author found in her observations of children in the home during their second and third years that empathic responses to others become more frequent during these years. However, the children also become more sophisticated concerning how to upset others. Such behavior shows that the children understand both how to hurt other people's feelings and also that such behavior is not acceptable to family members. The data make clear that by 24 months children's verbal comments show some grasp of the notion of responsibility and blame in relation to feelings and social rules. Evidence shows that the experience of growing up with a mother who explains and is concerned about others' feelings is associated with the development of conciliatory behavior.

84. Dunn, J., & Munn, P. (1986). Siblings and the development of prosocial behaviors. *International Journal of Behavioral Development, 9,* 265–284.

In a longitudinal study of siblings about 26 months older than their 18-month-old toddler siblings, there were significant correlations between prosocial behaviors of the siblings. The toddlers with older siblings who were more giving were more likely to be cooperative in turn. If the toddlers showed high levels of sharing, helping, comforting, and cooperating at 18 months, then six months later their older siblings showed higher cooperation. Thus, reciprocal prosocial behaviors of siblings influence the development of altruism in both members of the pair.

85. Eagly, A., & Crowley, M. (1986). Gender and helping behavior: A meta-analytic review of the social psychological literature. *Psychological Bulletin, 100,* 283–308.

Social-role theory proposes that the male gender role fosters helping that is heroic and chivalrous, whereas the female gender role fosters helping that is nurturant and caring. Results from a meta-analytic review of sex differences in helping behavior indicate that in general men helped more than women and women received more help than men. However, studies of helping have been primarily confined to short-term encounters with strangers. Three major explanatory factors emerged for the sex differences: (a) women perceived helping as more dangerous than men did, (b) men are more likely to help women if there is an audience present, and (c) if an individual was the only helper available, he or she tended to overcome limitations of sex-typed skills and vulnerability to danger.

86. Eckerman, C., Davis, C., & Didow, S. (1989). Toddlers' emerging ways of achieving social coordinations with a peer. *Child Development, 60* (2), 440-453.

Fourteen peer dyads were observed longitudinally at 16, 20, 24, 28, and 32 months of age to access developmental changes in social coordinations. Children were paired on the basis of birthdates (within two weeks of one another), lack of prior acquaintance, and a common meeting time. The actions of each dyad were videotaped from behind a one-way window while the children played. The predominant behavioral strategy enabling social coordinations throughout this age range was that of imitating another's non-verbal play actions. The authors propose that in the absence of verbal communication, toddlers *imitate actions* to facilitate the perception of being connected with another toddler, of the other being like oneself, and of successfully exerting social control over another's actions.

87. Edelstein, W. (Ed.) (1987). *Contemporary approaches to social cognition*. Frankfurt: Suhrkamp.

Contains: Blasi, A. (1987)

88. Eisenberg, N. (Ed.). (1982). *The development of prosocial behavior*. New York: Academic Press.

Post-1972 data and theory are presented. The chapters address theoretical issues, cognitive aspects and conceptualizations of prosocial and altruistic behaviors, research and theory relating to specific aspects of prosocial development, and the role of affect and cognition in the development of prosocial behaviors.

Contains: Feshbach, N. (1982)
Grusec, J. (1982)
Hoffman, M. (1982)
Underwood & Moore (1982a)

89. Eisenberg, N. (1983). Children's differentiations among potential recipients of aid. *Child Development, 54,* 594-602.

Age and level of prosocial moral development are related to children's willingness to help others portrayed as needing assistance. Moral dilemmas were presented to 125 children from 2nd, 4th, 6th, 9th, 11th and 12th grades. Responses were scored for willingness to help, uncertainty, and refusal to help, as well as the reasons for and against helping (e.g. whether person in need was familiar, seen but not known, of a different racial/ethic/religious background/or criminal). Children's willingness to help, despite different characteristics of potential recipients, increased with age. Controlling for age, those children with higher moral reasoning scores made fewer differentiations about whom they would help. Differentiations that seemed most influential were: those close to self (family/friends); dislike for an individual; and the potential recipient's "moral character". Eisenberg suggests that at higher levels of moral reasoning, children focus more on the value of the moral act itself rather than on their attachment to the person in need or on their own personal outcomes.

90. Eisenberg, N. (1986). *Altruistic emotion, cognition, and behavior.* Hillsdale, NJ: Lawrence Erlbaum.

The focus of this review of theories and researches is primarily on intrapsychic factors involved in prosocial responding. The author covers sympathy and emotions related to self-evaluative responses, which have been viewed as potential motivators for altruistic behaviors. She explores the relation of cognition and altruism, evaluates the degree to which various acts are considered altruistic, and relates altruistic values to accompanying cognitive processes basic to moral decision-making. Socialization and situational influences on altruism are addressed. Scoring systems are provided in detail both for moral judgment stages of Kohlberg and for Eisenberg's moral-reasoning categories. The latter include:

1. Obsessive and/or magical view of authority and/or punishment

2. Hedonistic reasoning: a) pragmatic orientation to gain for self; b) direct reciprocity with orientation to personal gain; c) affectional, friendship-related

moral reasoning

3. Non-hedonistic pragmatism (e.g. "I will help because I am strong")

4. Concern for others' needs: a) concern for others' material/physical needs; b) concern for others' psychological needs and what would make others happy

5. Concern with the human needs of others as living persons

6. Stereotyped reasoning: a) stereotypes of helping because it is nice or good versus bad; b) stereotyped images of what others would do, what would be the majority response; c) stereotyped images of others and their roles (e.g. give help because teachers are nice people)

7. Approval and interpersonal orientation (reasoning that others will like you if you help)

8. Overt empathic orientations: a) sympathetic orientation – being concerned about others; b) role-taking: trying to put oneself in another's place to see how another feels

9. Internalized affect: a) simple relation between positive affect and consequences (e.g. helping would make you feel good when you saw others out of danger of pain); b). internalized positive affect from self-respect and living up to internalized values and principles; c) internalized negative affect over consequences of behavior (feeling guilty if another person is hurt); d) internalized negative affect about self if "one does not do the right thing"

10. Other abstract or internalized types of reasoning: a) orientation to norms to uphold laws and take on duties and responsibilities; b) concern with the rights of others that might be violated if help is not given; c) generalized reciprocity – people would be better off if all people helped each other; d) concern with helping society as a whole be better through people behaving prosocially.

91. Eisenberg, N. (Ed.) (1989). *Empathy and related emotional responses.* San Francisco: Jossey-Bass.

The editor defines empathy as sharing the perceived emotion of another. Empathy involves differentiation between one's own and another's emotional state. Empathy is distinguished from 1) *affective perspective-taking,* where one can discern and identify others' emotional states; 2) *cognitive perspective-taking,* where one can grasp another's viewpoint; or 3) *sympathy,* which is an emotional response stemming from another's condition, but not identical to the other's emotion. Authors in this volume examine the origins and precursors of empathy, assessment and correlates of empathy, and how empathy is socialized.

> Contains: Kestenbaum, R., Farber, E. A., & Sroufe, L. A. (1989)
> Strayer, J., & Schroeder, M. (1989)

92. Eisenberg, N. (1991). Meta-analytic contributions to the literature of prosocial behavior. *Personality and Social Psychology Bulletin, 17* (3), 273–282.

Eisenberg discusses the use of applied meta-analytic techniques to the study of prosocial behavior. Meta-analytic procedures summarize across numerous studies, examine differences among subsets of studies that differ in critical ways, and test theoretically derived hypotheses. Eisenberg summarizes the findings of meta-analytic studies concerning: (a) the relation of sociocognitive capabilities such as role-taking and moral reasoning to prosocial behavior, (b) the relation of empathy and related emotional reactions to prosocial behavior, (c) the relation of general mood-- positive and negative--to prosocial behavior, (d) prosocial behavior in urban versus rural environments, (e) the effectiveness of the foot-in-the-door technique, and (f) gender differences in prosocial behavior.

93. Eisenberg, N., Boehnke, K., Schuler, P., & Silbereisen, R. K. (1985). The development of prosocial behavior and cognitions in German children. *Journal of Cross-Cultural Psychology, 16* (1), 69-82.

Both German and American preschoolers answered questions about whether a story protagonist should help the other character or not, and why. Preschoolers in both cultures used more hedonistic reasoning than did second-graders, who used less than fourth-graders. Fourth-grade students used more reciprocity and more "concern for humanness" reasoning. Second-graders described more needs-oriented reasoning.

94. Eisenberg, N., Cameron, E., Tryon, K., & Dodez, R. (1981). Socialization of prosocial behavior in the preschool classroom. *Developmental Psychology, 17,* 773-782.

Behaviors of 33 children (51 to 63 months) were videotaped and coded into three categories: social (playing together, asking for help); prosocial (sharing, comforting, giving assistance); and defensive (objecting verbally or physically to requests/initiations). Peers' and teachers' positive and negative reactions to prosocial behaviors were also coded. Teachers never responded positively to boys' prosocial behaviors, and reacted positively to girls between 11% (for spontaneous prosocial actions) and 5% of the time (compliance with asked-for behaviors). With peers, children tended to receive the types of reactions they gave (e.g., children who responded positively to others' prosocial behaviors received more positive responses in return).

95. Eisenberg, N., Cialdini, R. B., McCreath, H., & Shell, R. (1987). Consistency-based compliance: When and why do children become vulnerable? *Journal of Personality and Social Psychology, 52,* 1174-1181.

Children were taught to make puzzles so that they could later teach younger children to construct similar puzzles to give as gifts to hospitalized children. Some children were not given responsibility for teaching other children. Days and weeks later, those boys and girls who *had* been assigned responsibilities to *teach* others during the training donated more generously to needy children some of the gift certificates they had earned and also indicated that they would be willing to make more puzzles for sick children compared to the controls. Giving children early responsibilities for helping each other and assisting others less fortunate promotes early altruism.

77

96. Eisenberg, N., Cialdini, R. B., McCreath, H., & Shell, R. (1989). Consistency based compliance in children: When and why do consistency procedures have immediate effects? *International Journal of Behavioral Development, 3,* 351-367.

The effectiveness of a foot-in-the-door procedure on subsequent verbally reported prosocial intentions and enacted intentions was examined with 54 preschool and kindergarten children, 48 second-graders, and 44 fifth-graders. Children either did or did not experience a situation where they were induced to comply with an adult request to share prize coupons, and half of each group was then labeled or not labeled as helpful. The children were then asked about how they would behave in a number of situations in which prosocial behavior was an option. Girls who had been *labeled helpful* showed more consistency in prosocial intentions. The prosocial indices varied as a function of children's grade, their understanding of traits (such as helpful) and their belief that adults valued consistency in children.

97. Eisenberg, N., Fabes, R., Miller, P., Fultz, J., Shell, R., Mathy, R., & Reno, R. (1989). Relation of sympathy and personal distress to prosocial behavior: A multimethod study. *Journal of Personality and Social Psychology, 57* (1), 55-66.

Participants (66 second-graders, 69 fifth-graders and 69 undergraduate students) were shown two tapes, one showing a mother distressed because her children had been in a serious car accident and much in need of help with household duties. After viewing the tapes, the participants had an opportunity to help the mother - adults by volunteering time to help the mother do household chores and the children by giving up recess time to organize the homework for the injured children who were in the hospital. Sympathy and personal distress was assessed via facial and physiological indexes (heart rate) as well as self-report indexes. These measures were then related to the various indexes of prosocial behavior. Heart rate deceleration during exposure to the needy others was associated with increased willingness to help. For both children and adults, facial concern was positively related to the indexes of prosocial behavior. Facial distress was negatively related to prosocial intentions and behavior with children. Sympathy and personal distress may be differentially related to prosocial behavior.

98. Eisenberg, N., Fabes, R., Miller, P. A., Shell, R., Shea, C., & Traci, M. (1990). Preschoolers' vicarious emotional responding and their situational and dispositional prosocial behavior. *Merrill-Palmer Quarterly, 36,* (4) 507-529.

Preschoolers (N=53) viewed empathy-eliciting videotapes of children who accidentally fell from a treehouse and were hospitalized. Then the preschoolers had an opportunity to assist the hospitalized children by putting crayons in boxes for them, rather than playing with toys. Heart rate (HR) deceleration and facial sadness while viewing the tape were positively related to the children's prosocial helping; HR acceleration and facial personal distress were related to not helping. Compliant prosocial behaviors, particularly among boys, were associated with low facial concern. The authors note that "compliant and spontaneous prosocial behaviors are fundamentally different".

99. Eisenberg, N., Hertz-Lazarowitz, R., & Fuchs, I. (1990). Prosocial moral judgment in Israeli kibbutz and city children: A longitudinal study. *Merrill-Palmer Quarterly, 36,* (2), 273-286.

Children's reasoning about prosocial moral dilemmas (wherein the needs and wants of one person conflict with another but the role of authorities, laws, and punishments are minimal) is often hedonistic or needs-oriented (that is, primitive empathic reasoning whereby the child simply orients to the other's need). Israeli children (24 kibbutz and 28 city) were interviewed in third grade and later in sixth grade. Prosocial moral reasoning was assessed with four dilemmas (such as helping a child being beat up by a bully or helping a woman whose purse was being stolen). The children were asked to describe what the story protagonist would do and why. City children verbalized more pragmatic and hedonistic reasoning; kibbutz children verbalized more concern than city children with humanness (reflecting empathic concerns) and direct reciprocity reasoning (which reflects ideas of group membership and obligations). Children's prosocial reasoning matched their cultural milieu's values. Social contract reasoning increased with age, and needs-oriented reasoning decreased, but no sex differences were found.

100. Eisenberg, N., & Lennon, R. (1983). Sex differences in empathy and related capacities. *Psychological Bulletin, 94,* 100-131.

Sex differences between males and females in emotional responses to another's distress tend to disappear when physiological measures are used rather than the usual self-report measures, in which females consistently report more distress and empathy.

101. Eisenberg, N., Lennon, R., & Roth, K. (1983). Prosocial development: A longitudinal study. *Developmental Psychology, 19*, 846-855.

Developmental changes in prosocial moral judgment were examined for 33 children (seven to eight years) interviewed first at 36 and 18 months prior to the present study. From the preschool to elementary school years, needs-oriented (empathic) reasoning increased in frequency of use, whereas hedonistic reasoning decreased. Developmentally mature prosocial moral judgments were related to non-authoritarian, non-punitive maternal practices. Positive parenting discipline techniques enhance a child's chances to become more prosocial.

102. Eisenberg, N., Lundy, T., Shell, R., & Roth, K. (1985). Children's justifications for their adult and peer-directed compliant (prosocial and non-prosocial) behaviors. *Developmental Psychology, 21*, 325-331.

Middle-class preschoolers (N=61) between the ages of 45 and 64 months were observed at play in their preschool classrooms. When a child was observed to comply with a request, the researchers asked *why*, to assess possible differences in motives for compliance with peers or adults. Children used authority/punishment explanations more frequently to justify compliance with adults, while concerns for others' needs and affectional relationship justifications were used to explain their compliance with peer requests. This may reflect, in part, real differences in the types of requests peers and adults make. Only 32% of compliant behaviors to a teacher directly benefited another, whereas 76% of compliance behaviors in response to peer requests were prosocial.

103. Eisenberg, N., McCreath, H., & Ahn, R. (1988). Vicarious emotional responsiveness and prosocial behavior: Their interrelations in young children. *Personality and Social Psychology Bulletin, 14,* (2), 298-311.

Four- and five-year-old children (N=62) viewed a videotape of a distressing situation - for example: a peer is injured while playing on the playground. Afterward, the children played in pairs with a simple "jumping frog toy". Each child then watched a different "distress" videotape and answered questions and pointed to pictures to indicate how s/he felt. Self-reports of emotion were categorized as positive, undifferentiated, negative, sad, and fearful. Pointing responses were coded as happy, sad, angry/upset or neutral. Children who expressed anxiety during the "distress" tapes were more likely to ask for help during the play sessions. Expressions of sadness/concern were positively associated with spontaneous sharing.

104. Eisenberg, N., & Miller, P. (1987). The relation of empathy to prosocial and related behaviors. *Psychological Bulletin, 101,* 91-119.

The degree of positive association between measures of empathy and prosocial behaviors depends on the measure of empathy used. No significant relationship between frequently used picture-story measures of empathy and prosocial responding has been found. Empathy self-reports via questionnaire are positively correlated with prosocial behaviors for adults and children, while self-reports in simulated situations are unrelated to prosocial acts for children. Observer's reports of empathy and prosocial behavior are positively correlated. Physiological indices are positively correlated with feelings of anxiety and sadness, but the relation between these and prosocial responding has not been sufficiently tested. Experimental training procedures directed at enhancing empathy are effective in increasing prosocial responding.

105. Eisenberg, N., & Mussen, P. (1978). Empathy and moral development in adolescence. *Developmental Psychology, 14,* 185-186.

The relationship between empathy, volunteering, and moral reasoning was studied in 9th-, 11th-, and 12th-graders. Students completed an affective empathy questionnaire; were invited to assist the examiner voluntarily in an hour-long task at a different time; and were presented with four moral dilemmas where the needs/wants of the participants would conflict with those of the people in the story, but without any context of obligation, authority, or law.

Boys high in empathy volunteered more frequently than girls. Scores on empathy and the moral judgment dilemmas were significantly positively correlated for both sexes. Comparison of empathy scores and student perceptions of parental childrearing practices (assessed through questionnaire) revealed a positive correlation between high empathy in males and mothers who were non-punitive, non-restrictive, egalitarian, willing to discuss problems, and had high expectations for their sons (with respect to impressing others). No significant relationship was found for father-son childrearing practices or for either parent with daughters. The authors suggest that this may be due to girls' relatively high empathy compared to boys.

106. Eisenberg, N., & Mussen, P. (1989). *The roots of prosocial behavior in children*. New York: Cambridge University Press.

The roles of biology, culture, childrearing practices, the media, peers, personal characteristics, and situational determinants for the development of prosocial behavior are summarized in this fine text. Prosocial behavior can be learned according to these authors, and many ideas for enhancing prosocial development in children are shared.

107. Eisenberg, N., Pasternack, E., & Cameron, E. (1984). The relation of quantity and mode of prosocial behavior to moral cognitions and social style. *Child Development, 55,* 1479-1485.

Four-year-olds were observed, videotaped, and interviewed to determine the relationships between their social interactions, moral judgments, self-attributions and frequency of prosocial acts. Each child was videotaped during play to document the degree of sociability with peers. In addition, an observer circulated through the play room noting instances of prosocial behavior and asking the children why they had responded in that fashion. Finally, moral judgment data was gathered using stories portraying moral dilemmas. Frequency of *spontaneous* prosocial behavior related positively to degree of sociability with peers and children's own moral judgments, and related to a limited degree to types of self-attributions. Children frequently viewed a prosocial act as pragmatic--carried out when it cost them little. Frequency of *requested* prosocial responding was related to sociability only. Perhaps many prosocial acts are performed almost automatically, with little internal conflict or perceived cost to the actor.

108. Eisenberg, N., & Randall, H. (1988). Vicarious emotional responsiveness and prosocial behaviors: Their interrelations in young children. *Personality and Social Psychology Bulletin, 14,* 298-311.

Preschooler's (N=62, aged 46 to 68 months) sad/concerned and anxious facial/gestural reactions and self-report of emotion in response to others' distress were obtained. Prosocial behaviors (spontaneous and requested) were assessed in peer-interactions in a semi-naturalistic setting. Sad/concerned facial/gestural reactions were positively associated with sharing in a situation in which sharing was likely to be altruistically motivated (i.e., spontaneous actions) and, for girls only, with assisting when escape from the other's request was difficult (i.e., requested prosocial behavior). In addition, children who tended to express anxiety when viewing others in distress elicited more requests for assistance.

109. Eisenberg, N., Reykowski, J., & Staub, E. (1989). *Social and moral values: Individual and societal perspectives.* Hillsdale, NJ: Lawrence Erlbaum.

This collection of edited chapters provides viewpoints in the field of moral judgment by experts from different social contexts and geographical areas. Chapters address questions concerning the genesis and relativism of prosocial values, moral principles, and prosocial activism. Several authors discuss the relationships between self-theory, self-identity, and prosocial values. Issues of work, parental socialization values, and sociopolitical systems are also addressed in relation to prosocial learnings.

110. Eisenberg, N., Schaller, M., Fabes, R. A., Bustamante, D., Mathy, R. M., Shell, R., & Rhodes, K. (1988). Differentiation of personal distress and sympathy in children and adults. *Developmental Psychology, 24,* 766-775.

Third- and sixth-grade students (N=117) and college students (N=90) discussed neutral topics with the experimenter (routes they traveled to school); recalled and described an experience or event where they felt anxious or distressed; and remembered and described an experience where they felt sorry for someone else, but were not distressed or anxious (sympathy). Heart rates were recorded during all procedures, via electrocardiogram. Females demonstrated more sympathy and reported more distress than did males. Heart rates were higher during distress than in sympathy induction, and they returned to normal during neutral periods.

111. Eisenberg, N., Shell, R., Pasternak, J., Lennon, R., Beller, R., & Mathy, R. M. (1987). Prosocial development in middle childhood: A longitudinal study. *Developmental Psychology,*

23, 712-718.

Results of a previous longitudinal study were extended by five- and seven-year follow ups, yielding information on the development of prosocial moral judgment over a seven-year age span (four to eleven years). Children responded to four moral dilemmas, completed empathy and social desirability scales, and helped adults on brief tasks rated by "cost" of assistance to the helper. Hedonistic reasoning decreased with age, while needs-oriented (primitive empathic) reasoning increased with age until 7-8, then leveled off. More advanced forms of reasoning (role-taking, sympathetic) and pleasure related to consequences of a prosocial act increased with age.

112. Eisenberg, N., & Shell, T. (1986). Prosocial moral judgment behavior in children: The mediating role of cost. *Personality and Social Psychology Bulletin, 12,* 426-433.

Fifty-six preschoolers responded to four illustrated moral dilemmas where the needs or wants of the main story characters were in conflict with those of another. Children described what they thought the main character should do in this conflict and why. In addition, children had opportunities to donate objects to and help others. In the donation condition, children received either ten identical unattractive stickers (low-cost condition) or ten different attractive stickers of their choice (high-cost condition). Children could privately donate some of their stickers to poor children in the experimenter's absence. High-cost donating was negatively related to hedonistic moral reasoning, but positively related to needs-oriented reasoning. In the helping condition, children had the choice of playing with some interesting toys or sorting paper to be used in an activity by hospitalized children who "needed something fun to do" (high-cost condition). In the low-cost helping condition, no toys or alternative activity were available. Children helped less when the cost of helping was high.

113. Eisenberg, N., & Strayer, J. (Eds.) (1987). *Empathy and its development.* New York: Cambridge University Press.

Researchers and theorists examine significant aspects of empathy which Staub defines as "apprehending another's inner world and joining the other in his or her feelings" (p. 104). Contributors clarify the role of empathy in human survival, personal development, and as a source of moral principles. Empathy is enhanced by: affective synchrony in mother-infant play, the availability of empathic models for young children, secure early attachment, caregiver encouragement of the child's positive self-concept, perception of child as similar to others, and discouragement of excessive competition. Researchers review studies on: maladaptive parenting and its inverse relation to empathy, gender and age changes in the development of empathy, and measures of empathy.

Contains: Feshbach, N. (1987)

114. Eisenberg-Berg, N. (1979). The development of children's prosocial moral judgement. *Developmental Psychology, 15,* 128-137.

Elementary and high school, white middle SES children (66 males and 59 females) responded to four stories designed to tap prosocial moral reasoning. Subjects were asked what the story character should do and why he or she should act in the advocated manner. Elementary school children's reasoning tended to be hedonistic, stereotyped, approval oriented, interpersonally oriented and/or tended to involve labeling of others' needs. High school students used substantial amounts of reasoning which reflected strongly empathic and more abstract and/or internalized moral concerns.

115. Eisenberg-Berg, N. & Geisheker, E. (1979). Content of preachings and power of the model/preacher: The effect on children's generosity. *Developmental Psychology, 15,* 168-175.

For 8- and 9-year-old children, the effect of empathic preaching, which emphasized how happy and excited recipients of sharing would be, led to greater altruism than when the children were exposed to exhortations which urged normatively that people ought to share.

116. Eisenberg-Berg, N., & Hand, M. (1979). The relationship of preschoolers' reasoning about prosocial moral conflicts to prosocial behavior. *Child Development, 50,* 356-363.

Second-grade children were presented with same-sex story characters in moral conflict situations and the children's moral judgments and reasonings were elicited. Each of the children's responses was coded into one of the following categories:

Obsessive and/or magical view of authority and punishment
Pragmatic, hedonistic gain
Direct reciprocity
Affectional relationship

Non-hedonistic pragmatism
Concern for others' physiological needs
Concern for others' psychological needs
References to humanness
Stereotype of a good/bad person
Approval/interpersonal orientation
Role-taking
Simple internalized positive affect and
positive affect related to consequences
Internalized negative affect over
consequences of behavior
Internalized law, norm, and value
orientation
Generalized reciprocity

117. Eisenberg-Berg, N., & Lennon, R. (1980).
Altruism and the assessment of empathy in
preschool years. *Child Development, 51,* 552-
557.

The authors examined the relationship
between empathy and spontaneous prosocial
behaviors of 51 children (*M*=4-5 years). Four
stories depicting happy or sad events were
read to each child, who was then asked: to
state how she felt; how the main character
felt; and to point to the picture of the face
(sad or happy) that matched how the child felt
(non-verbal response). In addition, each child
was observed for 10 weeks in a free play
situation with peers for instances of
spontaneous sharing, helping, and offering
comfort. High empathic responding on the
stories was negatively correlated with
spontaneous prosocial behaviors, although the
relationship was slightly more positive for non-
verbal rather than verbal empathy scores. The
authors suggest that perhaps empathy scores
do not reflect empathy, but a desire to
respond in a socially approved manner. What
children say to gain adult approval and how
they act may not be highly correlated.

118. Eisenberg-Berg, N., & Neal, C. (1979). Children's moral reasoning about their own spontaneous prosocial behavior. *Developmental Psychology, 15* (2), 228-229.

No sex or age differences were found for 48- to 63-month- old preschoolers observed and questioned on the spot by a familiar experimenter about their spontaneous helping, sharing, or comforting behaviors over a 12 week period. The children justified their behaviors primarily with references to others' needs (25%) and pragmatic considerations (25%) and used little punishment or authority-oriented, approval-oriented, or hedonistic reasoning.

119. Elardo, R., & Freund, J. J. (1981). Maternal childrearing styles and the social skills of learning disabled boys: A preliminary investigation. *Contemporary Educational Psychology, 6,* 86-94.

Maternal childrearing styles were assessed in 15 homes of learning disabled boys with the Home Environmental Process Inventory (HEPI). A correlation of .83 between children's role-taking and mothers' press for consideration of others' needs suggests that mothers who value highly a child's sympathy and concern for other children and ability to get along with adults will have children who are successful at taking the role of another *despite* having a learning disability. Two measures of social skills, role-taking and interpersonal problem-solving, were administered to each child. The .61 correlation between children's role-taking scores and the STAUB subscale suggests that mothers *who encourage their children to be socially responsible by doing home chores* have children who can take the point of view of others, and be empathic. Mothers who reported: 1) *employing induction as a discipline technique,* and 2) *orienting their children to the consequences of their misbehavior for others*, facilitated the children's problem-solving skills in interpersonal conflicts.

120. Elias, M. J., Gara, M. A., Schuyler, T. F., Branden-Muller, L. R., & Sayette, M. A. (1991). The promotion of social competence: Longitudinal study of a preventive school-based program. *American Journal of Orthopsychiatry, 61* (3), 409-417.

Children in a two-year, intensive, elementary school-based prevention program (ISA-SPS) aimed at promoting positive social skills, were followed up five and six years later. Children in both regular and special education programs who learn the skills show improved social adjustment. The ISA-SPS curriculum has three phases. In the Readiness Phase, children learn self-control, group participation, and social awareness. In the Instructional Phase, the eight steps for social decision-making and problem-solving include: affect, problem analysis and goal-setting, means-ends thinking, and anticipation of obstacles. In the Application Phase, teachers are trained with specific lesson activities to ensure reinforcement and extension of SPS skills. Children in grades 9-11 who had two years of this program in grades 4 and 5, in comparison with control classes, showed less vandalism against parental property, less hitting or threatening parents, and less use of illegal substances. They "showed higher levels of positive prosocial behavior and lower levels of antisocial, self-destructive and socially disordered behaviors" (p. 415). Sex differences were strong. Control boys showed more alcohol use and control girls more tobacco use. The authors note that more continuity and reinforcement of skills in the students' home and peer social environments is needed and that teacher monitoring and support are crucial for the program to work.

121. Ember, N. P., & Rushton, J. P. (1974). Cognitive-developmental factors in children's generosity. *British Journal of Social Clinical Psychology, 13,* 277-281.

Sixty working-class children (7-13 years) attending a play center were asked to outwit an experimenter in a game, by preventing him from winning either of two coins concealed under two cups. They were told their opponent knew that they would try to fool him. Their choice of strategies, revealed through questioning, was a measure of role-taking ability. Piagetian stories were used to elicit children's concepts of distributive justice (for example, the sharing of food when one child has lost his portion). A bowling game was played and a "Save the Children Fund" bowl was available to donate won tokens. Sympathy-arousing cues were manipulated through describing the child shown on the Fund poster. In the non-sympathy condition, the poster child was matter-of-factly described. No sex differences were found. Increases in generosity with age are attributable to developmental transformations in children's concepts of distributive justice. No relation between role-taking capacity and generosity was found, or between sympathy manipulation and generosity. Changes in generosity may be related to changes in a child's understanding of moral norms rather than changes in the child's capacity to experience sympathy.

122. Emde, R. N., Johnson, W. F., & Easterbrooks, M. A. (1987). The do's and don'ts of early

moral development: Psychoanalytic tradition and current research. In J. Kagan & S. Lamb (Eds.), *The emergence of morality in young children* (pp. 245-276). Chicago, IL: University of Chicago Press.

The authors describe psychoanalytic and attachment theorists' ideas about how early parenting practices help a child develop affect sharing, affect attunement, and empathy. In the laboratory, *mutual referencing and sharing of positive affect* occurred frequently among twelve-month olds and their mothers, and this can facilitate striving to do what the parents do and approve.

123. Enright, R. D., Franklin, C. C., & Manheim, L. A. (1980). Childrens's distributive justice reasoning: A standardized and objective scale. *Developmental Psychology, 16*, 193-202.

The Distributive Justice Scale presents subjects with two dilemmas. Each dilemma is followed by 18 pairs of pictures. The subject is asked to point to the picture from each pair which best ends the story. There are three picture pairings per dilemma. This measure is applicable to preschoolers with low verbal skills. A significant increase in understanding of distributive justice was found for older children compared with preschoolers.

124. Erikson, E. (1964). *Insight and responsibility*. New York: Norton.

Erikson elaborates on his neo-analytic theory that the failure of the development of basic trust between infant and caregiver and the failure of harmonious mutuality between parent and child is the basis of pathogenic social development and the child's lack of development of moral and ethical characteristics and striving.

125. Fabes, R. A., Eisenberg, N., McCormick, S. E., & Wilson, M. S. (1988). Preschoolers attributions of the situational determinants of others' naturally occurring emotions. *Developmental Psychology, 24,* 376-385.

Fifty-three girls and sixty-one boys were observed in six preschool classrooms. When overt expressions of emotion occurred, observers recorded the emotions displayed, the sex of the child, and the situational factors that preceded (elicited) the emotion. If two or more children were involved, the child whose emotions were most obvious was selected as the target child. After the event, observers questioned a nearby child about the reason for the emotions the classmate displayed. If the emotion was negative (sad, angry), the child was asked to describe ways s/he could help the classmate to feel better. Children's strategies for intervening included: physical (hugging); verbal (saying "It's okay"); social (inviting the child to play); material (sharing a toy); or helping (fixing something). When describing ways to intervene in order to help their classmate feel better, children suggested physical or verbal strategies for sad or distress reactions, and material responses for angry displays.

126. Fabes, R. A., Fultz, J., Eisenberg, N., May-Plumlee, T., & Christopher, F. S. (1989). Effects of rewards on children's prosocial motivation: A socialization study.

Developmental Psychology, 25, 509-515.

Mothers' attitudes toward rewarding their 7-9 or 9-11 year-old children were assessed and then the 72 subjects were assigned to control or experimental conditions, which differed in whether children received rewards for helping and whether children engaged in helping tasks or watched other children help. Children were given an opportunity to help in a non-reward free-choice period. Children whose mothers felt positive about using rewards to promote prosocial behaviors showed *less* prosocial behavior in the free-choice periods. Their mothers reported that the children showed less spontaneous or requested prosocial behavior. Mothers who have very positive feelings about using instrumental rewards may *undermine* their children's internalized desire to behave prosocially by increasing the salience of external rather than internal rewards. Or parents of children who show fewer prosocial behaviors may feel that they need to use more rewards to get their child to behave prosocially.

127. Feshbach, N. (1975). Empathy in children: Some theoretical and empirical considerations. *The Counseling Psychologist, 5,* 25-30.

Is empathy a *cognitive* product mediated by emotional factors or an *affective* response mediated by cognitive processes? The author argues that an adequate understanding of empathy must take into account both cognitive and affective factors. Two of the components of empathy are cognitive and involve the person's discriminating the emotional capacity and responsiveness of other persons. While the cognitive dimension of empathy is important, it is the affective component that gives the empathy construct its uniqueness. A summary of research distinguishes two promising training techniques for increasing empathy in children. One is the use of role-playing and the second is to maximize the perceived similarity between the observer and the stimulus person.

128. Feshbach, N. (1978). Studies of the development of children's empathy. In B. Maher (Ed.), *Progress in experimental personality research*. New York: Academic Press.

No relationship was found between empathy (as measured by Feshbach & Roe's Affective Situation Test) and the sharing/helping behavior of six-to-eight-year-olds.

129. Feshbach, N. (1982). Sex differences in empathy and social behavior in children. In N. Eisenberg (Ed.), *The development of prosocial behavior*. New York: Academic Press.

The responses of 240 children aged 5 to 11 years (from five schools) of varying SES and ethnicity were used to develop a trio of empathy-related measures (the *affective matching measure, emotional responsiveness measure and Feshbach & Powell audiovisual test for empathy*). Prosocial behavior could not be used as the only criterion for empathy. The sex of child, the euphoric and dysphoric nature of the vicariously experienced affect (happiness and pride vs. sadness, fear, and anger) and the intensity of the child's affective experience – all influence empathy.

130. Feshbach, N. (1987). Parental empathy and child adjustment/maladjustment. In N. Eisenberg & J. Strayer (Ed.), *Empathy and its development*. New York: Cambridge University Press.

A theoretical model is presented in which parental empathy (that is neither intrusive nor smothering) plays a significant role in facilitating positive social competence in children. Research is summarized to support this model. Child-centered parents, who promote affectionate attachment and do not use physical punishment have children with more positive social skills. In a study, carried out with Carollee Howes, the author observed 117 mother-child pairs (abusive, non-abusive, and clinic clients) in a laboratory session. The mothers completed questionnaires measuring empathy, stress, and social support. On the Feshbach Parent/Partner Empathy Measure, a pencil and paper inventory, mothers indicate, for 40 statements in a Likert format, which are true always, usually, sometimes or never. Although the measure of child compliance was unrelated to the total empathy score, there was a significant correlation (r=.49) between mother's total empathy score and amount of self-control shown by the preschooler in the laboratory.

In a second study, 56 mothers and 41 fathers of 62 children (8-11 years) completed the Parent/Partner Empathy Measure, the Achenbach Child Behavior Checklist, and the Block. The greater the discipline discrepancy between parents, the lower was the maternal empathy score (r=-.55) and the paternal empathy score (r=-.54). Low parental empathy was also associated with more child behavior symptoms.

131. Feshbach, N., & Feshbach, S. (1969). The relationship between empathy and aggression in two age groups. *Developmental Psychology* *1*, 102–107.

The authors test the prediction that empathy should function as an inhibitor of overt aggressive behavior by using experimental measures of empathy and teachers' ratings of aggressive behavior for 40 6- and 7-year-olds and 48 4- and 5-year-olds. In the older age group, high-empathy boys were significantly less aggressive than low-empathy boys, while the converse was true for younger boys. There were no significant differences between high- and low-empathy girls at either age level. The contrasting relationship between empathy and aggression for boys at the two age levels appears to be a function of developmental changes in the role of aggression and social behavior.

132. Feshbach, S., & Feshbach, N. (1986). Aggression and altruism: A personality perspective. In C. Zahn-Waxler, M. Chapman, & M. Radke-Yarrow (Eds.), *Aggression and altruism: Biological and social origins* (pp. 189–217). Cambridge: Cambridge University Press.

The authors reason that the empathic child is likely to be sensitive to the feelings of others, more able to understand another child's perspective in a conflict, and more apt to act generously, cooperatively and be less aggressive than children low in empathy. Parent empathy (plus stimulation and reinforcement of the child's empathic behavior) is seen as an important link in the causal process, and empirical evidence is offered to support this linkage.

133. Flavell, J. H., & Markman, E. M. (Eds.)(1983). *Cognitive development,* Vol. III, in P. H. Mussen (Series Ed.), *Handbook of child psychology* (4th ed.). New York: John Wiley.

Contains: Rest, J. R. (1983)

134. Forge, K. L. S., & Phemister, S. (1987). The effect of prosocial cartoons on preschool children. *Child Study Journal, 17,* 83-88.

Children aged three to five (N=40) watched one of four 15 minute video programs: prosocial animated (The Get Along Gang); neutral animated (Alvin and the Chipmunks); prosocial non-animated (Mr. Rogers' Neighborhood); and neutral non-animated (Animal Express). Each child was observed immediately after for a three-minute period during free play in his/her classroom. Instances of sharing, cooperating, turn-taking, and positive verbal/physical contact were counted. Children who had watched one of the prosocial programs demonstrated significantly more prosocial behaviors.

135. Freeman, E. B., & Daly, J. (1984). Distributive justice in children: Its relationship to immanent justice and egocentrism. *Early Child Development and Care, 16* (Nos. 3 & 4), 173-184.

Twenty-one preschoolers and 24 second-graders completed the Distributive Justice Scale, responded to immanent justice stories, and participated in an adaptation of Piaget's mountain task (where a child in fixed position has to tell what view a doll has, when the doll is seated at different compass points). In this adaptation, the child selected from a series of drawings the one which represented a configuration of blocks that a stuffed animal would see from different vantage points. The Distributive Justice Scale presented a child with two dilemmas, followed by 18 pairs of pictures with each picture representing one of Damon's six stages. The child chooses from each pair the picture which best ends the story. Two Piaget story vignettes with cartoon illustrations represented a "bad" behavior followed by bad luck, and two of "good" behavior followed by good luck. A high score reflected a greater belief in immanent justice. Egocentrism scores were negatively correlated with immanent justice scores. There was no significant correlation between the two moral attributes, immanent justice (which relies on a child's cause-and-effect understanding) and distributive justice (which emphasizes fairness issues). No age trends were found in the distributive justice scores which suggests that even preschoolers understand fairness and equity toward others.

136. Friedrich, L. K., & Stein, A. H. (1973). Aggressive and prosocial television programs and the natural behavior of preschool children. *Monographs of the Society for Research in Child Development, 38,* (4, serial No. 151).

Ninety-three preschool children, enrolled in a nine-week nursery school session, saw one of three types of television programs: aggressive cartoons, neutral films, or prosocial programs (Mister Rogers' Neighborhood). The children were also observed in free play during and after exposure to the films which occurred *daily* during the middle four weeks of the nursery school session. Children who saw the prosocial programs daily showed higher levels of task persistence, rule obedience, and tolerance of delay of gratification. Additionally, children from low-SES families showed increased cooperative play, nurturance, and verbalization of feelings.

137. Friedrich, L. K., & Stein, A. H. (1975). Prosocial television and young children: The effects of verbal labeling and role-playing on learning and behavior. *Child Development, 46,* 27-38.

Seventy-three kindergarten children watched a television program and participated in a follow-up activity in one of five conditions: neutral TV and irrelevant training (individual games); prosocial TV and irrelevant training; prosocial TV and verbal labeling training (using a book which highlighted feelings and actions of characters in the program); prosocial TV and role-playing (with puppets); and prosocial TV with verbal labeling and role-playing. Children completed a content test for recall of characters and events from the programs, to assess their learning. Two tests of generalization and implementation of prosocial learning were used: puppet play (to assess spontaneous production of verbal and non-verbal prosocial behavior) and a behavioral helping measure (opportunity to assist an absent child by repairing that child's torn art work). Children who had viewed the prosocial TV program demonstrated greater knowledge of content than those who watched neutral TV. Prosocial TV with verbal labeling training increased helping behavior for girls, while role-playing was a more effective treatment for boys. Caregivers may need to *tailor* a variety of techniques in order to assist individual children in increasing prosocial interactions.

138. Friedrich-Cofer, L. K., Huston-Stein, A., Kipnis, D. M., Susman, E. J., & Clewitt, A. S. (1979). Environmental enhancement of prosocial television content: Effects on interpersonal behavior, imaginative play, and self regulations in a natural setting. *Developmental Psychology, 15*, 637-646.

Positive effects of prosocial TV programs were greater when other aspects of the environment were supportive. Head Start classrooms were assigned to 1) neutral TV with unrelated play items; 2) prosocial TV with unrelated play items; 3) prosocial TV with toys that related to the programs; or 4) prosocial teachers who were experienced in theme-rehearsal activities. Groups 3 and 4 were significantly more prosocial in their interactions after training. Prosocial TV by itself showed few behavioral effects. Only those children who watched prosocial TV and also rehearsed program themes (through acting them out) increased in prosocial interactions.

139. Froming, W. J., Allen, L., & Jensen, R. (1985). Altruism, role-taking, and self-awareness: The acquisition of norms governing altruistic behavior. *Child Development, 56*, 1223-1228.

This two-part study examined the relationship between self-awareness and altruism, as well as the possible contribution of role-taking abilities to facilitate altruistic behaviors. Three stages of altruistic development were postulated: (I) presocialization with sporadic altruism and lack of self-awareness; (2) realization that adults value altruistic acts, and such acts increase with adults present; (3) endorsement of altruistic norms, independent of adult presence.

In study 1, 222 children (grades 1-3) were given an opportunity to donate M & M's to absent peers with none, under these conditions: a) alone; b) with a non-evaluative adult; c) with an evaluative adult; d) alone but in view of a mirror reflecting child's actions. There was no effect of mirror. Six-year-olds showed no effect of adult presence but seven-year-olds showed perspective-shifting by donating more when adults were present.

In study 2, 143 children were asked to describe stories from another's perspective to assess their role-taking abilities. The same donation procedures were then used. Grade level and role-taking abilities were positively correlated. Role-taking facilitation is not sufficient for altruistic behaviors, since these also depend on the particular situation, such as public or private setting and child's age.

140. Fuchs, I., Eisenberg, N., Hertz-Lazarowitz, R., & Sharabany, R. (1986). Kibbutz, Israeli City, and American children's moral reasoning about prosocial moral conflicts. *Merrill Palmer Quarterly, 32,* (1), 37-50.

Prosocial moral reasoning of middle-class Israeli city children (N=36), kibbutz (N=29), and American third-graders (N=55) were compared on four moral reasoning dilemmas, in which the needs or wants of one person are in conflict with those of others in a situation with no pressure from rules, punishment, laws, and authority. One example dealt with a child going to a birthday party who, along the way, encounters a hurt peer who wants to have her parents notified. Should the child help and miss out on the party? What should the child do? Protocols were scored according to the reasoning categories of Eisenberg-Berg: Hedonistic, direct reciprocity, affectional relationship, pragmatic, physical needs-oriented, humanism, good/bad stereotypes, majority behaviors, focus on others' approval, role-taking, and internalized norms. Cultural differences were reflected in the children's judgments. Americans used more needs-oriented (primitive empathic) reasoning; Kibbutz children verbalized more concerns with the humanness of recipients and internalized laws; and Israeli city children used more reasoning based on explicit role-taking. American children differed somewhat from Israeli kibbutz and city children in using more needs-oriented reasoning in prosocial moral conflict problems. The Israelis used more reasoning related to direct reciprocity, prior relationships with others, internalized laws and norms, role-taking, humanness of potential recipients, and hedonistic concerns. Culture thus plays a role in prosocial moral reasoning. The kibbutz children live in a communal, egalitarian agricultural environment, in which many responsibilities, such as child care and material property, are shared.

141. Furman, W., Rahe, D. F., & Hartup, W. W. (1978). Rehabilitation of low-interactive preschool children through mixed-age and same-age socialization. Cited in H. McGurk (Ed.), *Issues in childhood social development.* Cambridge: Methuen.

An intervention experiment with young social isolates was carried on successfully in day care centers. The isolate played with a younger child, half of them with children 15 months younger and half with children 3 months younger. A control group received no treatment. Both experimental groups increased in sociability, but the one with younger therapist-playmates increased the most. Teachers can try pairing social isolate children with younger prosocial children in order to enhance the older child's positive social skills.

142. Gelfand, D. M., Hartmann, D. P., Cromer, C. C., Smith, C. L., & Page, B. C. (1975). The effects of instructional prompts and praise on children's donation rates. *Child Development, 46,* 980-983.

Kindergarten and first-grade children played a marble game where they earned pennies that they could exchange for prizes. The experimenter gave them many opportunities to donate to a peer who had poor luck in the game, and those who did not donate were urged to do so and then praised. Rewarded and urged generosity increased markedly. However, as soon as the praise was discontinued, the generosity also stopped. Effects of preaching or of forced generosity may be short-lived.

143. George, C., & Main, M. (1979). Social interactions of young abused children: Approach, avoidance, and aggression. *Child Development, 50,* 306-318.

Ten abused toddlers in day care more frequently performed the following behaviors than did matched controls from stressed families: harassed their caregivers, assaulted their peers, and avoided caregivers in response to friendly overtures. Abused toddlers showed markedly fewer prosocial interactions than non-abused toddlers with caregivers and peers.

144. Gergen, K. J., & Gergen, M. M. (1972). Individual orientations to prosocial behavior. *Journal of Social Issues, 28,* 105-130.

This research review cites findings on factors correlated with prosocial behaviors. The authors assert that a traditional search for single correlates, such as *age* or *social status,* is short-sighted. Their work with college students suggests that different personal dispositions are related in different ways to prosocial behaviors and that situational payoffs and interactions among predictors must be taken into account.

145. Gilligan, C. (1982). *In a different voice.* Cambridge, MA: Harvard University Press.

The author's thesis is that two different ideologies characterize the moral development of males and females. For boys, the morality of rights is based on equality and centered on understanding the concept of what is fair. The ethic of responsibility that females are more likely to develop rests on recognizing differences in needs and this understanding gives rise to compassion and care for others. Thus, *integrity/rights* and *intimacy/care* are two different perspectives that caregivers will have to help children develop in order that they become more adept at resolving the moral dilemmas that will arise in their lives.

146. Goelman, H. (Ed.) (1991). *Children's play in day care settings.* New York: State University of New York Press.

Contains: Honig, A. S., Douthit, D., Lee, J., & Dingler, C. (1991)

147. Gorn, G. J., Goldberg, M. E., & Kenango, R. N. (1976). The role of educational television in changing the intergroup attitudes of children. *Child Development, 47,* 277-280.

White Canadian preschool children who viewed a "Sesame Street" TV program with inserts depicting ethnically different children at play later showed greater preference for having these children visit their school than did children who were not given the opportunity to watch these TV segments of culturally different children at play.

148. Gove, F., & Keating, D. (1979). Empathic role-taking precursors. *Developmental Psychology, 15,* 594-600.

Preschool children (N=32) listened to stories accompanied by two picture cards depicting story characters (a boy and a girl). Two of the stories (situational inference stories) described an event that was objectively different for each story character (e.g., one won while the other lost a game). The other two stories relayed events that were objectively the same (e.g., each child received a puppy), yet visual cues in the pictures conveyed different emotional responses (one character smiles; the other shows fear). Children described how they thought each character would feel and why. Older children gave significantly more correct responses on the psychological inference stories than did younger children, who seemed to consider the emotions as part of the situation itself. When confronted with contradictory cues from the pictures, younger children reconstructed the stories to fit with different characters' expressions.

149. Grant, J. E., Weiner, A., & Rushton, J. P. (1976). Moral judgement and generosity in children. *Psychological Reports, 39,* 451-454.

Three sets of moral judgment stories and a measure of generosity were administered to 21 middle-class British girls aged 8-11 years. Children's conceptions of Piagetian intentionality, Piagetian distributive justice and Kohlbergian principles of morality were assessed. Generosity increased from age 8 to 11 years, although no age differences were found regarding moral judgment. The three sets of stories showed some degree of relatedness while the measure of distributive justice showed a positive (but marginal) relationship to children's generosity.

150. Green, F. P., & Schneider, F. W. (1975). Age differences in the behavior of boys on three measures of altruism. *Child Development, 45,* 248-251.

Lower-middle-class Canadian parochial school boys from kindergarten through grade 8 (N=100) were shown how to put together books to help poor children in school. The boys could volunteer to help from 1 to 5 days. The adult then "accidentally" knocked down pencils, and started slowly to pick them up. Pencil-pick up was the second measure of altruism. Each child was later given five candy bars for coming to see the experimenter, and told he could, if he wished, share some of them with other school children who would not be able to participate. There were no effects of age on volunteering to work for poor children. The amount of candy shared increased steadily across age. Among the two older groups, almost all the children helped the adult pick up pencils. Situationally relevant variables may be more salient once a

child has both learned to recognize and
appreciate others' needs and societal rules
for altruism.

151. Grieger, T., Kauffman, J., & Grieger, R.
(1976). Effects of peer reporting on
cooperative play and aggression of
kindergarten children. *Journal of School
Psychology, 14* (4), 307-312.

Researchers observed kindergarten children
(N=90) from two public half-day kindergarten
classes for aggressive acts and cooperative
play during 15-minute periods. During "Sharing
Time", children could report to their class the
cooperative or friendly behaviors of their
peers which had occurred during the day.
Children whose cooperative behavior was
reported by a peer received a happy face badge
as a reward. Later, only peer praise served
as a reward. Peer reporting of cooperative
play produced an increase in the cooperative
classroom play of kindergarten children. The
median percent of cooperative play rose from
42% during the baseline period to 55% during
the report and happy face phase. The median
number of aggressive acts decreased from 42
during baseline to 9 during *report* and *happy
face*. A reversal phase, in which unfriendly
acts were reported produced a decrease in
cooperation and an increase in aggression.
Peer reporting seems to be a natural and
inexpensive means of increasing prosocial
responses of children.

152. Grusec, J. (1981). Socialization processes
and the development of altruism. In J. P.
Rushton and R. M. Sorrentino (Eds.), *Altruism
and helping behavior: Social, personality,
and developmental perspectives* (pp. 65-90).

Hillsdale, NJ: Lawrence Erlbaum.

This survey of important altruism researches from the 1970's systematically analyzes the findings of researches in the following areas: mechanisms of acquisition in the growth of concern for others; response consequences in terms of rewards and punishments for prosocial behaviors; effects of models and model characteristics on children's donations and other altruistic acts (including researches on possible generalizing effects of modeling); effects of verbal persuasion and preaching methods; the effects of empathic sensitivity; and effects of attribution of prosocial characteristics on the enhancement of altruism.

Interest grew during the 1970's in the child's cognitions about the social world and in the mechanisms which might facilitate altruism. Researchers focused on "the child's ability to understand how others were thinking and feeling, and to explore the role of empathy as a mediator in the development of concern for others" (p. 66). Methodological innovations included: field experiments, observational studies of altruism in natural settings, continued interest in the assessment of altruism through interviews on child-rearing approaches and their effects, as well as evaluation of laboratory manipulations.

153. Grusec, J. (1982). The socialization of altruism. In N. Eisenberg (Ed.), *The development of prosocial behavior*. New York: Academic Press.

Altruism is defined as "behaviors such as helping, sharing, comforting, and defending, which occur independent of any external benefit to the altruist, and which may even include self-sacrifice" (p. 139). In these studies, mothers were trained to record helping acts by their children as well as situations in which altruism should have occurred but did not, and direct instructions to their children about concern for others. Subjects were 22 4-year-olds and 14 7-year-olds. During a home visit, the mother was to make two requests for altruistic behaviors of her child. According to the mothers' reports, the mean number of acts of altruism per day by 4-year-olds was .68 for boys and .62 for girls; for 7-year-olds it was .41 for boys and .43 for girls. In the vast majority of cases, the mother expressed pleasure, praised the act or the child, or thanked the child, regardless of child age. From maternal report, far more acts of altruism were offered by the 4's (154 acts) compared with the 7's (33 acts). Children who offered to help tended to be children who engaged more in spontaneous acts of altruism (rank order correlation=.41). Grusec suggests that caregivers more often accept children's offers of help so that children can gain feelings of competence and mastery that motivate them to perform other prosocial actions.

154. Grusec, J., Kuczynski, J., Rushton, P., & Simutis, Z. M. (1978). Modeling, direct instruction, and attributions: Effects on altruism. *Developmental Psychology, 14 (1),* 51–57.

Children aged seven to ten years played a bowling game for which they won marbles that could be exchanged for prizes. They were then given the opportunity to donate some marbles to absent "poor" children in one of three conditions: (1) the experimenter modeled donating, (2) told children to donate, or (3) both modeled and told them to donate. After the game, one-third of the children in each condition were given either no or one of several attributions about their sharing. The self-attribution was: "You shared because you like to help others." A two-week follow-up test showed no significant differences in effect for modeling or direct instruction (alone or combined). Children given self-attributions donated more than other groups, both immediately, and two weeks later.

155. Grusec, J. E., & Redler, E. (1980). Attribution, reinforcement, and altruism. *Developmental Psychology, 16,* 525-534.

In a research trailer parked in the school yard, 8-year-old boys and girls were told that they could donate winnings from their game to poor children if they wished. After they had shared their winnings, they received either a *positive attribution* (e.g. "You're the kind of person who likes to help others whenever you can") or a *social reinforcer* (e.g. the child was told verbally that it was good to share marbles with others and that is a nice and helpful thing to do). At the end of the session, the children were give a chance to donate (anonymously) some pencils they had been given to school-mates who would not be able to come to the trailer to play. One week later, the children returned. A stranger asked them to help fold some cardboard to make toy house roofs. After the children cooperated, the lady then either gave a further personal attribution to the children in the positive attribution condition or a social reinforcement comment to the children in that condition. A couple of weeks after that, a male stranger visited the children in their classrooms and asked them to make drawings and collect craft materials for sick children in the hospital.

Prosocial attributions and social reinforcements were equally effective in the promoting of the initial donations by children. However, on the various generalization tests, prosocial attribution continued to have a significant effect, but there was no longer any difference between the social reinforcement and the control children. In a second study with 4-, 5-, and 8-year-olds, the use of labeling only worked for the 8-year-olds. Children may need to have a certain level of thinking about themselves as possessed of enduring dispositional traits before they are sensitive to the effects of positive attribution. Cognitive capacity affects the outcome of some techniques to enhance altruism in young children. For 10-year-olds, positive attributions and social statements were found to be effective on the immediate post-test and the generalization tests. Cognitively, the 10-year-olds with superior thinking flexibility could infer that the social reinforcements implied positive attributions to them personally.

156. Grusec, J. E., Saas-Kortsaak, P., & Simutis, Z. M. (1978). The role of example and moral exhortation in the training of altruism. *Child Development, 49,* 920-923.

Children were exposed to two different kinds of exhortations - a general one which emphasized the importance of helping others whenever possible, and a specific one emphasizing the importance of sharing with others less fortunate (charity). Donating was modeled as the giving of tokens to a fund for poor children in order to purchase gifts for them. Children were observed (unobtrusively while they were alone) in terms of how many tokens they donated right after the training procedures and three weeks later. In a staged situation they had an opportunity to help an experimenter pick up some objects that she had "accidentally" knocked over. They could then share gifts (pencils) with children in their school who were not able to be a part of the research. More than a month after initial training, a stranger who visited the children's classrooms, asked them: 1) to make drawings to cheer up sick children; 2) to collect junk materials such as margarine tubs and pieces of fabric for sick children to make crafts while they were in the hospital.

Modeling had more effect than preaching in the immediate donation opportunity. Boys who had been exhorted to share specifically shared more pencils than boys just generally exhorted to help others, and they shared somewhat more than boys who received neither preaching nor modeling. The generalized exhortation led to children's collecting more craft items than did the control (no treatment) condition. But children who imitated the model in giving up game winnings for poor children were no more likely than controls to share pennies that they had won with other schoolmates or to collect craft materials. The effects of modeling may not generalize to situations other than those in the original training situation, even though donation and not other prosocial kinds of acts would still be involved.

157. Hampson, R. B. (1981). Helping behavior in children: Addressing the interaction of a person-situation model. Developmental Review, 1, 93-112.

Methodological factors in studying children's helping behaviors (such as rescue, donation, and direct assistance) and research findings with different techniques are discussed. Low correlations are sometimes found between different measures. Donation (which calls for giving tangible material goods to an absent other child) correlates poorly with other forms of helping. The relation between task assistance and sharing is very low. In training researches to enhance altruism, models who foster the greater changes are more special to the children, warm, expressive, and practicing the prosocial behaviors they are trying to teach. Helping is facilitated when children feel good about themselves. Friendship patterns are significant. Children were peer-rated on popularity, helpfulness and friendship and then observed on six different helping tasks. The more friends the children had, the more helpful they were. The more popular helpful children were, the more they helped peers more directly (e.g. volunteered to spend time with an unknown peer in distress). The less popular but helpful children engaged in more behind-the-scenes helpfulness (e.g. picking up papers for a peer). Both person *and* situational variables are implicated in children's helpfulness.

158. Hardin, G. (1977). *The limits of altruism: An ecologist's view of survival.* Bloomington, IN: Indiana University Press.

This philosophical essay looks at the ego-preserving roots of so-called altruistic behaviors, and finds that generosity in archaic societies was mostly socially coerced and obligatory. The author retells the story of Freud's children, who were horrified to learn that their servants, especially Nanny, worked for wages rather than pure love. When the child learned the truth, she broke into tears and wept for hours.

The author opts for acknowledging our parochialism and placing limits on generosity, so that altruism toward members of one's "in-group" is combined with judicious controls on antipathy toward other groups. Insisting that children learn to believe and act on universal brotherhood rather than on limited brotherhood may not be conducive to their developing altruism.

159. Hartmann, D. P., Gelfand, D. M., Smith, C. L., Paul, S. C., Cromer, C. C., Page, B. C., & LeBenta, D. V. (1976). Factors affecting the acquisition and elimination of children's donating behavior. *Journal of Experimental Child Psychology, 21,* 328-338.

When playing a game, 8- to 10-year-olds were fined if they did not donate some of their winnings to a charity when they were given the opportunity to donate. The children became more generous in later trials. However, they became less generous as soon as they were informed that they would no longer be fined for refusing to donate. Simple reward and punishment by caregivers may not induce attitudinal and motivational changes that lead to consistent prosocial patterns of responding.

160. Hartshorne, H., & May, M. A. (1928). *Studies in the nature of character.* New York: Macmillan.

This early study is included as a "classic", one (reported in three volumes) in which Hartshorne and colleagues examined responses of over 11,000 children to see whether they consistently displayed an altruistic personality across a variety of tests. The researchers tried to predict which children would cheat on a series of experimental tasks and disobey adult instructions by helping one another with answers. A low correlation was found between tests. The authors concluded that children's morality is contextually determined more by the specific situation than by any trait of honesty. The researchers had assumed that children who could recite moral standards such as the Boy Scout Code and the Ten Commandments would act more morally, but this hypothesis was disproved. Also, children may not view helping each other on a test as "cheating".

In this classic study, measures of altruism in which students were given opportunities to help others were called "service" tests. These included:

1. The self or class test. In a spelling contest, each student could compete for a class or individual prize but had to choose which contest to enter.
2. The money-voting test. The class voted what to do with won money, either in terms of buying something for some hospitalized child or dividing the money among members of the class.
3. The learning exercises. The amount of effort a child would make to work for the Red Cross, for the class, or for oneself was measured.
4. The school-kit test. Each child was given a kit of pencils as a "present from a friend of the school" and it was suggested that they give some away to make up kits for deprived children.
5. The envelopes test. The children had to find jokes, pictures, interesting stories, and the like, for sick children in hospitals, and the number of articles placed in the envelope given to each child was scored.

Similar procedures were used to study honesty, self-control, persistence and the ability to inhibit behavior. Since children's scores changed from test to test, the researchers concluded that there was situational specificity. When Rushton (see 1980 entry) combined scores on a *battery* of their items, however, he concluded otherwise, since he found evidence for a degree of generality in altruistic behavior.

161. Hartup, W. W. (1978). Children and their friends. In H. McGurk (Ed.), *Issues in childhood social development* (pp. 130–170). Cambridge: Methuen.

In this review of researches on developmental trends in friendship patterns among young children, Hartup notes that kind children are both more likely to have friends than unkind children and to be perceived as kind by their friends. He cites a correlation of r=.75 between children initiating positive overtures to peers and receiving same, and notes that rates of giving positive attention, approval, affection, and tangible objects increases significantly for 4-year-olds compared with threes.

162. Hay, D. F. (1979). Cooperative interactions and sharing between very young children and their parents. *Developmental Psychology, 15* (6), 647–653.

The purpose of this study was to document the very early occurrence of sharing and cooperation between 24 infants (12, 18, & 24 months) observed in a playroom with their parents. Coordinated interchanges were defined as: a) mutual involvement of the two partners; b) repetition of discrete actions, and c) taking turns. One 12-month-old, 7 18-month-olds and 7 24-month-olds participated in at least one cooperative exchange, such as ball games, pretend phone call or other representational game, pretend eating or drinking, give-and-take sequences, naming games and distinctive use of toys, such as showing and giving objects to the parent. Both cooperation and sharing increase in frequency markedly in the second year of life.

163. Hersh, R. H., Paolitto, D. P., & Reimer, J. (1979). *Promoting moral growth: From Piaget to Kohlberg.* New York: Longman.

This book explicates in detail the theories of Kohlberg and Piaget and the application of moral principles with upper level students in schools. A continuum of curriculum development is stressed, as well as use of books and of history. The authors stress opportunities for role-taking and the importance of relating issues to students' own lives. Kohlberg's Just Community Approach in a school is described.

164. Hetherington, E. M. (Ed.)(1983). Socialization, personality, and social development, Vol. IV, in P. H. Mussen (Series Ed.), *Handbook of child psychology* (4th ed.). New York: John Wiley.

Contains: Radke-Yarrow, M., Zahn-Waxler, C., Chapman, M. (1983)

165. Hinde, R. A., & Groebel, J. (Eds.) (1991) *Prosocial behavior, cooperation, and trust.* New York: Cambridge U. Press.

Contains: Stevenson, H. (1991)

166. Hinde, R. A., Perret-Clermont, A., & Stevenson-Hinde, J. (Eds.) (1985). *Social relations and cognitive development.* Oxford: Clarendon Press.

Contains: Shure, M. (1985)

167. Hoffman, M. L. (1975a). Altruistic behavior and the parent-child relationship. *Journal of Personality and Social Psychology, 31,* 937-943.

Classmates of 40 male, and 40 female middle-class, white fifth-graders responded on a sociometric questionnaire to the following items: "Which three boys (girls) in your class: A. are most likely to follow the rules even when the teacher is not around? B. care about how other kids feel and try not to hurt their feelings? C. stick up for some kid that the other kids are making fun of or calling names? D. blame themselves a lot if they do something wrong?" The altruism score was the total number of nominations received for items B and C divided by the number of children in the class. The parent measure consisted of 18 values described as "being important to men (or women) of your age". They included items such as "consideration for others"; "going out of one's way to help other people", and "going to church regularly". Discipline measures given to the parents consisted of situations in which a child harms another either with provocation, without provocation but with social support, and with no malicious intent and no support. Parents answered what they would have done if their child, e.g., "made fun of another child" at about age 5-6 years. Significant correlations were obtained between mother and daughter (but not son) altruistic values (r=.37) and father with both daughter and son (r=.34 and r=.35, respectively). High maternal value for victim-

centered discipline correlated (r=.50) with
altruistic values of sons but not daughters,
and high father value correlated with daughters
(r=.53) but not sons.

168. Hoffman, M. L. (1975b). Developmental
synthesis of affect and cognition and its
implications for altruistic motivation.
Developmental Psychology, 11, 607-622.

Hoffman describes a three stage sequence
of the development of intrinsic altruistic
motivation, shaped by evolution. Stage one (12
months of age) involves an empathic response
to cues about another person's feeling, a sense
of another person as a victim, and a desire to
assist to terminate the other's distress.
Although stage one children attribute their own
feelings to others, concern about own
discomfort gives way, in part, to concern for
the other. By age two (stage two), children
begin to differentiate, seeing others' feelings
as independent from their own, but not basi-
cally different. Helping initiatives are less
self-centered, with trial and error responses
to the other's needs. By ages six to nine
(stage three), children exhibit an awareness of
another's feelings as not only separate from
their own, but as related to the person's own
history and identity. The intensity of the
child's motivation to help relates to a
perception of the nature of the other's
distress.

169. Hoffman, M. L. (1977). Toward a
developmental theory of prosocial
motivation. In S. Cohen & T. J. Comiskey
(Eds.), *Child development: Contemporary
perspectives* (pp. 230-235). Itasca, IL:
Peacock.

An argument is made for prosocial behavior stemming from intrinsic motivation rather than from selfish motives or from reinforcement. Anecdotal data illuminate concepts of empathic distress, sympathetic distress, personal guilt, and existential guilt. Developmental levels for the four concepts are highlighted.

170. Hoffman, M. L. (1978a). Empathy, Its development and prosocial implications. In C. B. Keasey (Ed.), *Nebraska symposium on motivation* (Vol. 25) (pp. 169-217). Lincoln, NE: University of Nebraska Press.

Empathy is described as a vicarious affective response to others, where the vicariously aroused affect supplies inner cues to the observer that add meaning to the emotion inferred in another person. In the theoretical model proposed here, the process of empathy has three components: affective, cognitive, and motivational. Experimental research reviewed suggests that empathic distress is associated with a tendency to help, precedes and contributes to the helping, and diminishes in intensity following a helpful act.

Middle class preschoolers and kindergartners (N= 85 boys and 76 girls) played a simple game and received 30 plastic tokens later redeemable for prizes. The children were told that some children from another class would not be able to get prizes, but that they could share some of their tokens with the others if they wished. Children were randomly assigned to two groups a) encouraged to focus on the feelings of the less fortunate or b) encouraged to think about the less fortunate other children. Children in the empathy arousal condition, and also the older children, reported feeling significantly sadder and donated significantly more prize tokens. Adults need to encourage young children to empathize in order to enhance their charitable behaviors.

171. Hoffman, M. (1978b). Psychological and biological perspectives on altruism. *International Journal of Behavioral Development 1*, 323-339.

Hoffman argues for a biological basis for human altruism, and presents psychological evidence supporting this view. He explores the case for viewing altruism as an inherent part of human nature.

172. Hoffman, M. (1981a). Is altruism part of human nature? *Journal of Personality and Social Psychology, 40*, 121-137.

Drawing on psychological and evolutionary biological research, Hoffman proposes that the tendency to help others in distress is a universal human quality. Evidence suggests that empathy acts as a mediator of altruistic action since: it is reliably aroused in humans in response to the distress of others; it facilitates helping action; and it appears to have a neutral base, present early in human evolution. In addition to preceding and contributing to altruistic behaviors, empathic distress diminishes in intensity following the action of helping. Empathy is described as "bridging the gap" between egoism and altruism, having elements of both. Conceptualizing empathic distress as only egotistic ignores the conditions that arouse it (e.g. distress of another), while focusing solely on the satisfaction derived from the act of helping. Hoffman calls for research specifically designed to test the proposition that there is an evolutionary biological basis for altruism in humans.

173. Hoffman, M. (1981b). The development of empathy. In J. P. Rushton & M. Sorrentino (Eds.), *Altruism and helping behavior: Social, personality, and developmental perspectives.* Hillsdale, N.J.: Lawrence Erlbaum.

Hoffman argues for a developmental theory of altruism, rather than a social-learning orientation that seems to imply that the learning process whether based on conditioning, reward, or exposure to the words or deeds of models, is the same regardless of age. Behavioral evidence shows that (a) most people of all ages try to help others in distress, (b) social approval may not be the usual motive for helping since people are less likely to help when approval needs are aroused and more likely to help when approval needs are fulfilled, and (c) there is evidence for a speedy altruistic response by bystanders to another's distress. These behaviors are more compatible with the view that there may be a powerful action tendency or motive in humans that is triggered by appropriate stimuli.

When findings of research are arranged developmentally, a "neat" package emerges. Children below a year cry empathically in response to someone's being hurt. In the second year they cry less but show empathic distress in their facial responses and occasionally attempt to help; by 3 or 4 years they continue to show empathic distress and in most instances can be counted upon to make some attempt to help. Beyond the preschool years, people continue to respond empathically and with more consistently appropriate helping behavior. These findings fit a developmental theory.

174. Hoffman, M. (1982). Development of prosocial motivation, empathy, and guilt. In N. Eisenberg (Ed.), *The development of prosocial behavior.* New York: Academic Press.

A theoretical model of empathic arousal, its developmental course, its transformation into guilt and the implications for altruistic motivations are outlined. The model stresses both emotion and the interaction between affective and cognitive processes within a developmental framework. Although there are certain drawbacks to the model, it provides a broad integrative framework for understanding developmental knowledge concerning the motivation to consider others.

175. Hoffman, M. (1983). Empathy, guilt, and social cognition. In W. Overton (Ed.), *The relationship between social and cognitive development* (pp. 1–52). Hillsdale, N.J.: Erlbaum.

Empathy has been defined as *cognitive awareness* of another person's inner state and as a *vicarious affective response* to others. Hoffman's theory emphasizes the second proposition, and he discusses six distinct states of empathy arousal:

1. Primary circular reaction. The newborn cannot tell the difference between the sound of its own cry and another baby's. Baby expects distress in self when perceiving distress in another.

2. Classical conditioning. Facial and verbal expressions accompanying mother's distress may become conditioned stimuli that can evoke distress in the baby, almost contagiously.

3. Direct association. A distress cue from another reminds us of one's own past experience of pain.

4. Mimicry. Empathy is an innate isomorphic response to another's expression of emotion, and this creates inner kinesthetic cues so that a child can then understand and feel the same distress as the other.

5. Symbolic association. Distress cues from a victim symbolically indicate the victim's feelings.

6. Role-taking. In this most developmentally advanced mode, the person imagines how it would feel if he or she were in the place of the distressed other person.

The intermediate four modes do not form a stage sequence, but may operate throughout life. Even very young children, under two years, are capable of role-taking in highly motivating, natural settings. Hoffman describes four levels of empathic response: global empathy (even at nine months an infant can cry if another child acts hurt); egocentric empathy (efforts to help another by giving what the toddler finds most comforting, such as own doll or teddy); empathy for another's feelings (four-year-old children can accurately recognize happiness or sadness in others and respond with appropriate affect, and later they can empathize with several, contradictory affects at once); empathy for another's troubles (by late childhood, children can empathize with chronic distress, such as another child's being poor or having an incurable disease).

Hoffman discusses the implication of personal and existential guilt in supporting moral norms against harming others and for helping others in distress, including making reparations. He cites the example of a child who offered to give a ride on a swing to another child he had accidentally knocked down 15 minutes earlier. Hoffman concludes that "empathy and guilt may be the quintessential prosocial motives, for they may transform another's pain into one's own discomfort and make one feel partly responsible for the other's plight" (p. 36).

176. Hoffman, M. L., & Levine, L. E. (1976). Early sex differences in empathy. *Developmental Psychology 12,* 557-558.

Seventy-seven four-year-olds responded to an eight-slide picture sequence showing same age and sex children in situations designed to elicit happiness, sadness, anger, and fear. Children's answers to the question "How do you feel?" were scored for the degree to which they matched the emotions pictured. While no sex differences were found for accuracy of labeling the emotions depicted, girls gave more empathic responses and boys gave more instrumental (action-oriented) responses.

177. Hom, H. L., & Robinson, P. A. (Eds.) (1977). *Psychological processes in early education.* New York: Academic Press.

Contains: Bryan, J. (1977)

178. Honig, A. S. (1982). Research in review. Prosocial development in children. *Young Children, 37* (5), 51-63.

This review of research concerning prosocial development discusses theory, and surveys researches. Teachers and parents can encourage and enhance prosocial behaviors in young children if there are:

1. Consistent contacts with nurturing, individually attentive and responsive caregivers.

2. Opportunities for children to identify their own and others' feelings.

3. Challenges for children to consider the consequences of their actions with others.

4. Adult models of helping, altruistic concerned actions.

5. Opportunities for children to respond to real victims in situations of distress where the child can actively participate in helping.

6. Caregivers encouraging events for children to think about *alternative* possibilities that might resolve their distress/conflict situations.

179. Honig, A. S. (Ed.) (1990). *Optimizing early child care and education.* London: Gordon & Breach.

Contains: DeVries, R. & Goncu, P. (1990) Honig, A. S., & McCarron, P. A. (1990)

180. Honig, A. S., Douthit, D., Lee, J., & Dingler, C. (1992). Prosocial and aggressive behaviors of preschoolers at play in secular and church-based day care. In H. Goelman (Ed.), *Children's play in day care settings.* New York: State University of New

York Press.

Prosocial and aggressive behaviors during play were observed for 40 boys and girls ($M=4$ years) in both secular and church-based centers. Males showed no differences as a function of attendance at either a church-based or secular center. Birth order was unrelated to prosocial rates, but child gender made a significant difference. Girls showed significantly more prosocial behaviors: four times as many as males in the church centers and twice as many as males in the secular centers. Any effects of a specific moral philosophy (as indexed by church sponsorship) or a center may be confounded by differential rates of aggressions and prosocial behaviors of boys and girls.

181. Honig, A. S., & McCarron, P. A. (1990). Prosocial behaviors of handicapped and typical peers in an integrated preschool. In A. S. Honig (Ed.), *Optimizing early child care and education* (pp. 113-125). London: Gordon & Breach.

Six types of prosocial bids were recorded for 10 typical and 5 special (4 autistic, 1 multiply handicapped) children (mean age 4.4 years) in four activity settings. Setting had a significant effect. Most of the 110 prosocial bids occurred during free play, structured play and gym, and the fewest prosocial bids occurred during teacher-directed structured circle time. Sharing, cooperating, and helping were the most frequent and sympathy and praise were rare. No nurturing was observed. No directionality preferences were found. That is, typical children initiated twice as many prosocial bids (Mean=20) as handicapped peers (Mean=10.2), but no preferences or prejudices were found in status of the child toward whom the bids were directed. Contact with typical children *per se* did not build a high level of social skills among the handicapped children. Teachers and therapists must *specifically* model and facilitate the development of these skills among special needs children.

182. Honig, A. S., & Pollack, B. (1990). Effects of a brief intervention program to promote prosocial behaviors in young children. *Early Education and Development, 1,* (6), 438-444.

A classroom procedure was implemented for one month for one of two classes with 37 rural second-graders. For one week prior to and one week after the month, the children's sharing, helping, and cooperating were tallied in the classroom, lunch room line up, hall walk, and cafeteria. One class met each afternoon in circle time and the children told their classmates if they had done something nice for a peer or a peer had done something nice for them. One corroboration by another child was required. For each act, the whole class had a gold star pasted on a chart, no matter which child did the action. The other class served as a control. A significant increase in the number of prosocial acts (from 45 to 71) of the treatment class was tallied from pre- to-post-program compared with the pre- and post-control tallies (43.5 and 45.5 respectively). Children's verbal sharing of their prosocial behaviors with each other seems to increase their motivation to perform acts of kindness.

183. Honig, A., Wittmer, D., & Gibralter, J. (1987). *Cooperation compliance and discipline: An annotated bibliography* (Catalog #203). Urbana, IL: ERIC Clearinghouse on Elementary and Early Childhood Education.

The authors provide brief annotations of researches and practical guides to promote positive discipline strategies and more compliant child interactions.

184. Howard, J., & Barnett, M. (1981). Arousal of empathy and subsequent generosity in young children. *The Journal of Genetic Psychology, 138,* 307-308.

The effect of eliciting empathic arousal on the subsequent sharing behavior of 4- to 8-year-old children was explored. Children enrolled in preschool through second-grade classes (85 boys and 76 girls) were divided into two age levels: preschoolers and kindergartners (N=86) and first-and second-graders (N=75). The children had earned tokens and then were randomly assigned to one of two conditions in which they were either (a) encouraged to focus on the feelings of the less fortunate others or (b) encouraged to think about the less fortunate others, but with no mention of feelings. Each child was then given an opportunity to donate some prize tokens, in private, to the other children. The children's affective response to the plight of the needy was also assessed. The children in the empathy-arousal condition reported feeling significantly sadder and donated significantly more prize tokens than did children in the no-empathy arousal condition. Older children donated significantly more prize tokens than did younger children. No interaction of experimental condition and age was found. Teachers and parents may want to focus the attention of young children specifically upon the feelings of needy others.

185. Howes, C. (1987a). Peer interaction of young children. *Monographs of the Society for Research in Child Development, 53,* (1, Serial No. 217).

Howes followed forty-one children in full-time child care for three years and 223 children for two years to study differences in the early development of social competence with peers. Complementary and reciprocal social play emerged when the children were 1 year old, and social pretend play emerged at age 2. Children classified as *rejected* were rebuffed by their peers when they attempted to play with a group of children, and children classified as *withdrawn* were found to be less socially mature.

Children who stayed in the same child care center with the same peer group increased their proportion of complementary and reciprocal peer play more than did children who stayed in the same child care center but changed peer groups. Children who moved to a totally new child care center but with a portion of their peer group increased their proportion of complementary and reciprocal peer play more than did children who changed child care centers without members of their peer group. This research points out the importance of providing stable peer groups for very young children attending full-time child care in order to enhance the possibilities for increasing their social competence and pro-social behaviors.

186. Howes, C. (1987b). Social competence with peers in young children: Developmental sequences. *Developmental Review, 7,* 252–272.

The interactive achievements of familiar toddlers at play are complementary games with reciprocal roles for younger toddlers and cooperative social pretend play for older toddlers.

187. Howes, C., & Farber, J. (1987). Toddlers' responses to the distress of their peers. *Journal of Applied Developmental Psychology, 8,* 441-452.

Forty-three toddlers (16 to 33 months) played freely in their day care centers as they were observed for 16, five-minute periods. Observers recorded behaviors in narrative form, beginning with the target child's interaction with a peer, and continuing for the full five minutes whether or not peer contact continued. Narratives were analyzed for frequency and type of peer interaction, as well as causes of and peer responses to instances of crying. Ninety-three percent of peer responses to crying were prosocial in nature: looking at a peer, attempting to mediate, or consoling. Children were more likely to respond prosocially to peers previously identified by the teacher as "friends," despite the low proportion of play time the child actually engaged with friends as opposed to classmates. Children who cried themselves responded more to others' cries.

188. Howes, C., & Stewart, P. (1987). Child's play with adults, toys, and peers: An examination of family and child care influences. *Developmental Psychology, 23,* (8), 423-430.

Families who were the most stressed and restrictive selected the lowest quality child care arrangements for their children and were the most likely to change arrangements. These children had the lowest levels of competence during social play with peers. Children who had experienced high quality child care and supportive parents had acquired the ability to decode and regulate emotional signals. These children were the most socially competent in peer play.

189. Hudson, L., Forman, E. A., & Brion-Meisles, S. (1982). Role taking as a predictor of prosocial behavior in cross-age tutors. *Child Development, 53,* (5), 1320-1329.

Eighteen second-grade students identified as "high" or "low" role-takers taught two same-sex kindergartners to make construction paper caterpillars. Materials were limited to maximize the likelihood of conflict over sharing. The process was videotaped and analyzed using 16 categories of social behaviors such as comforting, sharing, talking, and problem-solving. High and low role-takers differed significantly on eight of 16 dimensions, including problem-solving and helping, but most significantly in responding to indirect requests for help.

190. Hughes, R., Tingle, B., & Sawin, D. (1981). Development of empathic understanding in children. *Child Development, 52,* 122-128.

Kindergarten and second-grade children (N=48) viewed slides and heard stories about children their age involved in happy or sad events. They then responded to questions about how the story characters felt and why, as well as how *they* felt and why. Younger children were more likely to describe concrete features of the situation ("She was sad because the dog ran away"), while older children made more inferences about the character's feelings ("Her dog is lost and she lost someone she loved."). However, younger children showed increased understanding after reflecting on their own feelings as if they were the story character.

191. Hull, D., & Reuter, J. (1977). The development of charitable behavior in elementary school children. *Journal of Genetic Psychology, 131,* (1), 147–153.

Sharing increased with age among 187 children from kindergarten through sixth grade. They were asked to rank seven types of candy according to preference, and were then given the opportunity to share candy with children described as similar to them or dissimilar and needy. Charitable behavior, defined as sharing significantly more with needy others, only emerged at about age 7 and increased significantly to age 10 years. This may have occurred because charity for the needy depends on cognitive skills, such as understanding the abstract concept of *neediness*. Also, the child has to have internalized the norm of social responsibility, that it is proper to give to someone who is needy.

192. Huston-Stein, A., Friedrich-Cofer, L., & Susman, E. (1977). The relation of classroom structure to social behavior, imaginative play, and self-regulation of economically disadvantaged children. *Child Development, 48,* 908–916.

Structure (the amount of adult-directed activity in preschool classes) was related to naturally occurring social behaviors in 13 urban Head Start classes containing 141 2-5-year-

olds. Subjects in high structure classes
engaged in less prosocial behavior to peers,
less imaginative play, and less aggression than
subjects in low structure classes.

193. Iannotti, R. (1975). The nature and
measurement of empathy in children. *The
Counseling Psychologist, 5,* 21-25.

Empathy, a motivator of altruism, refers to
the responsiveness of a person to the feelings
of another person. Highly empathic children
frequently and appropriately respond to the
feelings of *others.* In contrast, sympathy
emphasizes the feelings of the *observer.*
Empathy can be considered a mediator of
prosocial behaviors. It requires both an
emotional response from the observer *and* role-
taking skills that allow the observer to take
the perspective of the distressed one.
Measurement of empathy is difficult. What is
needed for assessment is that the subject be
able to indicate both his own and another
person's feelings when the expressions of the
other person are incongruent with the
situation. That is, can a child differentiate
emotions of the other from the context
presented? Possibly, a child's empathy
develops at different rates for some emotions
compared to others. The author has developed
a measure of empathy which requires both an
emotional response and role-taking skills. After
the presentation of incongruous illustrated
stories (as a sad boy at a birthday party), the
child is required to choose a face which best
represents the child's emotional response. This
measure of empathy does not have to rely on
the verbal skills of a young child.

194. Iannotti, R. J. (1978). Effect of role-taking experiences on role-taking, empathy, altruism, and aggression. *Developmental Psychology, 14,* 119-124.

The effects of two types of role-playing experiences were observed for 30 six- and 30 9-year-old boys. For the first group, each boy assumed the perspective of one character of a story. In the role-switching condition, the boys took on the perspectives of different characters by switching roles every 5 minutes. The same stories were read to control boys and questions were asked, but no role-playing skills were taught. Role-taking measures were stories in which a hypothetical moral or social dilemma was posed and the child was asked about how to solve the problem. Empathy was measured by each child's response to 16 pictures. A story was told about each picture and the boy was to indicate his own feelings and the feelings of the story character. The child was asked to point to drawings of faces labeled happy, sad, afraid, and angry. In the pictures, the emotional response of the character was incongruent with the situation (e.g. a sad boy at a birthday party). Only responses to the incongruent pictures were used to score empathy.

Altruism was measured at the end of the testing session. Either M & M's or raisins were given to each child. The tester talked about a poor boy whose birthday was approaching, and he suggested options to donate treats for the poor boy. The child was left alone to donate in private and eat whatever was left. No effect of training on altruism was found for the 9-year-olds. Six-year-olds with role-taking training donated more candy to the poor boy than did controls. The 6-year-old boys who had switched roles shared the most. Teachers and parents need to be aware that the preschool years may be particularly sensitive for promoting prosocial sensitivity.

195. Iannotti, R. (1985). Naturalistic and structured assessments of prosocial behavior in preschool children: The influence of empathy and perspective taking. *Developmental Psychology, 21,* 46-55.

Children , four to five years of age, were observed during five months for instances of sharing, cooperating, helping, comforting, and their antecedents. During the last month, children completed laboratory measures of perspective taking, prosocial behaviors and empathy. Cooperation, the most frequent behavior, usually occurred in response to teacher requests. Sharing was most likely preceded by a peer's request, while helping was spontaneous. Laboratory measures correlated positively with observations when tasks were structured similarly in each setting. Teacher ratings were not related to any naturally-occurring prosocial behaviors. The best single predictor of spontaneous prosocial behavior was a child's ability to infer another's emotions.

196. Isen, A., Horn, N., & Rosenhan, D. (1973). Effects of success and failure on children's generosity. *Journal of Personality and Social Psychology, 27,* (2), 239-247.

Effects of success and failure on children's charitable behaviors were examined in three studies. The effects of success, failure, and two control experiences on children's charitability and their evaluation of resources were examined for children from grades 3 and 4 in a suburban middle-income school. Positive affect generated by success led to greater generosity than that found among children in whom positive affect was not induced. However, failure also sometimes led to giving.

197. Israel, A. C., & Brown, M. S. (1979). Effects of directiveness of instructions and surveillance on the production and persistence of children's donations. *Journal of Experimental Child Psychology, 27,* 250–261.

Children from grades 2 and 3 (N=112) from a predominantly white, middle class public school earned tokens for correct size judgments and observed a model (who had previously earned tokens at the same task) donate some of her earnings. Children were subsequently given an opportunity to donate tokens to children from another school in the presence or absence of the experimenter after being presented with *directive* (you must give) or *permissive* (you can give if you want to) instructions.

Directives and surveillance both produced greater initial giving for all children. Over time, permissive instructions produced greater reductions in giving for boys than for girls. Directives produced greater initial giving; and donating persisted better under the more explicit conditions.

198. Israel, A. C., & Raskin, P. A. (1979). Directiveness of instructions and modeling: Effects on production and persistence of children's donation. *Journal of Genetic Psychology, 138,* 269–277.

Forty-eight boys and girls (from grades 1 and 4) earned tokens and were subsequently given the opportunity to donate (in the absence of an observer) following: 1) the presence or absence of observation of a model who had donated and 2) the receipt of either *directive* (would have to) or *permissive* (might want, but didn't have to) instructions to give. Approximately four weeks later (with no further modeling, instructions, or observers present) children were given a second opportunity to donate.

Modeling produced higher levels of giving in both sessions. Directive instructions produced donations by all children in the immediate situation and for first graders at the follow-up. For 4th graders, donating produced by directive instructions decreased to a level equivalent to permissive instructions.

199. Jacobson, J., & Willie, D. (1986).   The influence of attachment pattern on developmental changes in peer interaction from the toddler to the preschool period. *Child Development, 57* (2), 338-347.

Studies on infant-mother attachment all predict that secure attachment will promote greater peer competence and/or sociability. Toddlers (N=24) were observed from two to three years of age. Each child was paired with a same-sex, securely attached unfamiliar playmate. Eight of the focus children were securely attached, eight avoidantly attached, and eight ambivalently attached.   Although frequency of positive initiations did not increase with age, securely attached children became the object of positive initiations as the year progressed. Among the anxiously attached children, avoidant children were eliciting fewer positive responses, whereas ambivalent children were receiving more disruptive responses, agonistic initiations, and resistance from peers. Dyads in which both children were securely attached were the most interactive as preschoolers. Secure preschoolers spent less time in solitary play and more time in innovative, resourceful, and challenging activities which then made them more attractive as playmates.

200. Jennings, K. D., Fitch, D., & Suwalsky, J. T. D. (1987). Social cognition and social interaction in three-year-olds: Is social cognition truly social? *Child Study Journal, 17* (1), 1-14.

Since decentering (the ability to take the point of view of another) is a multi-dimensional process, a composite score based on a battery of perspective-taking tests provides a better assessment of the relationships of social cognition with prosocial behaviors. Ten minutes of play were videotaped and coded for 53 middle-class 3 1/2-year-old dyads in a playroom provided with many toys. The codes were grouped into five measures:

1. *Social participation*: These included: Parten's categories of solitary play, parallel with imitative play, associate play, cooperative play, onlooker, plus negative comments about peer, brief bids, and bossing/rough-housing.

2. *Social decentering.* An 8-point scale reflected the degree to which each child could accommodate to the partner's ideas and behaviors while simultaneously integrating his or her own ideas into joint play activities.

3. *Helping behavior.* Sympathy, generosity, and helping acts were tallied.

4. *Conflict behaviors.*

5. *Egocentric speech:* defined as verbalizations that failed to communicate, so that the peer asked for clarification. Social cognition was assessed with the Flavell Picture cubes test, the upside-down picture test, pointed stick, and gift choice test plus DeVries' "penny guessing game" and Borke's test of interpersonal perception. Teachers completed the Kohn Preschool Behavior Scale. The McCarthy Scales of Children's Abilities were administered, and girls scored significantly higher than boys on the McCarthy and on social participation, social decentering, and helping behaviors.

The dyadic social cognition score did not relate to social participation or social decentering, but only to helping. Thus, there seems to be little relationship between the young child as a knower socially and as a prosocial interactor in the social world. Children may need to be observed for a longer period of time to allow for more valid comparisons between the child's social cognition "scores" and social "behavior".

201. Johnson, D. B. (1982). Altruistic behavior and the development of the self in infants. *Merrill-Palmer Quarterly, 28,* (3), 379-388.

In a laboratory session with 24 upper-middle class infant boys and girls (*M*=20.9 months), an experimenter (pretending) forcefully struggled to take away a stranger's doll. The mother and infant had also earlier each been given a small stuffed doll. The stranger pretended to cry. On the way out, the experimenter dropped the doll a bit away from, but in sight of the baby. This distress scenario was then repeated with the mother having her doll wrested away. The child, with a red spot marked on the nose, was shown a mirror while the mother asked, "Who's that?" The measure of self-recognition was mark-directed touching. Infants were asked to find their own picture from a group of other Polaroid shots of babies. Home observations of the infant's response to others' distress were recorded by mothers during a two-week period.

The most frequent form of infant intervention in the lab was to retrieve and return the distressed person's doll (50% for the mother and 9% for the stranger). Some babies gave own doll to mother (9%) and some gave physical comfort (18% to mother, 9% to stranger). Somewhat over half the babies identified the self picture, and all but one completed the mirror task. In the naturalistic situations, on more than one occasion, 80% of the infants acknowledged distress and intervened directly while 13% intervened indirectly. These results provide strong evidence for infants' sensitivity to the emotions and needs of others. A positive relationship between self-recognition and comforting/helping mother in the lab supports Hoffman's hypothesis that self-other differentiation underlies prosocial development in infancy.

202.Jones, D., Rickel, A., & Smith, R. (1980). Maternal child-rearing practices and social problem-solving strategies among preschoolers. *Developmental Psychology, 16*, (3), 241-242.

The relation between child-rearing practices and one aspect of social cognitive ability, (the type of social problem-solving strategies used by preschoolers), was investigated. Preschoolers (N=72) and their mothers were involved. A modified version of the Preschool Interpersonal Problem Solving

Test (PIPS) was administered to each child. Two peer problems focused on what a child could do or say to get a chance to play with a toy (either a truck or a drum) that another child was using. Two other problems were concerned with the ways in which a child could avert a mother's anger for damaging her property (either burning a hole in her dress or breaking a window). The child was encouraged to think of as many ways as possible that a story character could solve the dilemma. The preschoolers' responses were grouped into nine categories representing conceptually distinct strategies. Maternal variables successfully predicted five out of nine strategies used. Maternal restrictiveness was positively associated with the evasion and negatively with personal appeal and negotiation strategies. Maternal nurturance was negatively related to reliance on authority.

203. Kagan, J., & Lamb, S. (Eds.) (1987). *The emergence of morality in young children.* Chicago: University of Chicago Press.

This textbook is an excellent introduction to moral socialization research, including developmental considerations, cross-cultural researches, and sensitivity to real-life applications of research findings.

Contains: Dunn, J. (1987)
Emde, R., Johnson, W., & Easterbrooks, M. (1987)

204. Kagan, S., & Madsen, M. C. (1971). Cooperation and competition of Mexican, Mexican-American, and Anglo-American children of two ages under four instructional sets. *Developmental Psychology, 5,* (1), 49-59.

Equal numbers of boys and girls from Mexican-American, Mexican, and Anglo-American preschools or schools were tested with a circle matrix board game, with seven one-inch circles connected by one-inch lines. The children, who worked in pairs, were informed that they would take turns moving a marker to adjacent circles, and that receiving a toy was contingent upon the marker moving to a different circle for each subject. If children helped each other over trials, then they could share toys. Competition was non-adaptive as neither child could win. Young children (4- and 5-year-olds) cooperated more than older children. Among the 7-9-year-olds, Mexicans were most cooperative, Mexican-Americans next most, and Anglo-Americans least cooperative. No sex differences were found.

205.Kalliopuska, M. (1984a). Empathy and birth order. *Psychological Reports, 55,* 115-118.

Research in Finland explored the relationship between empathy and birth order. A group of 194 children ranging in age from 9 to 12 years were given Mehrabian and Epstein's emotional empathy scale. In general, results showed that mean empathy scores by birth order did not differ significantly. There was a tendency for middle-born children (second and third borns) to be more empathic than first borns.

206.Kalliopuska, M. (1984b). Empathy in children and social class. *Psychological Reports, 54,* 840-842.

In contrast to previous studies, no significant differences were found between social classes on scores of empathy. The lowest and middle-social class children tended to be more empathetic than children of the highest social class. The children, attending elementary school in Helsinki, Finland, ranged in age from 9 to 12 years old.

207.Kalliopuska, M. (1984c). Empathy in orphaned children. *Psychological Reports, 55*, 12-14.

Feshbach and Roe's Affective Situation Test for Empathy was given to 4- and 5-year-old orphaned children (N=10) and 10 controls, living in Finland. No significant differences were found between groups on any measure. For all children, empathy and egocentricity scores correlated negatively and significantly. In other words, the more empathy a child displayed, the less self-centered were his or her thoughts.

208.Kalliopuska, M. (1984d). Relation between children's and parents' empathy. *Psychological Reports, 54*, 295-299.

For 215 Finnish children ranging from 9 to 12 years old, positive correlations were found between the empathy scores of 9-year-olds and their parents, but were not found for 12-year-olds and their parents. The author hypothesizes that the rebellious nature of the preteen 12-year-olds led to the negative correlation of the empathy scores of the children with those of their parents. There was a positive correlation between the empathy scores of the fathers and the children, thus not supporting the view that mothers have a greater influence on socialization for empathy than fathers.

209. Kalliopuska, M. (1991). Study on the empathy and prosocial behavior of children in three day-care centres. *Psychological Reports, 68* (2), 375-378.

Five-to-six-year-old children (N=101) who attended day care were given Feshbach and Roe's Affective Situation Test (FAST) for Empathy as a pre- and post-test. Teachers also gave their appraisals of the children's prosocial behaviors. The ten items were: understanding of others, considerate, encouraging, friendly and benevolent to others, helpful to others, sociable, polite, attempts to maintain common spirit, capable of taking another person's role, and responsible. The test scores were examined by sex, age, and whole-day care vs. half-day care. Girls did not differ from boys in empathy but differed in total prosocial scores and separate items -- encouraging, helpful to others, and polite. Six-year-old children were more helpful to others and more responsible than 5-year-old children. According to the teacher's ratings, the half-day children behave more prosocially than the whole-day care children. This was explained as due to the latter having more difficult social backgrounds.

210. Kaufman, J., & Cicchetti, D. (1989). Effects of maltreatment on school-age children's socioemotional development: Assessments in a day-camp setting. *Developmental Psychology, 25,* 516-524.

Measures of self-esteem, withdrawal, aggression, and prosocial interactions were obtained for 70 neglected, emotionally abused and/or physically abused children and matched non-abused peers in a day-camp situation. Counselor and peer ratings of prosocial behavior correlated positively with children's prosocial ratings. The counselors rated the maltreated children lower on self-esteem and prosocial measures and higher on the withdrawn behaviors scales.

211. Keane, S., Brown, K., & Crenshaw, T. (1990). Children's intention-cue detection as a function of maternal social behavior: Pathways to social rejection. *Developmental Psychology, 266,* 1004-1009.

Popular and rejected first-graders were shown 10 videotaped vignettes where a child provoked a same-sex peer by destroying a toy while exhibiting one of 5 intentions: hostile, prosocial, accidental, ambiguous, or merely present. Children were asked what the filmed child did, why, and what they would do if that happened to them. Mothers were asked what would you tell your child to do if this happened to him or her. Mothers of popular children provided more prosocial resolutions to conflict in contrast to mothers of rejected children, who provided more hostile resolutions. Rejected children focused more on damage; they said they would respond more aggressively to provocation. Popular children provided more prosocial behavioral responses; they focused more on intentions. A strong positive relation between mother and child's behavioral responses was noted. Maternal values and behaviors may well shape children's social functioning.

212. Keasey, C. B. (1978). *Nebraska symposium on motivation (Vol. 25).* Lincoln, NE: University of Nebraska Press.

Contains: Hoffman, M. (1978a)

213. Kegan, R. (1982). *The evolving self.* Cambridge, MA: Harvard University Press.

Psychoanalysis and developmental constructivism are used to explain therapeutic cases and to explicate the moral development systems of Piaget and Kohlberg. The author gives personal details of how difficult moral teaching is even with seventh graders, who believe that if you have been teased and hurt by older kids, then when you get older the Golden Rule means that it is fair for you to do the same to younger kids! He reveals the importance of peer interventions for developing more prosocial ideas of "fairness". One classmate helped some of the others understand that revenge goes on indefinitely, and that kindness depends on realizing how you were hurt and not wanting others to get treated as badly as you were.

214. Keller, B. B., & Bell, R. Q. (1979). Child effects on adult method of eliciting altruistic behavior. *Child Development, 50,* 1004-1009.

Twenty-four college students participated in four sessions with one of three nine-year-old girls. The girls had been trained to role-play either high or low "person orientation" (looking primarily at materials and waiting for three seconds before answering the adult). Adults were directed to elicit consideration of others from the child, using familiar play and work activities. Adult interactions with children high in person-orientation were characterized by reasoning about the consequences of their actions ("What will Sally do when she sees that you've knocked down her block tower?"). Commands or bargaining were used more frequently with children in the low person-orientation condition. Adults need to be aware of how *reactive* rather than *proactive* their behaviors may be if their specific program goals are to promote positive social skills in children.

215. Kestenbaum, R., Farber, E. A., & Sroufe, L. A. (1989). Individual differences in empathy among preschoolers: Relation to attachment history. In N. Eisenberg (Ed.), *Empathy and related emotional responses* (pp. 51-64). San Francisco: Jossey-Bass.

Empathy is defined as an emotional response to how another feels as well as vicarious experience of the aroused emotion. Twenty-four low-income male and female preschoolers (M=48.7 months) were videotaped unobtrusively during free play for one hour per day for fifty days. The attachment histories of the children had been assessed in infancy. Empathic and anti-empathic social interactions were coded on an empathy scale from 1-7, with 1 being "shows no apparent response" to 7 "intense, clear-cut affective involvement" with an attempt at helping, comforting, and distracting (for example, asking the child to come and play), nurturing, or going to get the teacher. Nursery school teachers also rated the children on the Block California 100-item Q-sort deck, and mega-item scores for empathy were tallied based on items reflecting considerateness, empathy, concern for others' welfare and tendencies to give, lend or share. Children who had secure attachment in infancy scored significantly higher on the empathy scale compared with children with anxious-avoidant attachment histories. Preschoolers with anxious-resistant attachment in infancy did not differ from the other two groups.

Of the 12 incidents of anti-empathy observed, 11 were by children with anxious attachment histories and 1 by a child with a secure attachment history. The correlation between teachers' ratings of empathy and average ratings from the empathy scale were r=.47. Thus, teacher ratings and experimentally observed and coded ratings were fairly well in agreement. Children seem to develop empathic responsiveness in the context of an early nurturant relationship with a caregiver. If not nurtured early, then preoccupation with own distress plus incorporation of parental models of inappropriate emotional responses may decrease children's ability to respond empathically.

216. Kitwood, T. (1990). *Concern for others: A new psychology of conscience and morality.* London: Routledge.

The central thesis of this psychotherapist's book is that securely attached children with supportive caregivers who validate and confirm them as persons, will experience concern and empathy for others, "have some idea of others as important, and thus be able to extrapolate into a broader benevolence". If not, depth therapy can foster awareness and acceptance of one's own feelings, worth, and agency, and this positive sense of self will cause "moral restoration" and permit the growth of empathy and altruism toward others.

217. Knight, G. P., & Chao, C. (1989). Gender differences in the cooperative, competitive and individualistic social values of children. *Motivation and Emotion, 13,* (2), 125-141.

Children (130 3-to 12-year-olds), distributed across age groups from a middle to upper-middle socioeconomic community, completed a social decision-making task individually. The children decided how many pennies to keep for themselves and how many to give to a peer. The peer was always referred to by name, but was not present during the task. Older children more often made equality decisions, while the younger children more often made individual decisions. Girls, more often than boys, preferred cooperative resource distributions (equality), while boys, regardless of age, most frequently preferred competitive superiority (preference for distributions that maximize one's own resources relative to those of a peer).

218. Knight, G., Kagan, S. & Buriel, R. (1982). Perceived parental practices and prosocial development. *The Journal of Genetic Psychology, 141*, 57-65.

Eight- to eleven-year-old Anglo-American and Mexican-American children, from both lower and upper-middle socioeconomic (SES) class schools, completed the Social Orientation Choice Card. This measures cooperative, competitive, and individualistic tendencies through a series of questions with a choice of three alternatives reflecting these tendencies. Students also completed the Parent Practices Questionnaire, a measure of their perceptions of parental socialization practices. Mexican-American children were more cooperative than AngloAmerican children, who were more individualistic and competitive. Lower socioeconomic class students generally perceived their parents as less supportive, and more punishing, than upper-middle class peers. The relationship of perceived parental practices to prosocial (cooperative) tendencies was not consistent across economic classes. Among lower SES children, prosocial tendencies were positively related to perceptions of parents as both more supportive and more punishing.

219. Knudson, K., & Kagan, S. (1982). Differential development of empathy and prosocial behavior. *The Journal of Genetic Psychology, 140,* 249-251.

Empathy and prosocial behavior did not correlate among 88 Anglo-American and Mexican-American children. Mexican-American children usually score more prosocial than Anglos on Knight & Kagan's Social Behavior Scale, which yields measures of altruism, equality, superiority, rivalry/superiority and overall giving. Empathy, as measured by the Feshbach and Roe Affective Situation Test (using slides of real children in different situations) did not correlate significantly with prosocial behavior, regardless of child age (66-109 months). Empathic knowledge of others can apparently be used to compete better, not just to behave prosocially.

220. Kohlberg, L. (1976). Moral stages and moralization: The cognitive-developmental approach. In T. Lickona (Ed.), *Moral development and behavior: Theory, research, and social issues.* New York: Holt.

Moral development is conceptualized as a strict stage model:

1. The child does not share in making rules, but understands that obedience brings freedom from punishment.

2. The child has a morality of egoistic exchange and returns favors for favors – which exchange may be mutually decided upon.

3. Through reciprocal role-taking, the child learns to understand the feelings of others and their ongoing interaction patterns. This creates a morality of interpersonal concordance (as in the Golden Rule: "Do unto others as they do unto you"), where children who are considerate and kind get along with others and want to be helpful and nice. Children can consider each other's point of view both simultaneously and mutually.

4. Children understand that there is a morality of laws and duty to the social order, and that everyone is protected by the law as well as obligated.

5. Societal pressures constrain morality, and one is obligated by formal due process procedures to fulfill responsibilities.

6. Ideal morality and human cooperation and altruism are created by rational, impartial people in a system whereby benefits for each human being are maximized.

221. Kohler, F., & Fowler, S. (1985). Training prosocial: An analysis of reciprocity with untrained peers. *Journal of Applied Behavior Analysis, 18,* 187-200.

The effects of a social skills training package on the play behaviors of three young girls, nominated by their teachers as candidates for social skills intervention were examined. The 5-year, 8-month-old girl was described by her classroom teachers as domineering. When peers did not comply with her directive statements, she frequently demanded that they leave the activity. The 6-year, 3-month-old girl often watched other children play, but rarely requested permission to join in their activities. A 7 1/2-year-old frequently dominated free play activities by obtaining control of the most attractive materials and allowing only one or two peers to join her play group. Uninvited peers were told that they weren't welcome to play. Baseline behaviors of the children were coded during free play: play invitations, child acceptance or refusal of play invitations, amenities, and negative behaviors. Two children received training concerning invitations and amenities while one child received training with invitations only. Daily 10-minute training consisted of instructions, modeling, behavioral rehearsal, and feedback. The two children trained to give play invitations directed more positive social behaviors to their classroom peers after training. The two children's play invitations were maintained in the later absence of experimental contingencies. Both target children received a greater number of play invitations from their peers during free play periods. Thus, play reciprocity training may facilitate the maintenance of more prosocial play invitations over time.

222. Krebs, D. (1970). Altruism: An examination of the concept and a review of the literature. *Psychological Bulletin, 73*, (4), 258-302.

Krebs analyzes altruism on three levels as it relates to the main goal of socialization, to a core attribute of personality, and to theories concerned with human nature. The research relevant to personality traits is criticized. Facts that have been found to

influence the altruistic behavior of a person
are sex, age, ordinal position, social class,
nationality in relation to benefactors,
friendship status, in-group affiliation, and
social class in relation to the recipient.

223.Krebs, D. L. (Ed.) (1978). A cognitive-
developmental approach to altruism. In L.
Wispe (Ed.), *Altruism, sympathy and helping:
Psychological and sociological principles.*
New York: Academic Press.

Theoretically, Krebs reasons, the ability to
predict helping behavior is considerably
improved if we consider personality variables
in interaction with situational variables. The
Piagetian and Kohlbergian cognitive-
developmental theories postulate *qualitative*
changes in the structures of reasoning about
moral issues. At Kohlberg's Stage 3, people
become able to adopt the point of view of
groups of other people, and to handle the ideal
of reciprocity – behaving as you would want
others to behave. Thus, young children will
help corresponding to the way they interpret
the situations they encounter. For example,
children feel most generous when they give
what *they* would like. Thus, the quality of
helping should improve at each stage in
children's development.

224.Krebs, D., & Gilmore, J. (1982). The
relationship among the stages of cognitive
development, role-taking abilities, and moral
development. *Child Development, 47,* 51-61.

A positive relationship between cognitive
development and role-taking ability was
established for children ages five to fourteen.
The results tended to support Kohlberg's claim

that cognitive development is a necessary but not sufficient condition for the development of role-taking abilities.

225.Kurdek, L., & Rogdon, M. (1975). Perceptual, cognitive, and affective perspective taking in kindergarten through sixth-grade children. *Developmental Psychology, 11,* 643-650.

Kindergarten through six-grade children completed tests in three aspects of perspective-taking: perceptual, cognitive, and affective. A perceptual task assessed the child's ability to assume another's viewpoint with respect to moving a tray holding three Disney figures to match the position of the experimenter's identical tray. The cognitive task required each child to retell a story previously read from picture cards as if he or she were an absent friend who had not heard the story before. However, some key pictures had been removed. Finally, affective perspective-taking required the child to describe how eight story characters felt in pictured stories where four characters showed expected feelings to familiar events and four demonstrated inappropriate feelings (happiness at being chased by a tiger). Perceptual, cognitive, and appropriate affective perspective-taking increased with grade level, while inappropriate affective perspective taking decreased.

226.Kurtines, W. M., & Gewirtz, J. L. (Eds.) (1984). *Morality, moral behavior, and moral development.* New York: Wiley.

Contains: Turiel, E., & Smetana, J. (1984)

227.Kurtines, W. M., & Gewirtz, J. L. (Eds.) (1987). *Moral development through social interaction.* New York: Wiley.

Morality is defined as justice and fairness. In the five sections of this book, the following perspectives are represented: developmental process, developmental constructivist, social constructivist, interpretive-hermeneutic and social process. These labels represent different emphases on social cognitive research.

Damon and Colby's studies show that cooperative modes of interaction help young children advance in moral reasoning. Selman & Yeates' chapter stresses the importance of biographical knowledge of the children and how "pair therapy" can help increase positive social exchanges between children. Youniss' chapter provides a definition of morality based on mutual respect among friends. Berndt describes ways in which friends differ from non-friends and how they communicate, interact, and demonstrate care and concern. Knowing how friendship dyads differ from non-friendship dyads can help us address the relationship between social experiences and social understandings.

Contains: Damon, W., & Colby, A. (1987)

228.Kurtines, W. M., & Gewirtz, J. (Eds.) (1989-1991). *Moral behavior and development: Advances in theory, research, and application* (Vol. 1-3). Hillsdale, NJ: Lawrence Erlbaum.

This set of three advanced texts is divided so that the first volume focuses on theories, the second on researches, and the third volume is devoted to programs to promote altruism and prosocial behaviors.

Volume 1 presents chapters on the Kohlberg legacy, including his work as a moral educator. Bandura's chapter is "The social cognitive theory of moral thought and action", and Enright's is on "The moral development of forgiveness". Gewirtz and colleagues write on an integration of Kohlberg's and Hoffman's theories of morality. Hann presents "Moral development from a social constructivist perspective", and Staub writes on the "Psychological and cultural origins of extreme destructiveness and extreme altruism".

The research volume contains a chapter by Bar-Tal on decision-making models of helping behavior. Eisenberg and colleagues discuss "Empathy-related responding and cognition: The chicken and the egg dilemma". Turiel, Smetana, & Killen explore "Social contexts in social cognitive development" and Walker's research is on "Sex differences in moral development".

The third volume in this series contains, among others, a chapter by Battistich, Watson, Solomon, Schaps & Solomon on "The Child Development Project: A comprehensive program for the development of prosocial character"; a chapter by Gibbs on sociomoral developmental delay and cognitive distortion, with implications for the treatment of antisocial youth; and a chapter by Higgins on Kohlberg's Just Community approach to moral education. Lickona discusses a program for moral development in the elementary school classroom.

Contains: Battistich, V., Watson, M., Solomon, D., Schaps, E., & Solomon, J. (1989)
Higgins, A. (1989)
Lickona, T. (1989)

229.Kutnick, P. J., & Brees, P. (1982). The development of cooperation: Explorations in cognitive and moral competence and social authority. *British Journal of Educational Psychology, 52,* 361-365.

Over a 6-week period, children in a sensitivity group that promoted trust-dependence through exercises showed fewer competitive and more cooperative behaviors on a cognitive task and more child sensitivity on a moral task than children trained in cooperative activities or simply given free play.

230.Ladd, G. W. (1981). Effectiveness of a social learning method for enhancing children's social interaction and peer acceptance. *Child Development, 52,* 171-178.

Third-grade children were coached on three communication skills: asking positive questions, offering useful suggestions or directions, and offering supportive statements. Eight coaching sessions, 40-50 minutes each, took place over a 3-week period. Coaches verbally instructed the children in the concepts, guided them through rehearsal of the ideas, let the children practice on their own with a classmate, and reviewed the concepts following practice. The review process (which included coaching in self-evaluation skills, assessment right after training and 7+ weeks later) showed significant improvement in 2 of 3 social skills taught, and on the Oden and Asbul self sociometric play rating measure of peer acceptance.

231.Ladd, G. W. (1990). Having friends, keeping friends, making friends, and being liked by peers in the classroom: Predictors of children's early school adjustment? *Child Development, 61,* 1081–1100.

During the kindergarten year, for 125 children, measures of positive peer relationships predicted gains in school performance. Children with a larger number of classroom friends during school entrance developed more favorable school perceptions by the second month, and if they maintained those friendships, they liked school better as the year progressed. Early lack of prosocial skills for making friends forecast lower performance levels over the school year.

These data suggest that kindergarten teachers may well need to make prosocial skill learning part of the early curriculum in order to boost the early learning careers of some youngsters.

232.Ladd, G. W., & Oden, S. (1979). The relationship between peer acceptance and children's ideas about helpfulness. *Child Development, 50,* 402–408.

In a posed task, lower cognitive problem-solving skills were found to predict less adeptness in generating group strategies with other children in order to help a peer. Students in third and fifth grades (N=68) described ways to help a same-sex peer depicted in cartoons as being teased/yelled at by classmates, or having an academic problem in class. Cartoons depicted both small group and two-person situations. In separate interviews, students responded to the situations from the perspective of helper or the person needing help. In addition, peers rated students on measures of friendship and the degree to which they liked to work or play with the student.

Children's responses to the helping situations were coded into 13 categories taken from the behaviors they would enact as the helper or would desire as the person in need of help. Responses were scored as "flexible" if they described a variety of alternatives, and "unique" if no other same-sex peer gave such a response. Peers agreed highly as to the types of responses considered helpful. In group situations, students would typically help by commanding peers to stop teasing/yelling. In two-person situations, students would help by consoling, comforting, suggesting alternative activities, or instructing. Flexibility was positively correlated with friendship and peer-liking ratings for boys, but not for girls. The number of unique responses was negatively related to peer ratings of liking and friendship, suggesting the existence of situational norms for helping.

233.Ladd, G. W., Lange, G., & Stremmel, A. (1983). Personal factors that mediate compliant helping. *Child Development, 54,* 488-501.

In a three-part study on helping, study one involved 72 first- and fourth-grade students. Each child went to a room where a group of simple tasks were shown in varying stages of progress: tasks were either tying knots in rope, or folding papers to make designs. Conditions varied in several ways. In the "help related" condition, children were either given previous instruction to insure knowledge of the task, or given no instruction. In the "need" condition, varying levels of completion of tasks were presented to assess effect of apparent need on helping behavior. Children were told that these projects belonged to other students who would probably appreciate help finishing if the children chose to help.

Need scores reflected the number of times children chose to help the peer with the *least* completed project. *Knowledge scores* were the number of times tasks were chosen based on prior knowledge of task. Each trial contained both familiar and unfamiliar tasks. Both first- and fourth-graders showed a marked preference to help on the basis of need rather than knowledge. Fourth-graders chose to help based on both familiarity and need, while first-graders helped only on the basis of need.

In part two, 80 first- and fourth-graders experienced the same condition as above, with an additional group given no suggestion of helping. After the trials, all children answered questions regarding which peers needed help most, and whether they knew how to do the task or needed to figure it out. Helping was scored by the amount of time on task and the number of tasks completed. Children in the high-need and high-knowledge conditions spent a greater proportion of time on task than did low-need or low-knowledge children. Older children scored higher than younger on all but the high-need, low/knowledge condition. Across grades, those children exhorted to help spent more time helping than those who received no suggestion to help. Ninety percent of children reported that they helped because the peer needed help.

Finally, in part three, 72 kindergarten, first-, third-, and fourth-grade students looked at 16 pairs of line-drawn pictures and listened to stories where the personal (dispositional) and situational information given varied regarding the story character's capability to solve the problem presented, the character's gender, as well as situational constraints such as time allotted for helping. Older children reported they would help more consistently than younger children. Younger children showed a preference for helping same-sex peers. When helping opposite-sex peers, decisions were based on dispositional rather than situational factors.

234.LaGreca, A. M., & Santogrossi, D. A. (1980). Social skills training with elementary school students: A behavioral group approach. *Journal of Consulting and Clinical Psychology, 48,* 220-227.

Social skills were taught in small groups to isolated or non-accepted elementary school children (8-to-10 years old), but no differences were found in social interactions after treatment. The sociometric status of the target children also did not improve, but the target children did increase in frequency of initiating social interactions.

235.Lally, J. R., Mangione, P., & Honig, A. S. (1988). The Syracuse University Family Development Research Program: Long-range impact of an early intervention with low income children and their families. In D. Powell (Ed.), *Parent education as early childhood intervention: Emerging directions in theory, research, and practice* (pp. 79-104). Norwood, NJ: Ablex.

A longitudinal follow-up of 65 disadvantaged children who had been in an omnibus enrichment program that began with parent involvement prior to the birth of the infant (continuing until the child was 60 months) and included high-quality child care from six months onward, contrasted the academic and personal-social functioning of the children with 54 youths who had participated since infancy in a carefully matched control group. A strong program component of the Family Development Research Program (FDRP) was to enhance positive family functioning, self-esteem, and prosocial development. Ten years after graduation, the *delinquency* rates of the program children were much lower. There were 4 cases (mostly PINS) among FDRP youth, and 12 cases (including more recidivism and more severe acts, such as rape, robbery, and assault) among controls. Program families reported more family closeness and pride in their children. Early intervention programs need an emphasis on prosocial relationships as well as cognitive skill building.

236.Larrieu, J., & Mussen, P. (1986). Some personality and motivational correlates of children's prosocial behavior. *The Journal of Genetic Psychology, 147,* 529-542.

Sharing, caring, and helping actions on the playground were observed for 76 male and female fourth-graders and sociometric peer nominations of their prosocial status were obtained with questions such as:

(a) "Which three boys (girls) care most about how others feel and try not to hurt their feelings?"

(b) "Which three most often stick up for some kid that the others are teasing or calling names?"

There were more intercorrelations of sociometrically measured prosocial variables for girls than for boys, but this could be due to halo effect in rating. Personal attributes and self-concept were measured by questionnaire. Assertiveness in girls was associated with caring, and the more important these values were, the greater the frequency of observed helping. For the boys, caring, sharing, and helping were separate domains, relatively independent of one another. For girls, there was more coherence in manifestations of prosocial tendencies. Caring and empathy were greater for girls than boys. Possibly this is due to differential socialization, where boys are more likely to be socialized for active instrumental roles and girls for more nurturing expressive roles.

237.Lawrence, B. (1984). Conversation and cooperation, child linguistic maturity, parental speech, and helping behavior of young children. *Child Development, 55,* 1926-1935.

Sixty children (aged 18, 24, and 30 months) participated with parents in completion of familiar household tasks, such as bedmaking and picking up books, in a laboratory setting. Parents' verbal and non-verbal behaviors were recorded both before and during tasks, while the length of children's spontaneous verbalizations were measured throughout. Time spent on task completion was measured for both parent and child. The length of child verbalizations was a better predictor of cooperative behavior than child age. Aspects of parental speech were significant only in *maintaining* helping behaviors once begun, with positive comments associated with continued cooperation, and excessive parental talking associated with a decrease in helping.

238.Leahy, R. L. (1979). Development of conceptions of prosocial behavior: Information affecting rewards given for altruism and kindness. *Developmental Psychology, 15* (1), 34-37.

Graduate students, first-graders, and fifth-graders were presented situations of kindness or altruism, with children allocating rewards. Younger children used an *additive* principle, allocating greater rewards for behavior that led to positive consequences or avoided negative consequences. Older children used a *discounting* principle, allocating greater rewards for behavior that initially led to no reward or occurred under the threat of harm.

239.LeCapitaine, J. E. (1987). The relationship between emotional development and moral development and the differential impact of three psychological interventions on children. *Psychology in the Schools, 24,* 372-378.

Seventy-two students, third- and fourth-graders, were randomly divided into three treatment groups. Both before and after treatment, all students completed Kohlberg's Moral Judgment Interview and the DuPont Affective Development Test. Activities for all groups consisted of: viewing filmstrips, role-playing, large and small group discussions, and brainstorming. Group One students focused on identification of feelings. Group Two activities stressed identification of conflicts/problems, generating alternative responses to the problem, and selecting a "best" course of action. Group Three students participated in activities combining aspects of both groups. All three groups showed a significant increase in general emotional development scores after treatment. Group Three students demonstrated a marked increase on Kohlberg Moral Maturity Scores, while both other groups showed only a slight increase. In general, emotional development scores were positively correlated with moral development scores.

240. Lennon, R., & Eisenberg, N. (1987). Emotional displays associated with preschoolers' prosocial behavior. *Child Development, 58,* 992-1000.

Two- to four-year-olds, grouped in same-sex, same-age triads, played in a familiar, empty room containing one "jumping frog" toy. Children's object-related actions were filmed for ten minutes. Actions were coded as sharing (spontaneous or requested) or defensive (saying no, pushing peer away, or removing toy). Emotions were coded for those who shared and those who were the recipients of sharing, both before and after each interaction. Categories included happy, sad, and angry. Those who shared showed more happiness before spontaneous sharing than requested sharing. Recipients displayed greater happiness after spontaneous than asked-for sharing, but more anger before asked-for than spontaneous sharing. Those who shared did so much more readily when their peers displayed happy as opposed to angry emotions (sadness was noted for only two interactions).

241. Lerner, M. J., & Meindl, J. R. (1981). Justice and altruism. In J. P. Rushton & R. M. Sorrentino (Eds.), *Altruism and helping behavior: Social, personality, and developmental perspectives.* Hillsdale, NJ: Lawrence Erlbaum.

This chapter explores the origins/motives of altruism and justice in adults and children using constructs of the Justice Motive theory which states that people act according to rules of "justice" if and when they believe them to be the most profitable and least costly way to behave. The initial stages of the development of the justice motive theory, (i.e., the psychosocial basis and the development of "personal contract" which seeks to maximize personal outcomes) are explored.

242.Levin, I., & Beckerman-Greenberg, R. (1980). Moral judgment and moral behavior in sharing: A developmental analysis. *Genetic Psychology Monographs, 101,* 215-230.

Children indicated if and why they would share pretzels with three kinds of children:

a. peers who had previously refused to share crayons with the child
b. a "bad" child who often disrupts the lessons, and
c. a poor and needy child.

The children also expressed whether they thought in general one should share with other children and why. Responses were coded into 6 levels of justification reasoning:

1. Moral egocentrism and lack of generosity
2. Immediate, automatic, generous reciprocity
3. Desire to be a "good" and generous child
4. Generosity depends on the relation between people
5. Child is generous through empathizing with others
6. Generosity is due to positive justice being regarded as a value that can enhance group social relations.

Older children were more likely to use less egoistic and more relationship justifications for generosity.

243.Levine, L., & Hoffman, M. (1975). Empathy and cooperation in 4-year-olds. *Developmental Psychology, 11,* 533-534.

Eighty four-year-olds responded to the Feshbach-Roe (1968) empathy measure (identifying happiness, sadness, anger, and fear through pictures) and two measures of cooperation. The first measure was an adapted version of Kagan and Madsen's (1971) cooperation board game. Whether each player's moves were gauged as cooperative or competitive depended on whether they continued or blocked the direction of their opponent's moves. The second measure consisted of two and one-half hour observations in regular nursery school settings, while children were engaged in cooperative work or play. Although girls obtained higher empathy scores than boys, empathy did not relate to cooperation scores. When asked why they had cooperated, only a few children answered in empathic terms; most referred to requirements of the game, friendship, or reciprocity.

244. Lewis, M., & Rosenblum, L. A. (Ed.) (1975). *Friendship and peer relations.* New York: Wiley.

This volume contains chapters on the origins of friendship, the beginnings of peer relationships, toddler peer interactions, apprehensions with unfamiliar peers, and comparative perspectives on interpersonal development among primates. Early peer interactions are important for advancing children's understanding of prosocial methods of interpersonal behaviors and this volume presents researches on the earliest peer interaction patterns.

245. Lickona, T. (Ed.) (1976). *Moral development and behavior: Theory, research, and social issues.* New York: Holt.

Contains: Kohlberg, L. (1976)

246.Lipscomb, T., McAllister, H., & Bregman, N. (1985). A developmental inquiry into the effects of multiple models on children's generosity. *Merrill-Palmer Quarterly, 31* (4), 335-344.

Generosity was studied among 87 kindergarten and 80 4th-grade children. The Full Circle Board game was used. Two canisters held winnings. On one was written *March of Dimes* and *My Money* on the other. A videotape informed the children about the game and the possibility to donate winnings. One model was a woman, one a man, and they modeled either generosity (donating pennies), selfishness, or inconsistency (first generous on one exposure, then selfish in the next exposure).

Kindergarten children donated significantly more when both models were generous compared with when one model acted selfishly and the other generously. The generosity of younger children was affected more by the models' behaviors. Older children exposed to a single selfish model two times also patterned their behavior after that of the model to a significant extent. Despite having internalized norms of generosity to those less fortunate, older children exhibited a significant disinhibitory effect toward selfishness.

247.Lovelace, V. (1988). The prosocial and educational impact of watching television. American Psychological Association Division 37. *Division of Child, Youth and Family Services Newsletter, 11*, pp. 2, 25.

This short concise summary of research describes the effects of prosocial television shows: to increase children's helping behavior, decrease aggression, and improve social interactions.

248.Macaulay, J. R., & Berkowitz, L. (Eds.) (1970). *Altruism and helping behaviors.* New York: Academic Press.

This edited book includes chapters focusing particularly on children's prosocial development. Bryan's chapter is entitled "Children's reactions to helpers: Their money isn't where their mouths are." Resenhan's chapter is entitled "The natural socialization of altruistic autonomy."

Contains: Aronfreed (1970)

249.Madden, N., & Slavin, R. (1983). Effects of cooperative learning on the social acceptance of mainstreamed academically handicapped students. *Journal of Special Education, 17,* 171-182.

Self-esteem increased and the rejection of academically handicapped grade-school children decreased after the initiation of cooperative learning strategies, although friendships were not increased.

250.Madsen, M. C. (1971). Developmental and cross-cultural difference in the cooperation and competitive behavior of young children. *Journal of Cross-Cultural Psychology, 2,* 365-371.

Madsen is the inventor of the marble-pull game. Children play in pairs sitting facing each other with the game board between them. The game board consists of an open-top box with a hole in the bottom at each end, facing each player. Two blocks, in the middle of the box, are hollowed out on one side and held together by magnetic tape. Each block has a string attached that runs through an eyelet in front of each player. The teacher places one plastic disc (of ten) at a time in the hollow space in the block. When a child pulls the string in front, the block moves the disc towards one side or the other until the disc drops into the hole and a small receptacle cup. If both children pull at once, the block pulls apart and the disc falls into neither player's hole. The teacher rejoins the block and more trials continue until all ten discs are used. Thus, children can try cooperation or competition. They can decide to share — to taken turns where each can win a disc.

251. Madsen, M. C., & Shapira, A. (1970). Cooperative and competitive behavior of urban Afro-American, Anglo-American, Mexican-American, and Mexican village children. *Developmental Psychology, 3*, 16-20.

Mexican boys from a small town were far less competitive in a Madsen board game than Afro-American, Anglo-American, and Mexican-American boys. The differences between the girls did not reach significance.

252. Maher, B. (Ed.) (1978). *Progress in experimental personality research.* New York: Academic Press.

Contains: Feshbach, N. (1978)

253.Main, M., & George, C. (1985). Responses of abused and disadvantaged toddlers to distress in agemates: A study in the day care setting. *Developmental Psychology, 21* (3), 407–412.

Ten abused toddlers and ten matched controls (1 to 3 years old) from families experiencing stress were observed in day care for response to distress, frights, or panic among their peers. No abused toddler showed concern in response to peer distress. They did show disturbing behaviors not seen in the controls, such as alternately attacking and attempting to comfort the distressed peers. Half of the non-abused toddlers showed concern, sadness, or empathy at least once while observing peer distress. On average, the disadvantaged toddlers from stressed but non-abusive families responded with concerned expression to one-third of the witnessed distress events. Abused toddlers may be mirroring parental behavior they have experienced.

254.Mant, C. M., & Perner, J. (1988). The child's understanding of commitment. *Developmental Psychology, 24* (3), 343–351.

The researchers asked 5–10-year-old children (N=120) to pass moral judgment on story protagonists for not carrying out an action that could have prevented a friend's misfortune. In the commitment story, the protagonist agreed to act; in the no-commitment story, the protagonist predicted he would act without understanding that his friend would then really count on him. Only children from 8 and 1/2 years onward showed improvement in understanding that it is good to keep a promise to a friend. The six-year-olds tended to judge the protagonists by the adverse result of their failure to act as planned. As "moral realism" in Piagetian theory would predict, the children focused only on objective results, without considering that if one child had made a promise to the other and then simply did not keep it, this was a worse action than if the child had been prevented by parental prohibition or had simply said they might come (to a pool with paid admission, where a friend was waiting). The youngest children understood a promise, even when they did not yet understand that one is only constrained to carry out an action if one has, indeed, *committed* oneself so that another is relying on you. Understanding reciprocity takes time to develop.

255.Marcus, R. F. (1987). The role of affect in children's cooperation. *Child Study Journal,* *17,* 153-168.

Pairs of children from two and one-half to six years of age (N=72) were observed in free play in their classrooms engaging in one of three types of cooperative play: dramatizing situations of adult life; working to achieve a common goal such as building a block construction together; or playing formal games. Observers collected running accounts of each cooperative episode, as well as the pair's expressions of emotion, verbalizations, and behaviors. Categories of emotion included: happy, sad, angry, afraid, and neutral. Language categories were: agreement, disagreement, joking, directing/demanding, and squabbling. Cooperation lasted longer when both children were judged to be happy. In addition, duration was significantly related to verbal expression of feelings, both positive and negative. Only squabbling was unrelated to the length of cooperative interaction.

256.Marcus, R. F., Telleen, & Roke, E. J. (1979). Relation between cooperation and empathy in young children. *Developmental Psychology, 15* (3), 346-347.

Cooperation among 32 preschool children (age 37-61 months) was measured during free play by coded observations and a 7-point rating scale of cooperation, which ranged from extremely cooperative and sharing to extremely individualistic. Empathy was rated by the Feshbach & Roe slide sequences, where children are asked "Tell me how you feel". Cooperation was greater for the older preschoolers. No significant relation between empathy and coded cooperation was found, but observed and rated cooperation measures were correlated (r=.30).

257.Maruyama, G., Fraser, S. C., & Miller, N. (1982). Personal responsibility and altruism in children. *Journal of Personality and Social Psychology, 42,* 659-664.

Children trick-or-treating on Halloween night were asked to donate some of the candy they received to children in hospitals. For some groups, there was a generalized request. For other groups, one group was arbitrarily designated as the collector for the group. In other groups, responsibility was given to each child directly ("I will be counting on you and you and you...") for the donations. The smallest donations were made in the groups where no one was given responsibility. The most generous donations were made by the groups in which *each individual child was given responsibility.*

258.McGrath, M. P., & Power, T. G. (1990). The effects of reasoning and choice on children's prosocial behaviour. *International Journal of Behavioural Development, 13* (3), 345-353.

Second- and third-grade children (N=48) were randomly assigned to groups where they were either asked or instructed to ("you must") donate one of two prizes to sick children who could not be in the study. Some children were told: "I'll be upset if you don't donate one of your prizes to the sick children, but it's up to you whether or not you donate one of your prizes" (adult-oriented reasoning/choice condition). In the beneficiary-oriented reasoning/choice condition, the experimenter said: "It's up to you whether or not you donate one of your prizes." In the no-choice beneficiary-oriented reasoning condition, the child was told she or he must donate, and that the sick children would be upset if a prize wasn't donated. All children donated one prize. They were then given the chance to copy words on a paper to help "other children who were having trouble with school" and to play with toys. More children in the choice conditions reported that they had a choice about donating, and choice earlier enhanced the occurrence of prosocial behavior in the later situation. Almost all the children reported that the sick children and the experimenter would be sad or mad if the child did not donate. The children already seemed to have internalized moral values related to sharing and helping, and superfluous reasoning actually reduced their prosocial behaviour.

259.McGurk, H. (Ed.) (1978). *Issues in childhood social development.* Cambridge: Methuen.

Contains: Furman, W., Rahe, D., & Hartup, W.
(1978)
Hartup, W. W. (1978)

260.Midlarsky, E., & Hannah, M. (1985).
Competence, reticence, and helping by
children and adolescents. *Developmental
Psychology, 21,* 534-541.

Two studies, using separate groups of
first-, fourth-, seventh-, and tenth-grade
students (N=256 for each) looked at children's
willingness to help an injured victim, as well as
reasons for not helping. In Study One, each
child had the opportunity to help another
(either a preschooler or a peer) who had bumped
into a table and fallen to the floor. The
child's response was scored for whether help
was attempted, the amount of help given, and
the time elapsed before helping.

In Study Two, the same scene was staged to
the point of injury. Groups of students then
completed a questionnaire on whether or not
they would help and what might prevent or
inhibit helping. Helping increased from first to
fourth grades, decreased from fourth to
seventh and increased again from seventh to
tenth. Girls gave significantly more help to
preschoolers than boys did, but were less
helpful when confronted with an injured peer.
All participants gave more help to a person
whose injury seemed more serious. Reasons for
not helping varied with age. First- and fourth-
graders described feelings of lacking
competence. Seventh-grade students noted fear
of social disapproval, while tenth-graders cited
fear that recipients might be embarrassed or
regard help as condescending.

261. Miller, D. & Smith, J. (1977). The effect of own deservingness and deservingness of others on children's helping behavior. *Child Development, 48,* (2), 617-620.

Fifth-grade students were given 70 cents for "testing" a miniature basketball game for experimenters described as working for a toy company. One-third of the students were told this was the usual proper payment for fifth-graders. One-third were told this was less than fifth-graders typically received and that they were underpaid; while the remaining third were told that 70 cents was more than fifth-graders usually received and that they were overpaid. Students were then given the opportunity to donate some of their earnings to others who either did not receive payment or lost their earnings. Students who were overpaid donated the most money, giving equally to both groups. Those who were properly paid donated more than underpaid students; both giving more to those children who did not receive payment than to those who had lost their earnings.

262. Miller, P., Kessel, F., & Flavell, J. (1970). Thinking about people, thinking about people, thinking about ...: A study of social cognitive development. *Child Development, 41,* 613-623.

Children from grades 1-6 (N=62) from a suburban elementary school described line drawing representations of talking and thinking similar to ones used in comic strips to trace the understanding of recursive thinking, e.g., "He is thinking that she is thinking that he is thinking...." Such thinking may be implicated in empathic/decentered responses. Although performance improved with increasing grade level, understanding of recursive thought was not nearly complete at grade 6. Group

performance and scalability of individuals
indicated progressive development:

    thinking about people
    thinking about action
    thinking about thinking
    thinking about thinking about thinking

263.Miller, P., & Lindholm, E. (1988).
Differentiation of vicariously induced
emotional reactions in children.
Developmental Psychology, 24, 237-246.

Preschoolers (N=39) and second-graders
(N=43) watched three short films designed to
generate vicarious feelings of: anxiety (a
thunderstorm); sadness (death of a pet bird);
and cognitively-induced sympathy (a disabled
child discussing physical therapy). After the
film, children described how they were feeling,
and pointed to the drawing of a child's face
that matched their feelings (choice of happy,
sad, afraid, sorry or neutral). Facial
expressions were coded on a five-point scale
from "no sign of emotion" to "exceptionally
strong" emotional display. Expressions were
compared to heart rates and self-reported
emotions. Children's heart rates accelerated in
response to the anxiety film, and decelerated
when watching the sad and cognitively induced
sympathy films. Facial expressions of fear, gaze
aversion and anxiety occurred during the
anxiety film; sadness/concern were evident
during both of the other films. Children
reported fear during the anxiety film and
sadness during the sad film. "Feeling nothing"
was the most frequently reported response to
the sympathy film. Older children differentiated
emotions more clearly than younger children.

264.Miller, R., Brickman, P., & Bolen, D. (1975). Attribution versus persuasion as a means for modifying behavior. *Journal of Personality and Social Psychology, 31*, 430-441.

Children who were told by their teachers and principal that they were neat and tidy persons reduced their littering more than children who were told that they ought to be neat and tidy or who were given no talks at all. Children, reminded often of how ecology-conscious they were, picked up more wrappers thrown on the ground in order to tidy the environment, compared with children not given such attributions. Children in the persuasion or moral exhortation group fell midway between the attribution and control groups.

265.Mischel, W., & Mischel, H. N. (1976). A cognitive social learning approach to morality and self-regulation. In T. Lickona (Ed.), *Moral development and behavior: Theory, research, and social issues.* New York: Holt.

Young children who are alerted *prior* to non-compliance can learn self-control better than children who are corrected after doing a non-acceptable action. Teachers can use this finding to teach prosocial responses prior to agonistic peer encounters.

266.Mischel, H. N., & Mischel, W. (1983). The development of children's knowledge of self-control strategies. *Child Development, 54*, 603-619.

Impulse control and delay of gratification for the self are important ingredients in prosocial behavior. This work traces the growth of self-control in young children. Two studies of preschoolers and third-graders asked children what would help them wait to get two marshmallows to eat rather than eat one after a much shorter delay. Findings were that preschoolers did not know any of the basic delay rules. By third-grade, children knew that it is preferable to wait with rewards covered rather than exposed, and to engage in task-oriented thinking rather than ideation about self-gratification (such as how good the marshmallows will be to eat). The older children anticipate that if delayed objects are exposed, they will be frustratingly aroused by them. The value of abstract thinking is important in helping children think about consequences that are short-term versus longer-term or that could be more beneficial rather than less.

267.Moore, B. S., Underwood, B., & Rosenhan, D. L. (1973). Affect and altruism. *Developmental Psychology, 8,* 99-104.

Students in the 2nd and 3rd grades were given the opportunity to donate money to absent children in one of four situations: after generating and thinking about happy or sad experiences (treatment groups); after counting to 30 or sitting quietly for 30 seconds (control groups). Children who thought about happy experiences contributed the most. Contrary to previous studies, children who focused on negative/sad experiences contributed the least. One difference may be that this study utilized *internally generated sad experiences*, where others have used externally controlled failure experiences such as those that occur in competitive games.

268.Moore, S. (1977a). Research in review. Considerateness and helpfulness in young children. *Young Children, 32,* (4), 73-77.

Although positive, friendly behaviors exceed negative aggressive ones in preschool researches, only a small proportion of the friendly interactions involve other-oriented acts of generosity, nurturance, or helping. Teachers need to encourage children to become both givers as well as receivers of help and affection.

269.Moore, S. (1977b). Research in review: The effects of television on the prosocial behavior of young children. *Young Children, 32,* (5), 60-65.

This review of prosocial television research in the 1970's suggests that children do seem to imitate the behaviors of some of the prosocial characters seen on TV. Mr. Rogers' Neighborhood is noteworthy in stressing the unique worth of each individual. Enhancement of a child's self-esteem may be one precursor for the development of prosocial attitudes toward others.

270.Moore, S. (1979). Research in review. Social cognition: Knowing about others. *Young Children, 34* (3), 54-62.

Moore reviews researches that address questions about the role-taking skills of young children, how they acquire and use social knowledge, how they infer the emotional state and intentions of others, and what childrearing factors enhance children's ability to acquire and use social knowledge. Research programs available for enhancing such acquisitions are described. These include Smilansky's dramatic play program where sociodramas are acted out by children and the children are encouraged to tell what they know about people, animals, and events through their role-taking and play themes.

271. Moore, S. G., & Cooper, C. R. (Eds.) (1982). *The young child: Reviews of research*, Vol. 3 (pp. 157-158). Washington, DC: National Association for the Education of Young Children.

Contains: Asher, S. R., Renshaw, P. D., & Hymel, S. (1982)
Rubin, K., & Everett, B. (1982)

272. Morris, W., Marshall, H., & Miller, R. (1973). Effect of vicarious punishment on prosocial behavior in children. *Journal of Experimental Child Psychology, 15,* 222-236.

The effect of punishment of a model's antisocial behavior was explored. First- and second-graders who witnessed a peer model being punished for refusal to share, shared more than a control group. Sharing was also increased, however, in a group who witnessed the model being punished for no apparent reason (non-contingent on behavior). These results support the hypothesis that the viewing of non-contingent punishment to a model results in a generalized inhibition against antisocial behaviors.

273. Mussen, P., & Eisenberg-Berg, N. (1977). *Roots of caring, sharing, and helping: The development of prosocial behavior in*

children. San Francisco, CA: Freeman.

This out-of-print easy-to-read textbook provides a summary of research findings related to prosocial actions. Such variables include: parenting practices, child mood, exhortation or modeling by adults, as well as television, peer, cultural, and situational influences.

274.Mussen, P., Harris, S., Rutherford, E., & Keasey, C. (1970). Honesty and altruism among preadolescents. *Developmental Psychology, 3,* 169-194.

Sixth-grade students completed a self-concept scale, an intelligence test, a sociometric questionnaire, and participated in two situational tests of honesty and altruism. The sociometric questionnaire was a 20-item "peer nomination" measure where students named peers who, for example, were most willing to share, likely to follow rules, or would never copy from another's test. A child's score on this measure was the number of nominations. In the situational test of honesty, students played a "shooting gallery" game by shooting a "ray gun" at a moving target. Scores were prearranged, and registered above the game. Prizes were promised for high scores, unachievable due to prearranged scoring. Since students played the game privately, the experimenter was (presumably) unaware of the accuracy of scores reported after the game. Performance on this measure was scored by whether the student reported an honest or dishonest score for the game. The situational test of altruism involved an electronic game played with a fictitious peer in a different room (actually, the experimenter). Players could either cooperate in choosing the sequence of moves in this game (and split the points), or compete and attempt to win the majority of points. The altruism score was the number of cooperative choices the student made.

Situational honesty scores were positively correlated with peer nominations on the sociometric measure. Honesty, for boys, was *negatively* related to parental behaviors sometimes considered to be linked to prosocial development. Honest boys were more likely than their less honest peers to feel more dissatisfied with themselves, anxious, inadequate and not likable.

275.Nadler, A., Romek, E., & Shapiro-Friedman, A. (1979). Giving in the kibbutz: Prosocial behavior of city and kibbutz children as affected by social responsibility and social pressure. *Journal of Cross-Cultural Psychology, 10,* 57-72.

It was hypothesized that children reared in a communal settlement such as a kibbutz should (a) espouse attitudes of social responsibility and (b) display prosocial behavior, more than a comparable sample of city children. Fifth-graders (N=123) were chosen for the study. Approximately half were from an elementary school in Tel-Aviv and half were from three kibbutzim. The children were asked to donate some or all of ten pens that had been given to them as a reward. The altruistic social pressure group children were told that children in a first group gave seven or more out of ten pens. In the egotistic pressure group, children were told that most of the children in the first group gave only two or less of their pens to the poor children. It was found that the Kibbutz children had higher scores on the social responsibility scale and were more generous than city children. Females had higher social responsibility scores, and gave more than males. The failure of the altruistic pressure to elicit the predicted higher rate of prosocial behavior with kibbutz children may be a result of ceiling effect. Kibbutz girls did not yield to the egotistic social pressure. It appears that the communal educational system which exerts pressure toward cooperative values affects the children's giving.

276.Naparstek, N. (1990). Children's conceptions of prosocial behavior. *Child Study Journal, 20* (4), 207-220.

The age at which children are capable of identifying different subcomponents or subconstructs of prosocial behavior was explored. Twenty children, from each of five age groups (second-, fourth-, sixth-, eighth-graders, and adult teachers) sorted and labeled statements that were constructed for each of the constructs of helping, sharing, comforting, and complimenting. The children were told to "make separate piles for the statements that seem to belong together because they share something important in common." The children were also told that they could make as many or as few piles or groups as they wanted. Older children, especially the 8th-graders, exhibited greater differentiation of the subconstructs of prosocial behaviors than younger children.

277.Norem-Hebersen, M., & Johnson, D. (1981). The relationship between cooperative, competitive, and individualistic attitudes and differentiated aspects of self-esteem. *Journal of Personality, 49,* 415-426.

When compared with competitive and individualistic situations, cooperative learning strategies for children in elementary school classrooms promoted greater feelings of support, more open and accurate communication of ideas and feelings, greater satisfaction from efforts to achieve, and greater ability to take the emotional and cognitive perspective of others.

278. Nucci, L. P., & Nucci, M. S. (1982). Children's responses to moral and social conventional transgressions in a free-play setting. *Child Development, 53*, 403-412.

Students in thirty classes (ten each at second-, fifth-, and seventh-grade level) were observed and interviewed during classroom and playground situations. Observers coded spontaneous events involving transgressions that were social-conventional or moral in nature. After the event, nearby children were interviewed individually about what they had observed, whether it was the right thing to do; whether a rule existed about this at school; and if a rule existed, whether it should always be followed. There was a high level of agreement between children of all grades and observers regarding classification of events as moral or social conventional, with many more conventional than moral transgressions observed.

Children responded more frequently to moral transgressions, with second-graders requesting adult involvement and older children responding with retaliation or ridicule of the transgressor. They responded to conventional transgressions with rule statements in second grade, while fifth- and seventh-graders used ridicule. Teachers were much less likely to respond to moral transgressions than to violations of school conventions. They may need more training in recognition of and response to *moral* versus *rule* transgressions in classrooms.

279.Nucci, L. P., & Turiel, E. (1978). Social
    interactions and development of social
    concepts in preschool children. *Child
    Development, 49,* 400-407.

    Preschoolers made distinctions between the
concepts of *moral rules* and *social rules*. In a
preschool setting, teachers were more likely to
initiate responses to conventional
transgressions (such as getting up out of a
seat). Both adults and children responded to
moral transgressions: adults by focusing on
feelings and reasons for behaving differently,
and children (typically the victims) by emotional
and physical expressions of injury or loss, or
by involving adults.

280.O'Bryant, S., & Brophy, J. (1976). Sex
    differences in altruistic behavior.
    Developmental Psychology, 12, 554.

    Seventy fifth-grade students had the
opportunity to donate tokens to absent
children and to give direct help to a younger,
same-sex child in a counting task. No
relationship existed between donating and
helping. Girls and boys were equally generous in
donating, but girls were significantly more
helpful than boys in assisting the younger
child.

281. O'Connor, M., & Cuevas, J. (1982). The
    relationship of children's prosocial behavior
    to social responsibility, prosocial
    reasoning, and personality. *Journal of
    Genetic Psychology, 140,* 33-45.

    In the *Prosocial Reasoning Test* a child is
presented with four pictured prosocial
vignettes with accompanying narratives in which
one child helps another of the same sex. An

example of a vignette is:

Mary and Amy were going to the school cafeteria at lunchtime. When they were in line, Amy discovered that she didn't have any money -- she had accidentally lost it. Mary offered to let Amy have part of her lunch.

After each vignette, the children read four possible reasons why the character in the story had offered help. On a 5-point scale they were to show how probable it was that the character had helped for each reason listed, (e.g. Mary thought that Amy might be more likely to share something with her later on, or Mary didn't want Amy to be hungry). The range of possible scores for both self-oriented and other-oriented reasons ranged from 8 to 40.

282.Oden, S., & Asher, S. (1977). Coaching children in social skills for friendship making. *Child Development, 48,* 495-506.

Third- and fourth-grade students rated by peers as socially isolated received coaching in social skills. Coaching consisted of: *instructions from an adult on skills in friendship making and playing games with a peer to practice these skills.* A post-play review session with the coach evaluated learning and performance. A second group played the same games with peers, but without coaching, while a third group played in a room without interaction. Children in the coaching group showed significantly greater increases on follow-up sociometric ratings compared with peer play or control groups, both immediately after coaching, and one year later.

283.Olweus, D., Block, J., & Radke-Yarrow, M.(Eds.)(1986). *Development of antisocial and prosocial behavior: Research, theories, and issues.* New York: Academic Press.

This volume of edited chapters contains a variety of approaches to study social development. Hinde reviews the implications of evolutionary theory and comparative data for the study of antisocial and prosocial behaviors. Others discuss the role of genetic factors and hormones. Rheingold describes nurturant acts of toddlers. Several chapters relate infant-parent attachment patterns and child-interaction patterns in the home with preschool prosocial and antisocial behaviors. Authors also review the contributions of sex-role patterns, impulse control, siblings, and the role of television in the development of prosocial/antisocial behaviors.

Contains: Pulkkinen, L. (1986)
Radke-Yarrow, M., & Zahn-Waxler, C. (1986)
Water, E., Hay, D., & Richters, J (1986)

284.Overton, W. (Ed.) (1983). *The relationship between social and cognitive development.* Hillsdale, NJ: Lawrence Erlbaum.

Contains: Hoffman, M. (1983)
Turiel, E. (1983b)

285.Park, K., & Honig, A. S. (1991). Infant child care patterns and later teacher ratings of preschool behaviors. *Early Child Development and Care, 68,* 89-96.

Preschool teachers (blind to infant care status, rated 105 middle class preschoolers (M= 53 months) on the 30-item Preschool Behavior Questionnaire and the Preschool Behavior Rating instrument. Group 1 had begun full-time care prior to 9 months, Group 2 after 9 months. Group 3 had no full-time care prior to 36 months. Teachers reported no differences in cooperativeness with adults, no difference in social assertiveness, and no differences in positive peer interactions as a function of infancy care patterns. Group 1 children were slightly more likely to be rated as antisocial rather than prosocial in peer interactions, but also as more successful at problem-solving and ability to abstract. Aggression behaviors were predicted more by quality of child care and by current mother-child attachment than by group membership. Caregivers may need to be particularly careful to have well-planned and specific activities comprising a prosocial curriculum for infants in full-time care in the first year of life. They can also provide developmentally appropriate information/support materials and talks for full-time employed parents of very young babies in child care.

286.Park, K. A., & Waters, E. (1989). Security of attachment and preschool friendships. *Child Development, 60,* 1076-1081.

Mother-child attachment patterns (measured by the Waters Q sort) related to the social nature of play between good preschool friends. Of the 40 friend pairs, those who were securely attached to their mothers played together happily, shared readily with each other, negotiated peacefully to settle issues between them, and settled them fairly. Those dyads where one friend was securely attached and the other insecure showed more partner rejection when angry, more grabs for toys, and more verbal rejection of the partner. Securely attached children were more prosocial in their interactive *style* with peers.

287.Parke, R. D., & Bhavnagri, N. P. (1989). Parents as managers of children's peer relationships. In D. Belle (Ed.) *Children's social networks and social supports.* New York: Wiley.

Parental supervision was more important for 2 to 3 1/2-year-olds to sustain prosocial peer interactions compared with 3 1/2- to 6-year-olds. The younger children could not sustain positive social skills without parental support. Parental competence in teaching turn-taking was positively related to toddlers' ability to act simultaneously on toys together with a peer, and to play longer and more cooperatively.

288.Paulson, F. L. (1974). Teaching cooperation on television: An evaluation of Sesame Street social program goals. *AV Communication Review, 22,* 229-246.

Children from 10 day care centers were assigned to view or not view Sesame Street episodes daily in which characters modeled cooperative strategies of interaction. Six test situations subsequently replicated problems in cooperation that had been viewed and a seventh situation was added to assess generalization of cooperation to new situations. Viewers scored significantly higher on cooperation solutions that had been modeled on the program segments aired and on general cooperation (not previously modeled on the TV episodes). But the children did not differ in a free play observation, which was however, extremely brief, and may not have assessed social interactions sufficiently.

289.Payne, F. D. (1988). Children's prosocial conduct in structured situations as viewed by others: Consistency, convergence, and relationships with person variables. *Child Development, 51,* 1252-1259.

Prosocial behaviors clustered together according to whether the recipient was an unknown peer (donating and helping) or an actual classroom peer (cooperating and sharing). The relationship of the child to the recipient may determine the *consistency* of various prosocial interactions.

290.Pearl, R. (1985). Children's understanding of others' need for help: Effects of problem explicitness and type. *Child Development, 56,* 735-745.

When distress is expressed subtly and non-verbally, four-year-olds have a difficult time recognizing that the person needs help. When distress was expressed more explicitly, then fours could recognize the problem. Nine-year-olds had no difficulty recognizing even very subtle cues of distress in others.

291. Perry, D. G., Perry, L. C., Bussey, K., English, D., & Arnold, G. (1980). Processes of attribution and children's self-punishment following misbehavior. *Child Development, 51,* 545-552.

The researchers argue that children anticipate and experience heightened self-criticism when they fall to live up to positive dispositions attributed to them. Based on their interaction with some children, the experimenters told them that they believed them to be capable of carrying out instructions, following rules, working hard, and avoiding distraction. Other children were not provided with these moral attributions. The children had to perform a boring task and not be distracted by exciting cartoons shown. When children yielded to temptation, they were told they might not be deserving of all the tokens to be given for participation in the task. Children who had been told that they were the kind that could resist temptation, but had failed, kept fewer of the tokens for themselves. When they are told that they possess desirable attributes, children's self-image changes and they make higher demands of themselves. Adults can help children develop high expectations of themselves and feel dissatisfied unless they live up their "good" (helpful, kind, etc.) attributions.

292.Peterson, L., & Gelfand, D. M. (1984). Causal attributions of helping as a function of age and incentives. *Child Development, 55,* 504–511.

Ten males and ten females from first-, fourth-, sixth-grades, and college, responded to a series of 16 tape-recorded vignettes describing a child with a familiar adult in need of help with a simple task, for example, picking up spilled groceries, or buying milk at the store. Stories provided one of eight reasons for the child's helping: empathy, reciprocity, praise, tangible reward, helping norm, criticism, physical punishment, or no reason. Students rated the degree to which the story character liked to help and would help again, if given the chance. Girls and women tended to rate the character as more likely to help than did boys and men. College students rated the actor overall as liking to help less than did first-, fourth-, and sixth-graders, who did not differ from each other on this rating. Regardless of age, students rated actors who helped out of fear of punishment or criticism as less likely to want to help than those who helped because of empathy or anticipating praise.

293.Peterson, L., Hartmann, D. P., & Gelfand, D. M. (1977). Developmental changes in the effects of dependency and reciprocity on children's moral judgments and donation rates. *Child Development, 48,* 1331-1339.

Two studies investigated the effects of dependency and reciprocity cues on the moral judgments and donation rates of kindergarten through third-grade children. In experiment 1, 47 children heard six pairs of stories, each of which involved a child who shared toys or candy with, or who contributed work or effort to another child. The recipient's need or prior generosity differed. Forced to choose, the children overwhelmingly saw more merit in the actions of the donor who gave to a needy child as compared with a donor returning a favor.

In experiment 2, each child (N=63) played a marble-drop game in which he or she could earn pennies toward purchase of a prize. Periodically the children could donate a penny to assist a same-sex peer whose marble became stuck inside the game for up to 30 seconds. Out of 40 marble drops, there were 10 opportunities to help. Next, the child was given a chance to receive donations (for a stuck marble) from another child. The game timing was then manipulated so that some children thought they were being helped each time and others thought they were not helped at all. Control children were told that the donation slots were not working. Next, baseline conditions were reinstated.

In experiment 1, the older the children, the more they devalued reciprocal helping. In experiment 2, the older the child, the more willingness to be of help when their previous generosity was not reciprocated. Thus, the norm of *social responsibility* seems to become increasingly salient with child age in relation to the *norm of reciprocity*.

294.Pettit, G., Dodge, K., & Brown, M. (1988). Early family experience, social problem-solving patterns, and children's social competence. *Child Development, 59*, 107-120.

The origins and patterns of children's social problem-solving competence were explored with 63 disadvantaged 4- and 5-year-olds. From photos, children selected liked most and liked least classmates and rated their peers on a 5-point scale ("How much do you like to play with ---?"). Children named three classmates who "cooperate, take turns, and are nice to play with" and three who "start fights, say mean things, and don't share". Teachers completed a checklist for each child on aggressiveness and social skill. Children responded to 8 videotaped vignettes in which one boy clearly provoked the other, and to 4 stories with ambiguous provocation.

Children responded to items on Rubin's Social Problem Solving Test, such as getting a balloon from another child and making friends with a new child. Prosocial solutions to friendship initiation were scored as well as aggressive responses. Mothers were interviewed about discipline and responded to child misbehavior vignettes. Peer- and teacher-rated social skills were significantly predicted by family experience. The social problem-solving measure remained significantly related to early experience even after the child's classroom competence was partialed out. Social competence, social problem-solving, and social experience in family are related in complex ways. The authors suggest that family-based *preventive* interventions should be implemented before children behave non-prosocially and experience the negative consequences of peer rejection.

295.Phinney, J. S., Feshbach, N. D., & Farver, J. (1986). Preschool children's response to peer crying. *Early Childhood Research Quarterly, 1,* (3), 207-219.

Causes of crying, and peer and teacher responses to crying were observed for 3 hours among 37 lower-middle class, ethnically diverse children in day care. Peers responded to child crying under 1/4 of the observation time. Teachers made a higher proportion of punitive responses to boys than to girls and a higher proportion of consoling responses to girls than boys. Teachers provided a model of less consoling for males. With the sample divided into children high or low on numbers of friends, responsiveness to peer crying was higher for boys with more friends. Prosocial peer responses were more likely to occur if a child was crying alone than when with a peer. Children who were frequent criers were more likely to respond if a peer cried.

296.Piaget, J. (1965). *The moral judgment of the child.* New York: Free Press.

Using children's marble-playing games and his clinical concentric method of asking questions of children to find out how they are thinking, Piaget examined the relation between the practice of game rules and the consciousness of rules. He traced the gradual evolution of rules as something "obligatory and sacred" to something subject to the children's own choices. As children develop cognitively, their moral judgments move from heteronomy toward autonomy. For young children, every command from a respected adult is the starting point of an obligatory rule (e.g. about not telling lies or hurting others). A morality of good, a product of children's peer cooperation, then develops alongside the morality of right or duty. An intermediate step is when the child obeys a rule. Finally, the child discovers through interactions with others, for example, that "truthfulness is necessary to the relations of sympathy and mutual respect." Reciprocity seems to be the determining factor of autonomy in the child's developing ideas of justice.

297.Poresky, R., & Hooper, D. (1984). Enhancing prosocial play between handicapped and non-handicapped preschool children. *Psychological Reports, 54,* 391-402.

Effects of social toys on social play of three preschool handicapped children was examined in a teacher-mediated comprehensive treatment for 25 days over 12 weeks. Three areas were available: creative activities, manipulatives, and book/toy. Baseline data were taken on level of social interaction without and with the toy areas, and data were taken during the full program which involved prompting, reinforcement contingent on appropriate social interaction, environmental structure, and a cooperative lesson plan. A return to program with just toys, plus a reimplementation phase, allowed graphing of the real effect of the full program. Parent play classifications were noted as well as teacher behaviors. The teachers presented more prompts and verbal reinforcement in the repetition than in the first comprehensive phase. That is, when teachers were shown the effects of their behavior on the children, then they gave even more verbal prompts and specific reinforcements for parallel and cooperative-associative play in the second phase. To enhance positive social interactions, teachers of handicapped children need specific techniques and encouragement.

298.Potter, J., & Ware, W. (1989). The frequency and context of prosocial acts on prime time TV. *Journalism Quarterly, 66* (2), 359-366, 529.

The authors analyzed the content of prime time television to determine the frequency of certain contexts in which prosocial activity is portrayed. They included: types of prosocial acts, the context of the acts occurring, the reward for the prosocial act, the justification of the prosocial behavior, the motivation of the character, and how the character is portrayed. All regularly scheduled dramatic programs on the three commercial television networks were recorded during prime time for two randomly selected weeks. Excluded from the sample were non-fiction programs, movies, mini-series, sporting events, award shows, and other special programs. From the sample of 88 hours of television programs, a total of 1,780 acts were identified as prosocial. Of this total, 1,486 were in the symbolic category and 294 were in the physical category. The average hourly rate of prosocial activity was 20.2 acts. Episodic series had the highest rate of prosocial acts while the action/adventure category had the lowest. When characters commit an act of helping, sharing or altruism, they almost always do so out of a genuine desire to please, and they almost always get rewarded in some way.

299.Poulds, R., Rubinstein, E., & Leibert, R. (1975). Positive social learning. *Journal of Communication, 25,* (4), 90-97.

A code was developed for evaluating regular broadcast TV according to 7 categories of prosocial behavior. Thirty first-graders were then randomly assigned to 3 viewing conditions: a prosocial "Lassie" program, a neutral "Lassie" program, and "the Brady Bunch" comedy. Subjects were then asked to monitor the care of puppies in a distant kennel by listening through earphones. Subjects had to choose between pushing a "help" button for the puppies or earning points in a game they were playing. Those subjects watching the prosocial program helped significantly more than those watching the other two shows.

300.Powell, D. (Ed.) (1988). *Parent education as early childhood intervention: Emerging directions in theory, research, and practice.* Norwood, NJ: Ablex.

Contains: Lally, J., Mangione, P., & Honig, A. (1988).

301. Power, F. C., Higgins, A., & Kohlberg, L. (1989). *Lawrence Kohlberg's approach to moral education.* New York: Columbia University Press.

Kohlberg's experiments in moral education (the attempts to promote moral stage development among sixth-graders through weekly classroom discussions of hypothetical moral dilemmas) are described. Subsequently, Kohlberg and his colleagues implemented this procedure through integrating classroom discussions of moral dilemmas into the curricula of humanities and social studies classes. Next, Kohlberg tried to change the school's moral culture – not simply by developing students' moral reasoning, but by building the power of the collective while protecting the individual rights of each student. He drew on the model of the Israeli kibbutz. He founded his first "just community" in 1974, and this book describes the social functioning of three schools implementing the model.

The key to the just community school is a kibbutz-like weekly community meeting – a gathering of students and staff to decide school policies and practices. The just community educator's role is similar to that of the kibbutz *madrich* (youth leader). The sense of community solidarity allows the peer group to function in order for alternative conceptions of the good, (such as respecting other's rights and property) to emerge. The students address caring and fairness issues. The democratic schools were significantly higher than control high schools on all moral culture variables, and the average moral stage scores were also higher. No gender differences were found.

302.Presbie, R. J., & Coiteux, P. F. (1971). Learning to be generous or stingy: Imitation of sharing behavior as a function of model generosity and vicarious reinforcement. *Child Development, 42,* 1033-1038.

Children from grade one (N=64) were randomly assigned to a model who was either stingy (one who gave away few marbles) or generous (one who gave away many marbles). Praise following generous behavior accentuated child sharing. Praise following stingy behavior increased the stinginess of the subject. Culturally acceptable or unacceptable behaviors are both affected by vicarious reinforcement. The study provides implications for the genesis of antisocial and prosocial behaviors in children: praise and modeling both boost child generosity.

303. Press, B., & Greenspan, S. (1985). The Toddler Group: A setting for adaptive social/emotional development of disadvantaged one and two year olds in a peer group. *Zero to Three, V,* (4), 6-11.

During a 12-month playgroup, disadvantaged toddlers did not exchange words, display smiling, joyfulness, or "friendliness", or participate in "roly-poly" or "roughhousing" play as their middle-class peers have been found to do in similar situations. Case studies highlight how a therapeutic playgroup can help isolated, avoidant toddlers to enjoy and participate in positive social relationships.

304. Puka, B. (1983). Altruism and moral development. In D. Bridgeman (Ed.), *The nature of prosocial development: Interdisciplinary theories and strategies* (pp. 185-204). New York: Academic Press.

Kohlberg's moral stage theory portrays justice as the highest level of moral cognition, and he defines the role of morality as ordering competing claims and resolving conflicts of interest among persons. Altruistic motivations do not, in his theory, demonstrate superior levels of moral understanding, but "merely particular desires to go beyond the call of duty" (p. 187). The *structure* or logic of caring, compassion and altruism must be contrasted with Kohlberg's stage of *deontological justice*, which sets minimal standards of acceptable behavior but does not guide the formation of values or "good" actions. The author describes Kohlbergian levels of preconventional, conventional, and postconventional moral judgment in detail and then suggests that this theoretical rubric must be supplemented with significant rationales for promoting altruistic values.

305. Pulkkinen, L. (1986). The role of impulse control in the development of antisocial and prosocial behavior. In D. Olweus, J. Block, M. Radke-Yarrow (Eds.), *Development of antisocial and prosocial behavior: Research, theories, and issues* (pp. 149-206). Orlando, FL: Academic Press.

The psychoanalytic concept of *impulse control* describes a way that the ego can mobilize resources and functions in order to act on reality to reduce drive and tension safely. Other theorists equate impulsivity with temperament or as a cognitive style. Both prosocial and antisocial motivations can be characterized by adequate or inadequate controls of impulsivity. But strong behavioral control may frequently be associated with prosocial development.

306. Putallaz, M., & Sheppard, B. H. (1990). Social status and children's orientations to limited resources. *Child Development, 61,*

2022-2027.

A study of the relation between first-grade children's sociometric status and their responses to hypothetical limited resource situations revealed that generosity is linked to high sociometric status. After sociometric questionnaire scoring, 22 high-status pairs and 10 low-status pairs of children were given an opportunity to try out each of three toys, a soft indoor basketball and hoop, then a computer space game, and then a bean bag toss game, with five minutes per toy per pair. More *low-status pairs competed* with each other for the toy; more *high-status pairs collaborated* to find some solution that satisfied the needs of both. This often involved mutual commentary and rule invention as well as compromising.

307.Radke-Yarrow, M., & Zahn-Waxler, C. (1984). Roots, motives, and patterns in children's prosocial behavior. In E. Staub, D. Bar-Tal, J. Karylowski, & J. Reykowski (Eds.), *The development and maintenance of prosocial behavior: Interpersonal perspectives on positive behavior* (pp. 81–99). New York: Plenum.

This chapter summarizes research on the origins, contingencies, and correlates of prosocial interactions.

308.Radke-Yarrow, M., & Zahn-Waxler, C. (1986). The role of familial factors in the development of prosocial behavior: Research findings and questions. In D. Olweus, J. Block, & M. Radke-Yarrow (Eds.), *Development of antisocial and prosocial behavior: Research, theories, and issues* (pp. 207–234). Orlando, FL: Academic Press.

Parental modes of influence on prosocial development are intentional (through instruction, provision of experiences and disciplining) and non-intentional (through their modeling). Researches have shown positive effects of 1) child participation in cooperative learning experiences and prosocial interactions and 2) the requirement that they take responsibility to maintain prosocial standards. This chapter summarizes research evidence on facets of parental rearing that influence prosocial development.

309.Radke-Yarrow, M., Zahn-Waxler, C., & Chapman, M. (1983). Children's prosocial dispositions and behavior. In P. Mussen (Series Ed.), *Handbook of child psychology* (Vol. 4) (pp. 469-545). New York: Wiley.

In this superbly thorough review of prosocial researches, the authors concisely survey prosocial researches up through 1982. Researches are grouped under domain of inquiry, such as parent-childrearing techniques, cross-cultural studies, effects of socioeconomic class, etc. The authors observe that the concept of prosocial behavior embraces behaviors that differ enormously in the psychological processes, properties, and capacities that are involved. Overt prosocial behaviors are of many kinds and include:

Sharing of goods or opportunities, participating in cooperative endeavors, giving help in rescuing or protecting a dependent or endangered person, giving sympathy and comfort. These behaviors can be graded in intensity, benefit, degree of sacrifice (e.g. from picking up paper clips to searching the park for a lost child). They can be differentiated in terms of underlying motives (e.g. love, fear, duty, personal gain) (p. 529).

The authors conclude that there is a need for more description of how prosocial responding is rooted in a child's personality and person-life experiences.

310. Raviv, A., Bar-Tal, D., & Lewis-Levin, T. (1980). Motivation for donation behavior by boys of three different ages. *Child Development, 51,* 610-613.

Middle-class Israeli boys (N=111) from grades 4, 6, and 8 from Tel Aviv were put into situations where they had an opportunity to donate money for crippled children. Children who did not donate in a situation corresponding to a higher stage (i.e., without any prompting or cues) were given opportunities in situations corresponding to a lower stage (i.e., the examiner would attempt to motivate a child to donate with decreasing levels of subtlety). Children were queried as to their motives of donation. Results indicated that (a) the older the children, the greater the percentage of them donating in the more advanced experimental situations; and (b) the more advanced the experimental situation of donation, the more advanced the level of motivation expressed for the donating behavior.

311. Rehberg, H. R., & Richman, C. L. (1989). Prosocial behavior in preschool children: A look at the interaction of race, gender, and family composition. *International Journal of Behavioral Development, 12,* 385-401.

Preschoolers (N=146) from both father-present and father-absent homes were taken to play in a toy room with an experimenter quietly busy in a room. Then another adult entered with some blocks, pretended to drop them, and appeared to become upset. Father-absent males had the highest scores for offering comfort. Comforting behavior was correlated with a single parent's dependency on the child for emotional support. *Children required to do chores at home showed the highest helpfulness in the laboratory situation.* Children from smaller families had higher comforting scores than those who came from large families.

312. Rest, J. R. (1983). Morality. In J. H. Flavell & E. M. Markman (Eds.), *Cognitive development,* Vol. III in P. H. Mussen (Series Ed.) *Handbook of child psychology* (4th ed.). New York: Wiley.

Piaget's, Kohlberg's, and Eisenberg's theoretical stages are explained in detail. Eisenberg's prosocial moral dilemmas are ones "in which the individual must choose between satisfying his own wants, needs, and/or values and those of others, particularly in contexts in which punishment, and formal obligations are irrelevant or deemphasized" (p. 606). In prosocial dilemmas, helping another person is in direct opposition (high cost) to helping oneself. It means self-sacrifice. These are in contrast to Kohlberg's dilemmas where rules or laws frequently dominate to constrain or prohibit prosocial action (as in the Heinz story, where a man would have to steal a life-saving drug to heal his wife).

313. Reykowski, J. (1982). Motivation of prosocial behavior. In V. Derlega & J. Grzelak (Eds.), *Cooperation and helping behaviors: Theories and research* (pp. 355-375). New York: Academic Press.

Motivations for prosocial behaviors are discussed theoretically. Persons may cooperate prosocially because they have internalized societal or family norms or out of deference to societal demands. These are *normative values.* Or, a prosocial act may be valued on the basis of its need-gratification characteristics or its instrumental role in need-gratification. These are *utilitarian values.* How a person is motivated to behave prosocially depends on iconic, linguistic, cognitive operations, and also on "deep structures" where personal values of objects (such as one's child or friend or parent) are encoded. Representations of such objects develop in a highly complex structure that functions according to Piaget's principle of equilibrium.

Thus, if the personal value of another is very high, there is *intrinsic prosocial motivation* toward altruism if that other is in distress. Another mechanism is *generalization of personal standards.* In this process one compares the situation of the other with the standards of well-being for the self. Some forms of self-concentration – namely concentration on one's own moral standards and their importance for self esteem – can have a positive impact on prosocial behavior. A second way of involving the self in the regulation of prosocial behavior is by eliciting a feeling of closeness to the person in need.

Since the self plays a mediating role in the regulation of prosocial behavior, high self-esteem and intelligent thought may help arouse prosocial acts. Smolenska, in a Polish dissertation, found that gifted pupils were more egocentric than pupils from regular schools, but also more sensitive to cues about similarities of persons, and thus more easily able to activate mechanisms for generalizing personal standards of moral behavior. The *value attribution process* plays a crucial role in prosocial behavior.

314. Rheingold, H. L., Hay, D. S., & West, M. J. (1976). Sharing in the 2nd year of life. *Child Development, 47,* 1148-1158.

In a home-like laboratory room, younger (15 months) and older (18 months) toddlers helped their own parents and the experimenter pick up spilled groceries and messy items. Helpfulness and sharing were frequent even in the youngest group. Prosocial characteristics are developed by early toddlerhood.

315. Richman, C. L., Berry, C., Bittle, M., & Himan, K. (1988). Factors related to helping behavior in preschool-age children. *Journal of Applied Developmental Psychology, 9,* 151-165.

In the first of two studies, 49 preschool children who were four and one-half years old participated in a helping game. Participants were grouped by gender and race, with approximately equal numbers of black females, black males, white females, and white males. A confederate was selected from each group, and trained for participation in the experiment. Children were individually escorted by an adult to a separate room within the school, and allowed to play with a collection of interesting toys while the adult "worked" nearby. After one minute, the confederate entered the room carrying a large stack of blocks; as the blocks fell, the confederate said, "Oh, no!" and feigned distress. The adult observed and recorded the potential helper's behavior. Black males showed more comforting/helping than all other groups, with white females second, and black females and white males helping the least. Prosocial

behaviors were more evident when the helpers
and confederates were the same gender and
race than when they were different.

Study Two replicated the above design with
98 children (four to five years). Again
participants were equally divided into groups
by race and gender. An additional variable,
adult presence or absence within the
experimental room, was introduced in Study Two.
For half of the events, the adult left the
room, observing and recording through a hidden
window. Black males remained the most helpful
group. Across groups, children were more likely
to help when the experimenter was present than
when absent.

316. Rodd, J. (1989). Is preschoolers' helping
behavior egocentric or altruistic?: The
effects of cost and need. *Australian Journal
of Early Childhood, 14,* (4), 37-42.

Children's helping behavior may involve a
cost, or sacrifice, or may occur in order to
avoid personal cost or discomfort. Thus
helping behavior may be egocentric or
altruistic. In Melbourne, 96 preschoolers were
paired with a peer for a game in (a) high and
low need and (b) high and low cost conditions. A
pencil box with a hinged bottom that permitted
colored pencils to drop out when the box was
lifted up had either 5 pencils (low need
condition) or 30 pencils (high need). The pair
went to the preschool office where "The
Repeater", an exciting perceptual motor game,
was located. The helpee child was told to bring
the pencil box to the experimenter. Cost to
the helper was specified because if help were
given to pick up the spilled pencils, the game
playing would have to be delayed (cost
condition). In the no-cost condition, the game
was omitted. Children were interviewed about

why help was or was not given. An intelligence test was given one week later.

Cost and need determined helping, for males. Higher help for boys was given in the low-cost need and none in the cost-high need situations. Intelligence did not affect helping. The least helping occurred when cost was high. Helpee children may have signaled the need for help through behavioral cues. Caregivers should emphasize personal and situational cues which can signal to young children the appropriateness of concern for another in naturally occurring helping situations.

317. Roe, K. V. (1980). Toward a contingency hypothesis of empathy development. *Journal of Personality and Social Psychology, 39,* 991-994.

The empathy level of 42 normal 9- and 10-year-old children from a Greek island was negatively related to their fear of physical punishment from parents, particularly from fathers, even though the children reported that their mothers spanked them more. A contingency model of empathy development might argue that if a child has a strong prior positive relationship with a parent, as is the case with the Greek mother, the effect of occasional use of physical punishment or power assertion by that parent will not impair the development of empathy.

318. Rogers, D. (1985). Relationships between block play and the social development of young children. *Early Child Development and Care, 20,* 245-261.

Kindergarten children playing with both large hollow and unit blocks exhibited much higher incidences of positive social behavior than negative social behavior. These children seldom threatened, hit, or threw blocks at another child. There was almost no crying or screaming and they never engaged in physical fights. Comparing a composite of behaviors classified as prosocial (comfort, help, and give) to a composite of behaviors classified as aggressive (hit, threat, and take), prosocial behavior was three times as likely to occur as aggressive behavior during large hollow block play and twice as likely to occur as aggressive behavior during the children's play with unit blocks.

319. Ross, D. D., & Rogers, D. L. (1990). Social competence in kindergarten: Analysis of social negotiations during peer play. *Early Child Development and Care, 64,* 15-26.

In a kindergarten block play situation, data from 12 hours of child interactions revealed large individual differences in children's ability to negotiate positive peer interactions, to get others to accept their ideas, to play with them, and to protect their own rights. The numbers and kinds of social strategies did not differ, but children's ability to establish mutually satisfying interactions through negotiation of elements of the social order did differ. When a child was aware of the needs and desires of the other, rather than struggling, for example, to be "in charge", then the child could suggest actions acceptable to a peer and joint lines of action were easily established. *Teachers need to help children gain competence in "reading" another child's social interactions, and negotiating common meanings and interests in order to play cooperatively.*

320.Rotenberg, M. (1974). Conceptual and methodological notes on affective and cognitive role taking (sympathy and empathy): An illustrative experiment with delinquent and nondelinquent boys. *The Journal of Genetic Psychology, 125,* 177–185.

Sympathy and empathy refer "to the ability or tendency to put oneself in the other's place, imaginatively, and to feel like him or with him, or merely to identify his feelings, thoughts, or moral viewpoint." Reviews suggest that *many empathy measures are unrelated to one another.* Some measures assess opinion about empathic personalities but don't measure actual empathic ability in ongoing interactions. Delinquent and non-delinquent youth, age 13–17 (N=73), were arranged into dyads, and a questionnaire was given to the "guesser" partner who was asked to report how he thought his partner would respond to a number of social interactions (e.g. "What would he say if you told him you lost all the money you have saved?"). The number of correct guesses, as compared with partner's actual answer was the CRT (Cognitive Role Taking) score. Not many differences were found between delinquents and peers, except a suggestion that black delinquents perceive their early childhood relations with parents and peers as warmer than do whites.

321. Roush, C., & Hudson, L. (1985). Quantitative versus qualitative dimensions of prosocial development: Age-related contributors to children's donating behavior. *Child Study Journal, 15,* (3), 157–165.

Four situations were presented in which 60 boys and girls from second-, fourth-, and sixth-grade (who had played a game of sequentially depressing a key to move the hand on the face of an electronic timer) donated some of their 12 penny earnings in the following order of levels of moral development: A) Altruism: children donate voluntarily from moral convictions; B) Normative donation in response to adult saying "It is nice when children share with children who are sick"; C) Concrete Reward: Adult says "I forgot to tell you that children who donate some of their pennies to the children who are absent will get a chance to win a prize"; and D) Compliance/Controls "Wouldn't you like to give some of your pennies to the absent children?" Older children were more likely to donate in response to both higher level moral appeals and to repeated presentations of the altruistic cue. All 6th-graders donated prior to the compliance condition. Repetition of the altruistic appeal had no effect on the second-graders, 90% of whom failed to donate at all after four presentations. The amount donated in response to lower level appeals did not differ as a function of grade level.

322.Rubin, K., & Everett, B. (1982). Social perspective-taking in young children. In S. Moore & C. Cooper (Eds.), *The young child: Reviews of research, Volume 3.* (pp. 97-113) Washington, D.C.: NAEYC.

The authors review the research on topics such as: how egocentric are young children, assessing children's spatial, cognitive, and affective perspective-taking skills, the role of perspective-taking in social skills, experiences contributing to growth in perspective-taking, and implications of researches.

323.Rubin, K., & Schneider, F. (1973). The relationship between moral judgement, egocentrism, and altruistic behavior. *Child Development, 44,* 661-665.

   Seven-year-old students completed measures of intelligence, perspective-taking, sharing and helping. Scores on the Peabody Picture Vocabulary Test placed all children within the range of normal intelligence. As a measure of perspective-taking, students played a matching game with an adult seated across a table holding a visual screen. Children described a series of ten "nonsense" figures to their partner, attempting to match the figure described with an identical one held by the partner. Descriptions were scored for the number of distinctive features they contained. After the game, children had the opportunity to donate candy to absent "poor" children represented in photographs, and/or keep candy for themselves. The number of candy boxes shared was the first measure of altruism. In a second session, altruism was measured through the opportunity to help a younger child finish a task which was grouping tickets in stacks of five. The younger child received more tickets, insuring that s/he would finish last. Both children were promised a chance to play with nearby toys when their jobs were done. Scores consisted of the number of stacks the older child helped the younger complete. Finally, each seven-year-old responded to six moral dilemmas, yielding a moral judgment score. Measures of altruism were significantly positively correlated with the measure of perspective-taking and level of moral judgment.

324.Rubin, Z. (1980). *Children's friendships.* Cambridge, MA: Harvard University Press.

   Chapters in this book explore in some depth different aspects of children's friendships -

the beginning of the earliest friendships, the description and definition of friends, skills required to make friends, effects of the loss of a friend, group conformity, segregation of sexes, cross-age friendships and last but not least, the impact of the physical, economic and cultural environment on a child's friendship patterns.

325. Rushton, J. P. (1975). Generosity in children: Immediate and long term effects of modeling, preschooling, and moral judgement. *Journal of Personality and Social Psychology, 31,* 459-466.

Working class boys and girls 7- to 11-years-old (N=140) were told Piagetian stories with a standard set of questions to elicit concepts of moral justice. Children were shown attractively arranged prizes. Then they played an electronic bowling game. On a table with tokens to win was a bowl beneath a "Save the Children Fund" poster depicting poorly clothed children. A caption read "Please give". The experimenter introduced an adult model as a possible future teacher in the school (this was to make the model seem powerful) who was interested in playing the game also. The experimenter suggested that the model should play the game first and instructed the subject to watch. The model then played the game and either donated to the poster child or kept all tokens for himself. There were three other conditions: generous preaching (teaching that one should share tokens with the poster child); or selfish preaching that one should not share; or neutral preaching --- simply noting that the game was fun. The child played the game while the model left. After his turn, the experimenter asked the subject to indicate his view of the model as very nice, just okay, not so nice, or very bad, and further, how much he would like to be in the model's class.

Children with higher moral scores donated more and those with a generous model donated more. In a two-month post-test, modeling was still highly significant and preaching had a significant effect. *When preaching was consistent with modeling, more donations were given.* Children with a high moral judgment score rejected the selfish preacher while those with a low moral judgment score did not.

326.Rushton, J. P. (1976). Socialization and the altruistic behavior of children. *Psychological Bulletin, 83,* 898-913.

Categories of altruism include a) normative, as when a child shares a toy because it is expected by another; b) reciprocal, when a child shares in the hope of later borrowing from the peer, c) principled, when a child shares in order to live up to an inner rule, and d) fairness or justice, when a child shares a toy in order to restore a specific equitable situation within the self. This paper reviews researches on differing *measures* of altruism, such as donating to a charity, helping and rescue behavior, consideration for others in competitive game situations, teacher and peer sociometric techniques, and naturalistic observations of helping and sharing. In some researches, measurement differences result in little or no correlation. That is, altruism as measured by a sociometric factor has been reported as unrelated to altruism measured in a ray gun resistance-to-temptation game situation. Characteristics of models and situations that affect children's altruism are methodically discussed in terms of research findings.

327. Rushton, J. P. (1980). *Altruism, socialization and society.* Englewood Cliffs, NJ: Prentice-Hall.

This book is about altruism and some of the biological, individual, and societal factors that influence it, and how society can increase the socialization of altruism. The author takes the social learning perspective that children abstract standards and rules of how to behave from the environmental contingencies they encounter.

In recalculating the intercorrelations from the Character Education Enquiry studies from the 1920's (see Hartshorne & May, 1928) Rushton found that if the original measures are combined into a battery, they correlate +.61 with the measures of the child's altruistic reputation among his teachers and classmates. These data also reveal that teacher and peer perceptions of a child's altruism agree highly (r=.80). Rushton concludes that there is a "trait" of altruism. Some people are consistently more generous, helping, and kind than others.

From the researches reviewed, Rushton notes that there is a strong relationship between nurturing parents and altruistic offspring. He expresses concern that the family, due to rapid technological progress, "is increasingly a less effective socializer of children in North American society and that unless we soon take active steps to find alternatives, we are in danger of producing a generation of undersocialized children" (p. 126). He specifically recommends support systems for families, such as enabling parents to be home for prosocial interactions when children come home from school. The social welfare system needs revision, as it may inadvertently be encouraging illegitimate births to single parents. He also recommends strong attention by schools and media to increasing specifically altruistic learning. High school social studies courses should teach understanding of human society and encourage classroom cooperative work. Moral education includes: inculcation, moral development, analysis, clarification, and action learning.

328. Rushton, J. P., & Sorrentino, R. M. (Eds.) (1981). *Altruism and helping behavior: Social, personality, and developmental perspectives.* Hillsdale, NJ: Lawrence Erlbaum.

Appropriate for graduate students and professional researchers, this collection of papers represents the major approaches to altruism at that time. The seven parts of the book include:

1. Introduction: an historical background to the study of altruism.

2. The Development of Altruism: examines the influence of both genes and socialization on the origins of altruistic behavior.

3. Internal Mediators of Altruism: discusses how role-taking, empathy, egoism, and emotional states affect or relate to altruism.

4. Individual Differences in Altruism: a re-examination of developmental evidence from over 50 years concluding that there is strong evidence for "an altruistic person-ality".

5. Social Constraints on Helping: examines how social constraints (such as group size and urban density) impede, facilitate, or direct the amount of altruism shown.

6. Consequences of Helping: the mixed consequences of aid on the help recipient are explored.

7. Overview: the major theoretical issues are discussed.

Contains: Grusec, J. (1981)
Hoffman, M. (1981b)
Lerner, M. J., & Meindl, J. R. (1981)
Schwartz, S. H., & Howard, J. A. (1981)
Staub, E. (1981)
Strayer, F. (1981)

329.Rushton, J. P., & Teachman, G. (1978). The effects of positive reinforcement, attributions, and punishment on model-induced altruism in children. *Personality and Social Psychology Bulletin, 4,* 322-325.

Social reinforcement increased sharing (the adult says "Good for you" or "That's really nice of you") among children even afterward, when the experimenter was no longer present.

330.Rushton, J. P., & Wiener, J. (1975). Altruism and cognitive development in children. *British Journal of Social and Clinical Psychology, 14,* 341-349.

Highly significant differences were found between 7- and 11-year-olds (N=60) in cognitive complexity, conservation, and role-taking ability, as measured in a snake-and-ladders type of game where the other player was blind-folded and the child had to explain the board and the counters to him. Also played were a racing game and an electronic bowling game in which the child won tokens which could be either exchanged for prizes or donated to a boy pictured on a "Save the Children" poster. The child exchanged however many tokens he had for a prize, 24 candies, a bag with his name, and another bag with the name of his best friend, to whom he could thus give some of the sweets. The number of sweets given to the friend, out of the possible 24, constituted the generosity score. Effects of age and IQ were highly significant, and when partialed out, then generosity to a friend correlated (r=.24) with generosity to a charity and negatively (r=-.55) with competitiveness. In general, there was a lack of relationship between the cognitive and behavioral measures, which suggests that altruistic behavior is not mediated by age changes in cognitive development. There may be *limited generalization of altruistic behavior across situations.*

331. Rutherford, E., & Mussen, P. (1968). Generosity in nursery school boys. *Child Development, 39,* 755-765.

This classic study of generosity among middle-class 4-year-olds (N=63) classified those who scored low or high on a situational test of generosity. Generous boys viewed their fathers as warmer and more sympathetic, and the boys were also rated as kinder, less hostile, and less competitive. "Generosity appears to be part of a pattern of moral behaviors acquired through the boy's identification with his father" (p. 755).

332. Sackin, S., & Thelen, E. (1984). An ethological study of peaceful associative outcomes to conflict in preschool children. *Child Development, 55,* 1098-1102.

In two different preschools, conflicts of 20 5-year-olds were observed naturalistically for 100 hours. Most ended in submission by one child and pair separation. When children played peacefully afterward, a conciliatory gesture had been offered by one partner (mostly same-sex) and accepted. Females gave significantly fewer conciliatory bids to males and received far fewer from them (when the males terminated responses). Cooperative propositions were the most frequent kind of conciliation offered (37%), followed by offers to share an object (31%), and grooming (22%). Adults can help children become aware of conciliatory behaviors that permit peaceful resolution of conflict and continuation of play.

333.Sagotsky, G., Wood-Schneider, M., & Konop, M. (1981). Learning to cooperate: Effects of modeling and direct instruction. *Child Development, 52,* 1037-1042.

Pairs of children in grades 1-3 either viewed films showing adult models discussing and practicing cooperation, received direct instructions to cooperate, or were in a control group. On an immediate assessment, all treatment conditions produced more cooperation than the control group. Results 7 weeks later indicated that for older children, but not for younger, greater cooperation was found for the treatment group.

334.Schaffer, H. R. (1984). *The child's entry into the social world.* New York: Academic Press.

Chapter 7, "Socialization through interaction", describes how very young children (under 3 years) grow up more cooperative if their parents use subtle control techniques, such as "indirect directives ("Would you bring the teddy bear over here?"). *Timing* of interventions needs to ensure that the toddler's attention is appropriately focused on a toy before action with toy is requested. Non-verbal devices (such as prompting cooperation by holding out a ring stack for a toddler to put a ring on or moving a toy within a toddler's reach, or presenting a toy attractively) ensured more toddler cooperation than purely verbal controls. Thus, the baby progresses from other-control to self-control and spontaneous compliance with parent.

335.Schantz, C. U. (1975). The development of cognition. In E. M. Hetherington (Vol. Ed.), P. Mussen (Series Ed.) *Review of child development research* (Vol. 5), Chicago, IL: University of Chicago Press.

In summarizing the role-taking literature, the author cautions that preschoolers' abilities to make accurate inferences about others' emotions, intentions, and thoughts in social situations may be underestimated in research. Assessment tasks used by investigators may involve cognitive abilities that preschoolers may not have mastered such as listening carefully to a story and remembering about each character. Perhaps even young children can be good role-takers in the natural environment of home and preschool where situation and persons are familiar to them, and the social problems to be resolved are not hypothetical but personal and meaningful for the child.

336.Schantz, C. U. (1983). Social cognition. In J. H. Flavell & E. M. Markman (Vol. Eds.), in P. H. Mussen (Series Ed.), *Handbook of child*

psychology: Vol. 3. Cognitive development,
4th Ed. (pp. 495-555). New York: Wiley.

This research review includes studies on
children's conflicts, friendships, attributions
of intentional behaviors, inferences about
psychological states and processes, and the
relation of social influences to social
behaviors. The expected relations of
perspective-taking and empathy with assorted
kinds of prosocial and antisocial behavior have
been found only in some studies. "It may be
that children differ in the degree to which
their social behavior is determined by situation
or person aspects" (p. 529).

337.Schenk, V. M., & Grusec, J. E. (1987). A
comparison of prosocial behavior of
children with and without day care
experience. *Merrill-Palmer Quarterly, 33,* (2),
231-240.

Three- to five-year-old children, half of
whom had been in full-time day care for 11
months or more and half cared for totally at
home, accompanied an unfamiliar adult to a room
for individual assessment. Children listened to
and answered questions on six stories depicting
individuals in need of help. Four behavioral
events designed to elicit prosocial behavior
were interspersed with the stories, where the
adult "accidentally" overturns a large box full
of materials; bangs her knee against a table,
uttering a cry of distress; offers a choice of
two uneven piles of sticks telling the child
that one is for the child and the other for an
absent peer; and describes an opportunity to
donate some stickers to hospitalized children.
Children's responses to story-questions and
behavioral events were recorded and scored.
Story responses were scored for stating a
prosocial response to questions, and indicating

a reason for the response. Behavioral events were scored for whether or not children acknowledged and/or responded to the incidents.

On the story measure, there was no difference between the two groups of children in their knowledge about appropriate behavior and the reasons for it. Scores on the four behavioral measures were negatively correlated with "knowledge" scores on the story measure. Home care children behaved more altruisticly with the adult by expressing concern/comfort for her "injury", while day care children behaved more altruistically in the peer context by sharing stickers with an absent peer.

338.Schneider, B., Rubin, K. H., & Ledingham, J. (Eds.) (1985). *Peer relationships and social skills in childhood: Vol. 2. Issues in assessment and training.* New York: Springer-Verlag.

Contains: Weissberg, R. P. (1985)

339.Schneider, B. H., & Byrne, B. M. (1987). Individualizing social skills training for behavior disordered children. *Journal of Consulting and Clinical Psychology, 55,* 444-445.

In an application of cognitive-behavioral therapy, training that was *individualized* for each disturbed child's particular difficulties, proved superior to standardized training in enhancing children's cooperative play, although not in reducing their aggression. Therapists may need to tailor prosocial training to individual children rather than use standard therapeutic models.

340. Schwartz, S. H., & Howard, J. A. (1981). A normative decision-making model of altruism. In J. P. Rushton & R. M. Sorrentino (Eds.), *Altruism and helping behavior: Social, personality, and developmental perspectives* (pp. 189–211). Hillsdale, N.J.: Lawrence Erlbaum.

The decision-making process by which personal and social norms mediate the influence of general values on altruistic and/or helping behavior includes a five stage sequence:

1. Noticing the other's need and feeling capable of helping.

2. Motivation – an internalized value system, for example, that one should help relatives and friends but not strangers.

3. Evaluation – the potential moral and non-moral costs of helping.

4. Defenses – these may weaken a sense of moral obligation by changing one's perception of: the need for potential action, one's ability to help, or the relevance of one's moral values to this particular situation.

5. Behavior – overt prosocial action or inaction.

341. Schweinhart, L. J., Weikart, D. P., & Larner, M. B. (1986). Consequences of three curriculum models through age 15. *Early Childhood Research Quarterly, 1*, 15–45.

Children from low-income families who attended preschool programs that provided many opportunities for children to initiate their own activities (traditional nursery school curriculum and the High/Scope curriculum) reported less juvenile delinquency in their teenage years than comparable youngsters who attended a preschool program with a direct instruction curriculum (Distar). High/Scope researchers, in a 19-year, longitudinal comparison study of three curricula, report that children who attended the direct instruction program fared less well on measures of delinquency and other indicators of social competence than children who attended two other programs that encouraged children to initiate many of their own activities.

342.Seegmiller, B., & Suter, B. (1977). Relations between cognitive and behavioral measures of prosocial development in children. *Journal of Genetic Psychology, 131,* 161–162.

Children's cognitive *understanding* of the concept of "kindness" is related to their *performance* on tasks that require cooperative and helping behavior. Understanding of prosocial behavior was measured among 184 preschoolers, kindergartners, and fifth- and sixth-graders by the Baldwin Kindness Picture Story Instrument, which consists of 10 pairs of stories. The children must choose the story involving kindness and explain the reason for their choice. In the cooperation task children must open a box which required four hands to open, and both children are rewarded. In the helping task only one child is reinforced. The more kindness choices for all age groups, the more cooperative behavior (the fewer seconds needed to open the box). Helping behavior did not relate to the number of kindness choices, regardless of child age.

343.Selman, R. (1971). Taking another's perspective: Role-taking development in early childhood. *Child Development, 42,* 1721–1734.

Four-, five-, and six-year-old children participated in two role-taking tasks. Task one involved *perceptual role-taking* (predicting what another person who was seated in a different position in the room could see, with barriers placed to obstruct the child's direct view). In addition, a *conceptual role-taking* task required the child first to sort a series of three toy sets by category, then predict how another child, missing part of the set, would categorize the objects. Task two used DeVries' guessing game where pennies are hidden in the experimenter's hands and success or failure at guessing is controlled.

Children's responses on the two role-taking tasks were coded into four levels. At Level A, the child may have a sense of the other, but fails to distinguish between the perceptions and thoughts of self and other. Level B children distinguish between self and other, but are unable to predict the others' thoughts/perceptions. At Level C, a child can assume the other's perspective, but attributes thoughts similar to his/her own. Level D children are aware that others have a different perspective, but based on different ways of reasoning. Age was positively correlated with role-taking level on all measures.

344.Selman, R. (1981). The child as a friendship philosopher. In S. R. Asher & J. R. Gottman (Eds.), *The development of children's friendships* (pp. 242–272). New York: Cambridge University Press.

Selman presents a dilemma for children to reason about. Should a target child go with a new friend to a special event that is scheduled at the same time as a previous engagement with a long-time best friend? The two peers do not like each other. Six issues in children's reasoning about friendship are explored: friendship formation, intimacy, trust and reciprocity, jealousy, conflict resolution, and ending. The matrix of conceptions about these issues defines stages as follows: Stage 0 occurs in children younger than 7 years and is labeled momentary physicalistic playmate (a friend is someone who lives nearby and with whom one plays). A close friend in Stage 1 is someone whose likes and dislikes one knows better than other children's, and the focus is on specific actions of the friend that meet the child's own wishes. Stage 2, somewhere between 6 and 12 years, is labeled fairweather cooperation, and involves the notion of coordinating and adjusting both one's own and the friend's likes and dislikes. In Stage 3, friends have intimate and mutually shared relationships (usually between 9 and 15 years of age).

This system seems to suggest that teachers who help children become aware of and skilled at the coordination of their viewpoints and desires with those of playmates can help assure that children will be able to find friends.

345.Selman, R., & Byrne, D. (1974). A structural-developmental analysis of levels of role-taking in middle childhood. *Child Development,* *45,* 803-806.

Five males and five females at ages four, six, eight, and ten (N=40) responded to two open-ended moral dilemmas presented on film.

Each dilemma involved two main characters (children) and others who acted as spectators. For example, one dilemma depicted a girl who had promised her father she would not climb a tree, but was faced with the problem of a friend's cat stuck in a tree. Children answered questions about how each of the characters might feel and why. Age was significantly positively correlated with role-taking skills. The four skill levels are: Level 0 (age four) showed no evidence of differentiation between characters, therefore no coordination of perspectives. Level 1 (age six) involved a differentiation of perspectives, but no ability to understand that one person's view can influence another's reciprocally. Level 2 (age eight) involves sequential, reciprocal perspective-taking. At level 3 (eight to ten-years), children can also assume the role of spectators to an action and see each party's point of view simultaneously.

346.Shure, M. (1985). Interpersonal problem-solving: A cognitive approach to behavior. In R. A. Hinde, A. Perret-Clermont, & J. Stevenson-Hinde (Eds.), *Social relationships and cognitive development* (pp. 191–207). Oxford: Clarendon Press.

The ICPS (Interpersonal Cognitive Problem Solving Skills) program teaches children a) alternative solution thinking; b) consequential thinking; and c) means-ends thinking and planning as well as role- or perspective-taking. A 3- or 4-month sequenced program script for 4-year-olds, for kindergarten, and grade school children revealed that negative impulsive and inhibited behaviors were reduced. Positive qualities, such as awareness and concern about peer distress increased, and as youngsters learned to consider the needs of others they gained greater peer acceptance.

347.Siegal, M. (1982). *Fairness in children: A social-cognitive approach to the study of moral development.* New York: Academic Press.

A good review of theorists' positions on moral development is provided, including: Piaget's stages, the social-learning theorists' work emphasizing the role of imitation and reinforcement in identification with prosocial behaviors, the psychoanalytic views on identification, and Kohlberg's cognitive development stage theory. The author reviews the relationships of attachment or deprivation of parenting and the effects of poverty, culture group, and parenting style on children's development of fairness ideas and behaviors. One chapter is devoted to the role of adults in promoting sharing, cooperating, self-direction and friendliness in peer groups.

348.Siegal, M. (1985). Mother-child relations and the development of empathy: A short-term longitudinal study. *Child Psychiatry and Human Development, 16,* 77–86.

In keeping with the feminine stereotype of nurturance and warmth, empathy is said to be indicative of the "expressive" role played by the mother in her affectional responsiveness and concern for others. One purpose of this study was to examine longitudinally the relation of empathy to identification and gender constancy. First-graders (45 boys and 49 girls) from middle-class suburbs in Brisbane, Australia were studied. The children were given questions on gender stability (for example, "When you were a little baby, were you a boy or a girl?") and gender consistency (for example, "If you wore [opposite sex of subject, i.e., girls' or boys' clothes] would you be a boy or a girl?"). The children were also given three parental identification items and an empathy index. They were asked to say whom they admire, whom they would want to be as grown-ups, and whom they mostly take after. The children's capacity for empathy was related to identification with their mothers.

349. Simmons, C., & Zumpf, C. (1986). The gifted child's perceived competence, prosocial moral reasoning, and charitable donations. *The Journal of Genetic Psychology 147*, 97-105.

Intellectually gifted four-, five-, six- and seven-year-olds (N=38) were given the Eisenberg-Berg prosocial moral reasoning stories. They were tested with the Harter & Pike Perceived Competence and Acceptance Scale. In return for completing the scales, the children were given 15 pennies and their attention was called to a poster about donating money for gifted children. Some donation to the jar of pennies was made by 68% of the children and the average contribution did not differ by age or sex of child. The children showed some categories of moral reasoning (such as abstract internalized reasoning) that did not appear until older ages in the normative groups (e.g. gifted fours and fives used less hedonistic and more mutual needs reasoning). Gifted children may move through the stages of moral reasoning more quickly than do average children.

350. Sisk, D. A. (1982). Caring and sharing: Moral development of gifted students. *The Elementary School Journal, 82,* 221-229.

Sisk states a need to emphasize moral education among gifted children in view of their high level of reasoning, critical sensitivity, and fund of information, in order to enable them further to develop and utilize their capacities to reason. One of the major problems gifted students may have is their inability to get along with others, hence they are often labeled as having social skill deficits. The emotional needs of gifted children and their potential for cognitive development as well as selective strategies for enhancing moral development are discussed.

351. Smetana, J. G. (1985). Preschool children's conceptions of transgressions: Effects of varying moral and conventional domain-related attributes. *Developmental Psychology, 21,* 18-29.

Children aged three to six years (N=57) responded to two stories, each describing some type of transgression within familiar settings such as home, nursery school, or playground. The children were randomly assigned to story conditions where events portrayed transgressions either in the moral domain (such as stealing another's snack) or conventional, for example, talking during naptime, or unspecified in nature. Unspecified story events used nonsense words for the transgression, forcing children to rely on event context for information. After the stories, children answered questions on the rightness or wrongness of the act, the usefulness of rules and contingencies regarding the transgression, the permissibility of the act in other settings, the seriousness of the act, and their reasons for labeling acts as transgressions.

Children in the moral condition judged events as less permissible, more wrong in the absence of rules, more generalizable and more serious than other groups. Children in the conventional condition reasoned that acts were wrong on the basis of "disorder," while those in the moral condition gave reasons relating to effects on others' welfare. Children in the event-unspecified condition often did not know why an action was wrong, but were more likely to reason about effects on others' welfare for stories where a child cried after the transgression.

352. Smetana, J. G., Killen, M., & Turiel, E. (1991). Children's reasoning about interpersonal and moral conflicts. *Child Development, 62*, 629–644.

The researchers systematically varied stories with conflicts between justice and interpersonal concerns. One story theme was:

Initial situation: Bob brings candy to share with everyone. His close friend George does not want Bob to give candy to Tim. George and Tim do not get along and Tim has been picking on George.

Interpersonal condition: Acquaintance: Bob is asked by an acquaintance (who does not get along with Tim) not to share with Tim.

Interpersonal condition: Sibling: Bob is asked by his brother (who does not get along with Tim) to not share with Tim.

Greater Need condition: Bob, who is in charge of distributing lunches, does not give one to Tim because he had picked on George.

Physical Harm condition: Bob inflicts physical harm on Tim to please George (p.632).

Both boys and girls (in 3rd, 6th, and 9th grades) considered interpersonal relationships and justice, welfare, and rights in making their judgments and giving reasons. Children did not rigidly apply concepts of justice and rights; they also took interpersonal loyalties and obligations into account. They recognize potential conflicts between justice/rights concepts and interpersonal friendship obligations. Thus, there are not clear-cut sex differences in children's moral reasoning, as Gilligan has suggested.

353. Smilansky, S., & Sheftaya, L. (1990). *Facilitating play: A medium for promoting cognitive, socio-emotional and academic development in young children.* Gaithersburg, MD: Psychosocial and Educational Publications.

Research and experiments in many countries demonstrate the effectiveness of facilitating children's progress in sociodramatic play. Sociodramatic play is spontaneous, voluntary, characterized by personal freedom of action and imaginative elements, with language used to plan, develop and maintain the play. There is intrinsic discipline imposed by the themes and roles chosen, and organization along a space-time continuum. The author discusses socioeconomic differences in sociodramatic play and its adaptive function as a "cooperative group enterprise requiring social sensitivity" (p. 17). The Smilansky Scale for Evaluation of Sociodramatic Play of Children Ages 3-8 years is offered as a tool to enable adults to discern play elements where children may need teacher help to learn to play more cooperatively.

354.Smith, C. L., Gelfand, D. M., Hartmann, D. P., & Partlow, M. Y. (1979). Children's causal attributions regarding helpgiving. *Child Development, 50,* 203-210.

In a research on the effects of material vs. social reinforcement, 7- and 8-year-old children who had been praised for sharing or verbally chastised for not sharing were likely to attribute their sharing to a desire to help or a concern for the welfare of the child with whom they later shared. The children who had instead been given penny rewards or fined, reported that they had shared in order to get a reward or to avoid losing money. Social consequences may be a more effective tool for promotion of prosocial actions if the child sees altruistic acts as compelled by an inner value system. On the other hand, children for whom material fines or reinforcers are used may attribute any altruistic actions they do only to external pressure from adults. Thus, *social reinforcers ought to be more effective in promoting children's internalization of prosocial values compared with material rewards or deprivations.*

355.Smith, C. L., Leinbach, M. D., Stewart, B. J. & Blackwell, J. M. (1983). Affective perspective-taking, exhortations, and children's prosocial behavior. In D. L. Bridgeman (Ed.), *The nature of prosocial development: Interdisciplinary theories and strategies* (pp. 113-134). New York: Academic Press.

The effects of verbalization exhorting prosocial behaviors were studied with 4- and 5-year-old children. Opportunities to behave prosocially were introduced by experimenters verbalizing needs. For example, when dropping objects apparently accidentally, the adult would say, "Oh, I dropped the sticks!" Or when the adult would need materials to be used, moved or cleaned up the adult might say, "I'd like to plant these seeds, but I don't have a cup". Teaching opportunities occurred when one of the experimenters revealed that she did not know how to do a simple task (such as a glitter picture) that the child had just been taught by another experimenter. One of the experimenters also feigned accidental injury to herself and said, "Oh, I bumped my knee. It really hurts." Each child participated in 3 sessions several days apart. In Session 1, no comments were made if the child did or did not respond prosocially.

In session 2, half of the children were given *power-assertive* statements, such as "When I play with you I want you to help." The others were given *inductive* statements, describing the person's need and the consequences of helping: e.g. "Jenny doesn't have any candy kisses. If you share yours, then she'll have some too." Two more prompts for prosocial behavior were given after the first attempt did not succeed in eliciting any. Session 3, with staged actions, took place one week later with two unfamiliar adults. At session 3, children who were exhorted to behave prosocially displayed significantly more prosocial behavior than controls.

Children who were given inductive reasons to share or help were just as prosocial as those commanded to do so. Children in both exhortation groups showed significantly more sharing and teaching in the delayed session 3 than control children who had not had any verbal communications. The helping scores of boys in session 3 did not differ from controls. The researchers "are convinced that adults can enhance the helping, sharing, teaching, and comforting behaviors of preschool children by furnishing them with exhortations to behave prosocially and opportunities to rehearse, or practice, the behaviors" (p. 132).

356.Smith, G. (1985). Facial and full-length ratings of attractiveness related to social interactions of young children. *Sex Roles, 12,* (3-4), 287-293.

Thirty-eight preschool children were observed for aggressive and prosocial interactions. More prosocial behaviors and fewer aggressive behaviors were directed at attractive girls than unattractive girls. There were no differences between attractive and unattractive boys concerning number of prosocial or aggressive advances.

357.Smither, D. (1977). A reconsideration of the developmental study of empathy. *Human Development, 20,* 253-276.

In this theoretical essay, the results of a conceptual analysis of empathy are presented by considering the nature of different forms of emotional expression. Research on developmental changes in sociocognitive processes and social relations is related to the analysis of the conditions of empathy. The nature of the processes and skills involved in any specific case of empathy depend upon particular dimensions of the situational context, the nature of the emotions involved in the empathee's feeling state, and the manner in which those feelings are expressed.

358.Solomon, D., Watson, M. S., Delucci, K. L., Schaps, E., & Battistich, V. (1988). Enhancing children's prosocial behavior in the classroom. *American Educational Research*

Journal, 25 (4), 527-554.

A program designed to enhance children's prosocial development was implemented in 3 suburban elementary schools for 5 years, along with intensive teacher training. The school-wide program creates a milieu to support the classroom program with family events, school-wide service, helping activities, buddies activities (where classes from different levels pair up and older children help younger ones) and a tutoring program. Observers were blind to the status of the program and comparison schools. Multivariate analysis confirmed that the teachers in the program classrooms were actually implementing the program.

Observational data for children moving from kindergarten through fourth grade revealed higher scores for program than comparison classrooms on:

1. Cooperative activities,
2. Developmental discipline (participation in rule-development, problem-solving class discussions, students working out own methods of learning and problem-solving,and students solving minor interpersonal problems),
3. Activities promoting social understanding,
4. Highlighting prosocial values, and
5. Helping (students working independently in groups with other students' help).

As well, program students were superior on two indices of interpersonal behavior: supportive, friendly behavior and spontaneous prosocial behavior.

359.Spangler, G. (1990). Mother, child, and situational correlates of toddlers' social competence. *Infant Behavior and Development,*

13, 405-419.

In a longitudinal study, 24 German mother-toddler dyads were observed in at-home play, with a stranger modeling toy play such as "telephoning" at some point, and requesting the toddler to perform. Temperament ratings from the first year were available. Children's play was coded as "high-interest" when they were busily engaged with toys, or "low-interest". When mothers demonstrated high-quality responsiveness to the toddlers during periods of low-interest play, the children were found to be highly socially competent and show a high level of cooperation in interaction with a stranger. Cooperation was particularly high for children with mothers who had been highly responsive to their toddlers' negative moods or displays. Mothers who had perceived their children as difficult were less likely to be responsive during this second year of life. The development of social competence is seen as a mutual process between child and mother.

360.Sparkes, K. K. (1991). Cooperative and competitive behavior in dyadic game-playing: A comparison of Anglo-American and Chinese children. *Early Child Development and Care, 68,* 88-98.

A modification of Madsen's marble-pull game was used to explore the dyadic game-playing behavior of 3- and 4-year-olds in preschools in Taiwan and the USA. A majority of the children, who played the game in pairs, showed equality or near equality in their scores, indicating that they had cooperated. Ethnic but no clear age differences were observed. Chinese female pairs showed a high degree of competitiveness and American female pairs a low degree. Fewer of the mixed sex pairs obtained equal scores. This supports the idea of dominance/submission, with boys pulling the cord in order to win more often, compared with the situation when girls played in same sex dyads.

361. Sparks, A. D., Thornburg, K. R., Ispa, J. M., & Gray, M. M. (1984). Prosocial behaviors of young children related to parental childrearing attitudes. *Early Child Development and Care, 15,* 291-298.

Prosocial behaviors of 3-6 year old young children were related to parental childrearing attitudes. The preschoolers with the lowest level of prosocial behaviors had mothers with scores representing a high need for adult control while the fathers' scores were below the mean.

362. Sprafkin, J. M., Liebert, R. M., & Poulds, R. W. (1975). Effects of a prosocial example on children's helping. *Journal of Experimental Child Psychology, 20,* 119-126.

First-graders watched either an episode from "Lassie" television programs in which a boy risked his life to save a dog, while control groups watched a "Lassie" episode without altruism or a family situation comedy. The children who had viewed the altruistic episode gave significantly more help to puppies in distress than the other children. Helping the puppies had actually cost the children who did so, because their helping meant that they had to withdraw from playing a game in which the children could win valuable prizes. Prosocial TV programs can influence altruistic behaviors of children, although some researchers suggest that this can only happen when accompanied by opportunities to play or enact prosocial behaviors.

363.Sprafkin, J., & Rubinstein, E. (1979).Children's television viewing habits and prosocial behavior. *Journal of Broadcasting, 23,* 265–276.

Children of grades 2, 3, and 4 (N=500) from two elementary schools were administered the Television Viewing Habits Questionnaire and a prosocial behavior measure which was the proportion of classmates who "voted" for a child on an item. The child's sex, grade, social class and academic achievement were included as control variables.

The amount of television a child watched and the level of prosocial content on favorite programs were related to the degree to which the child behaved prosocially in school – the less television a child watched and the more prosocial his/her favorite program, the more prosocial the child was likely to behave. However, each of these variables accounted for only 1% of the variance in prosocial behavior. Also, girls and children whose parents were highly educated constituted the greatest proportion of the prosocial programming audience.

364.Stanhope, L., Bell, R., & Parker–Cohen, N. (1987). Temperament and helping behavior in preschool children. *Developmental Psychology, 23,* 347–353.

Children aged three to five responded to four opportunities to help an adult with simple tasks such as picking up spilled objects and opening a trunk. Helpfulness was rated according to the amount of time and number of prompts given before the child began assisting. Helping scores were compared to teacher and parent ratings on sociability, social adaptability, and helpfulness. Parent rating of helpfulness did not correlate with sociability, but social adaptability showed a strong positive correlation to helpfulness.

365.Staub, E. (1970). A child in distress: The influence of age and number of witnesses on children's attempts to help. *Journal of Personality and Social Psychology, 14,* 130–140.

Children from grades 1, 2, 4, 6, and kindergarten (N=132) tested alone or in same-sex pairs, heard sounds of a child's severe distress and crying from an adjoining room after the experimenter left the room. In explanation to the target child, the experimenter pretended that a child was playing alone there and might climb on a chair and then might fall off. The oldest children made fewer attempts to go next door to help. The sixth graders' verbal reports suggested that fear of disapproval for possibly inappropriate behavior (they were "expected" to stay in the test room when the examiner left briefly, and it was during that time alone that the cries were heard) may have inhibited the older children's willingness to initiate helping actions.

Pairs of younger children tended to help significantly more than children alone, but this was no longer true for fourth- and sixth-graders. Among younger children, the presence of a peer may reduce fear or stress and lead to a more galvanized action to help. Additional analysis showed that birth order mattered. Children who were the youngest in the family tended to help less than children with younger siblings.

366.Staub, E. (1971). A child in distress: The influence of nurturance and modeling on children's attempts to help. *Developmental Psychology, 5,* 124-132.

To help someone in distress, a child must overcome fear or stress from the distress cues. An experimenter interacted with 64 kindergarten children, half boys, half girls, in a bowling game, either in a warm, friendly, nurturant manner or in a neutral task-oriented manner. Subjects then saw the experimenter go into an adjoining room, either to check on a child, since sounds of distress (faked by a tape-recorder) were heard, or to pretend to help a child. Thus, half the children received prosocial modeling of helping behavior. The other half were told that there was a child in the next room whom the experimenter would go check on. After returning, the experimenter told the child she would be leaving for a short time, and that there were extra crayons in the adjoining room if needed. After leaving, there was a tape of the sound of a crash and severe sobbing by a 7-year-old girl from the next room. The earlier modeling significantly increased the chances that a child would try to go next door to help or would tell the returning experimenter about the (presumed) trouble. Prior nurturance by the experimenter enhanced the helping scores of boys and girls. Children who came from larger families helped less than children from smaller families.

367.Staub, E. (1974). Helping a distressed person: Social, personality, and stimulus determinants. In L. Berkowitz (Ed.), *Advances in experimental social psychology,* (Vol. 7, pp. 113-136). New York: Academic Press.

A series of related experiments describing the multiplicity of influences promoting and/or inhibiting the giving of aid to those in physical distress are outlined in this chapter. The motives for helping (and not helping) others, the situation and person as determinants of helping behaviors and the effect of characteristics of the stimulus for help and of the surrounding conditions on helping behavior were explored. Sources of people's motivation for helping others vary greatly from expected external rewards (or avoidance of punishment) to self-reward and empathic reinforcement i.e., satisfaction gained from another person's increased well-being. The nature of distress cues, circumstantial conditions, and personality characteristics also influence helping behaviors.

368. Staub, E. (1975a). *The development of prosocial behavior in children.* Morristown, NJ: General Learning Press.

Staub presents his early researches on children's willingness to help in this pioneer volume on prosocial development.

369. Staub, E. (1975b). To rear a prosocial child: Reasoning, learning by doing, and learning by teachers and others. In D. J. DePalma, & J. M. Foley (Eds.), *Moral development: Current theory and research.* Hillsdale, NJ: Lawrence Erlbaum.

A set of three experiments was carried out with 5th and 6th grade students to determine effects of indirect instruction, positive induction, and participation in responsible action on subsequent prosocial behavior. *Teaching others, induction* and *participation in prosocial behavior* – all had some effects later, mostly enhancing prosocial behavior. Staub argues that a pattern of child-rearing practices and other socializing influences rather than a single influence affect a child's prosocial development.

370.Staub, E. (Ed.) (1978). *Positive social behavior and morality: Social and personal influences* (Vol. 1). New York: Academic Press.

Staub, E. (Ed.) (1979). *Positive social behavior and morality: Socialization and development* (Vol. 2). New York: Academic Press.

These two volumes contain an *excellent* assortment of research and theoretical articles on the state of knowledge in the early 1970's about prosocial development and morality.

The chapters in Volume 1 include:

* Prosocial behavior: Definitions, significance, and relationship to morality
* Genetic origins of altruism
* Why people behave prosocially
* Personality influences
* Stimulus characteristics that affect helping
* Social influences (this includes researches on modeling, on motives, on vicarious reinforcement)
* Sex differences and helping behavior
* Exchange and reciprocity in positive and negative behavior
* Cooperation in intimate relationships

Chapters in Volume 2 include:

* Positive social behavior, morality, and development
* Major approaches
* Developmental trends with age

* Parental control styles and socialization practices (including conditioning, learning through observation, and inductive reasoning)
* Peer socialization practices that promote prosocial development

371. Staub, E. (1981). Promoting positive behavior in schools, in other education settings, and in the home. In J. P. Rushton & R. M. Sorrentino (Eds.), *Altruism and helping behavior: Social, personality, and developmental perspectives* (pp. 109–133). Hillsdale, NJ: Lawrence Erlbaum.

Some adults worry that teaching children to be prosocial may be "counterproductive" to promotion of the child's own interests. Staub argues that a child can be helped to become a kind, prosocial person while also developing personal motives to promote the self. Extensive research shows that a positive relationship between adults and children – warmth, affection, nurturance, and love- promotes positive behavior. How to learn to move a child from aggressive or disruptive behaviors to more positive social transactions is a difficult and important adult role in training children.

Three steps in verbal communication can be effective: *first advise the child of a prosocial action* (such as sharing marbles so that other children can continue to play in the game). *Then use induction* to explain how another child feels when you share and he or she can continue in the game. *The third step attributes prosocial motives and feelings to children by telling them that they are kind and generous for having shared.* Prosocial actions can be advanced by naturally inducing children to participate in activities that benefit others.

Role-playing "as-if" participation can help. Modeling by adults and positive television models also helps. In the peer group, reciprocity and complementarity operate. Children who act prosocially toward others will tend more to receive positive actions by others. School size affects positive social actions. In smaller schools more children are participants in cooperative school and after-school activities.

Staub provides a variety of other techniques for teachers to help them foster prosocial activities among children. For example, teachers need to find "meaningful activities for children to benefit others in need." Older children in mixed age groupings can help younger ones; some children who know a skill can teach others how.

372.Staub, E., Bar-Tal, D., Karylowski, J., & Reykowski, J. (Eds.) (1984). *The development and maintenance of prosocial behavior: International perspectives on positive morality.* New York: Plenum Press.

Research and theories are reviewed concerning prosocial behavior – its motivations, consequences, interaction patterns, and the factors that promote or discourage acts of kindness, generosity, and cooperation. "Embedded induction" may be most effective in promoting prosocial behaviors. That is, induction, together with some positive behavior that children are engaged in, permits them to associate the thoughts and reasons provided by the adults with their ongoing behavior. Such a combination of verbal communication with a child's own actions may usefully call the child's attention to the reasoning technique, particularly for a child who is used to more authoritarian adult methods.

Attributing characteristics or behavioral
tendencies to children which persuade them that
the reason they have carried out a prosocial
or positive behavior is because they are
generous or kind or helpful was found to
increase later prosocial behaviors. Induction
may provide a "cognitive network", so that
thinking is stimulated about the relation of
one's own actions and others' needs as well.
Such thinking can then serve as an internal
self-guide for prosocial actions, particularly
if the inductive statements of the adults have
emphasized people's feelings. Extensive
inductive statements, however, while more likely
to increase girls' prosocial behaviors,
sometimes even decreased boys' positive
actions.

Contains: Radke-Yarrow, M., & Zahn-Waxler,
C. (1984)

373.Staub, E., & Sherk, L. (1970). Need for
approval, children's sharing behavior, and
reciprocity in sharing. *Child Development,
41,* 243-252.

Fourth-graders filled out questionnaires
that evaluated their need for approval,
friendship choices, and candy preferences.
Based on friendship choices, randomly selected
children were paired with a preferred
companion. One member of each pair was
selected as the "giver" (controller of candy)
while the other was designated the receiver.
Givers were given bags containing nine pieces
of their favorite candy for "helping" a book
publisher by responding to questions about a
tape-recorded story. Receivers, who joined
their partners after the candy had been
distributed, received none. During the story,
the experimenter withdrew behind a one-way
mirror to record the number of candies

receivers requested, the number givers ate, and the number of offers and refusals.

After the story, children were asked to draw a picture from the story. They were each given a blank paper, but only the receiver was given a crayon. Again the experimenter withdrew to record the length of time each child had the crayon, as well as the number of requests for sharing. The number of candies givers ate in the receivers' company was negatively related to givers' need for approval, while the length of time the crayon was shared was unrelated to the receivers' need for approval. However, receivers' crayon-sharing was significantly positively related to the number of candies shared by givers. When givers were selfish, receivers shared the crayon less.

374. Stevenson, H. (1991). The development of prosocial behavior among Chinese and Japanese children. In R. A. Hinde & J. Groebel (Eds.), *Prosocial behavior, cooperation, and trust.* New York: Cambridge University Press.

Asian and Western sources of prosocial development in children are contrasted. In China and Japan, parents and teachers, rather than religious leaders, are responsible for ensuring that children develop a high moral character. Group orientation is emphasized, as evidenced in the motto on playroom walls in Chinese preschools: Cooperation (friendship) first, competition second. The ancient and modern model of Confucian thought is not to inculcate moral principles through abstractions, but through concrete behaviors that can be imitated in the group. Maoist goals were taught to Chinese children through stories written for the teachers and transmitting prosocial messages (such as: a child repairs a torn page of another child's textbook, washes another child's handkerchief, gives up a bus seat to an old worker, or carries a heavy parcel for an elderly person). Textbook tallies reveal the strong theme of altruism in stories for schoolchildren. Such themes are prominent in Taiwan texts too. Group relationship and status is powerful, and includes even aggression with prosocial goals, such as defending the in-group against an enemy. In Japan each class is split into small groups of from 4 to 8 children, the *han*, and their responsibility is to help each other for their group to succeed. The high level of academic achievement of Chinese and Japanese children is postulated by the author to stem from their cooperative attitudes toward teachers.

375.Strain, P., Guralnick, M., & Walker, H. (Eds.) (1986). *Children's social behavior: Development, assessment, and modification.* San Diego: Academic Press.

This excellent resource book includes articles concerning the social environment, peer relationships, assessment methods, how best to design childhood interventions that promote mental health and social skills training. Trends occurring within the social interaction arena include 1) the development of comprehensive multicomponent intervention strategies; 2) the extension of social skills training efforts to more disabled groups of children; 3) the use of intervention procedures in increasingly complex naturalistic settings; and 4) the use of systematic procedures to enhance skill maintenance across time and generalization to new persons and settings.

Contains: Barton, E. (1986)

376.Strayer, F. (1981). The nature and organization of altruistic behavior among preschool children. In J. P. Rushton & R. M. Sorrentino (Eds.), *Altruism and helping behavior: Social, personality, and developmental perspectives.* Hillsdale, NJ: Lawrence Erlbaum.

The researchers tallied naturally occurring altruistic activity among preschoolers in three preschool groups. Fifty-four children (ages 3-6) were observed for four types of prosocial interactions: object, cooperative, helping, and empathic activities. Extensive descriptions and illustrations of these four categories and the sub-categories are included. The four sub-categories of cooperative behavior (giving, sharing, offering, and play) comprised the majority of prosocial activity in each group. Although the pattern of association between the four categories indicates that a high score on one prosocial measure is correlated with a higher rate of responsiveness for at least one other form of activity, the overall results do not justify the creation of a unitary altruistic index reflecting a generalized disposition to engage in prosocial activity.

377.Strayer, F. F., Waring, S., & Rushton, J. P. (1979). Social constraints on naturally occurring preschool altruism. *Ethology and Sociobiology, 1,* 3-11.

Social interactions among three-to-five-year-olds (N=26) were videotaped during free play and analyzed for identification of altruistic exchanges. Sixty percent of observed altruism was directed towards peers and 40% towards teachers. The degree of generality in children's altruistic behavior strongly depended on whether such activity was directed towards peers or teachers and on whether the peer was a friend. Children directed most of their altruistic activities and actions towards a member of their peer group. Furthermore, a strong relationship was evident between individual rates of initiated and received altruistic behavior.

378.Strayer, J. (1980). A naturalistic study of empathic behaviors and their relationship to affective states and perspective-taking skills in preschool children. *Child Development, 51,* 815-822.

Preschoolers (10 boys, 4 girls) (M=59 months) were observed naturalistically over an 8-week period. Event sampling was used to record the frequency of empathic behavioral interactions, defined as the presence of a prosocial response to a peer's display of one of four categories of affect – happy, sad, angry or hurt. Two perspective-taking tasks were administered to each child individually midway through the observations and a donating task was performed at the end. Of the naturally occurring affect displays, 39% were met with either affect-matching or instrumental displays, indicating empathy. Happy displays occurred more frequently and were responded to significantly more than other affect displays. Also, children with more frequent happy displays were more likely to display empathic responses toward others.

379.Strayer, J., & Roberts, W. (1989). Children's empathy and role-taking: Child and parental factors, and relations to prosocial behavior. *Journal of Applied Developmental Psychology, 10* (2), 227-239.

Issues examined in this research include (1) how children's empathy relates to other child factors, specifically, cognitive role-taking, imagination, and ego resiliency, (2) the associations between children's empathy and role-taking, and reports of children's prosocial behaviors in family and school contexts, and (3) whether children's empathy is related to familial factors such as parents' empathy and parents' perceptions of their children as empathic and prosocial in the family context. Fifty-one children ranging in age from 72 months to 85 months were interviewed. Role-taking was positively related to both assessed empathy and parents' reports of children's empathy. Children's performance on an imaginative, divergent thinking task and teachers' assessments of their creative, imaginative thinking were both related to scores on emotional empathy and role-taking. Ego resilience correlated significantly with parents' assessments of children's empathy and children's role-taking, but not with assessed empathy. Prosocial behaviors at home were associated with children's empathy, especially as assessed by parents' reports, while prosocial behaviors at school were associated with imaginative skills and (to a lesser extent) role-taking. The importance of *cognitive* factors (imagination and role-taking) for prosocial behaviors at school points to possible home-school differences that need to be understood when factors which contribute to children's prosocial responses are assessed.

380.Strayer, J., & Schroeder, M. (1989).Children's helping strategies: Influences of emotion, empathy, and age. In N. Eisenberg (Ed.), *Empathy and related emotional responses* (pp. 85-106). San Francisco: Jossey-Bass.

Three groups of children viewed 30-minute emotional evocative vignettes. Group 1 consisted of 15 boys and 18 girls (4.4-5.7 years old); group 2 consisted of 20 children from 8.3-9.7 years; group 3 consisted of 20 children 12.2-13.6 years. One vignette showed three children sneaking into a yard to peek into a house. A looming shadow of a man appears, and the children run away. Another showed a father and daughter at a circus that has stopped in town for one night. The girl jumps and laughs with excitement. Another showed a physically disabled girl practicing with a cane while she jokes with her physiotherapist. The children described each vignette and identified the characters' kind and intensity of emotions as well as self-experienced emotions. Empathy was scored on the Feshbach & Roe and on the Strayer Empathy continuum scale, which has seven levels of matches in kind and intensity of emotion reported for self and character. The children were asked if they felt like helping any character and how: instrumental, verbal reassurance or reasoning, social, material, aggressive or other.

Girls reported significantly more total helping strategies than did boys, and offered more help for happy characters than did boys. Young children with higher Empathy Continuum scores showed significantly greater willingness to help (r=.42). The younger children used instrumental strategies most often, aggressive strategies next most often. The oldest proffered verbal and instrumental strategies the most. Others' happiness and anger were responded to with the fewest offers of help. Helping was proposed most often in response to characters' fears (71% of all fear attributions) and sadness (56% of all sadness attributions). Fear was the only emotion of the four examined for which willingness to help and helping strategies increased significantly with age. The authors conclude that children probably learn prosocial responses to sadness at young ages.

381. Strein, W. (1986). Sex and age differences in preschool children's cooperative behaviors: Partial support for the Knight/Kagan hypothesis. *Psychological Reports, 58,* 915-921.

Knight and Kagan (1981) hypothesized that sex differences are in fact due to differences in individualism (the preference for maximizing one's own gains irrespective of the gains of others), with girls showing a greater preference for individualistic alternatives than boys. Knight and Kagan predicted that girls will appear to be more cooperative than boys on measures which confound individualistic and cooperative alternatives but will appear to be less cooperative than boys on measures in which individualistic and competitive alternatives are confounded. The purpose of the present study was to investigate the Knight/Kagan hypothesis on a younger sample of children with respect to two measures of children's cooperative behavior. Thirty four- and five-year old children, representing an ethnically and racially mixed group were chosen. When the results were interpreted dichotomously (cooperative vs. competitive), the results support traditional findings: girls were more cooperative than boys on one measure while younger children were more cooperative than older children on both measures. When interpreted trichotomously (cooperative/individualistic/competitive) partial support emerged for the view that girls are more individualistic than boys.

382.Thomas, D. (1978). Cooperation and competition among children in the Pacific Islands and New Zealand: The school as an agent of social change. *Journal of Research and Development in Education, 12,* (1), 88-96.

An urban sample of 48 children from grades 7 and 8 in Western Samoa, the Cook Islands, Fiji, and New Zealand played with the Madsen Cooperation Board for 4 one-minute trials. A pen in a central penhold can be drawn to any part of the paper on the board as each of four children appropriately manipulates a string passing through an eyelet near each of the children and through the penholder. The child who could draw a line through a circle near his or her eyelet was promised a coin. Some children were able to see that only cooperative behavior will be successful in maximizing the rewards for all the players, and some children tried verbally to get the other three players to cooperate. The majority of the Cook Island and New Zealand children were maladaptively competitive. The Samoan and Fiji children managed to obtain some coins each in cooperative group efforts.

No rural-urban differences were found, nor preferences for doing school work individually or in groups. Cook Island children preferred cooperation for non-school activities compared with the other groups. Polynesian teachers are encouraged to help children balance cooperative, competitive and individual goals, but to emphasize cooperation in learning.

383.Tietjen, A. (1986). Prosocial reasoning among children and adults in a Papua New Guinea society. *Developmental Psychology, 22,* 861-868.

Residents of Papua New Guinea, a small, traditional collectivist society, responded to four moral reasoning stories adapted from Eisenberg. Respondents varied in age: 69 elementary age children, 8 adolescents, and 24 adults. Stories conveyed moral dilemmas understandable to the Papua residents; for example, sharing the village harvest with a nearby community that had been flooded. Respondents indicated whether or not they would help, and why. Answers were analyzed and mental maturity scores calculated using the categories of reasoning derived from Eisenberg: hedonistic, needs-oriented, approval, interpersonal or stereotyped orientation, and self-reflective empathic or internalized.

Physical needs-oriented reasoning was used most frequently by the children, adolescents, and adults. Adults used psychological needs-oriented reasoning next most frequently; for all other groups hedonistic reasoning was second. Use of authority and punishment-oriented reasoning was very low at all ages. Results yielded support for cross-cultural use of Eisenberg's categories of reasoning, with adaptations in sequence and ultimate levels of moral reasoning influenced by cultural values.

384. Turiel, E. (1975). The development of social concepts. In D. DePalma & J. Foley (Eds.), *Moral development: Current theory and research*. Hillsdale, NJ: Lawrence Erlbaum.

Turiel's interviews with older children produce a series of levels of children's reasoning about social regulation. At Level 0 children confuse rules, conventions, customs, and personal habits and wishes arising from the child's own desire. Social regulation is not consistent and the child distorts prosocial norms, for example, to conform to his own wishes. At Level 1, a child begins to recognize the potential conflict between own desires and social norms. Rules and conventions (such as asking nicely rather than hitting and grabbing a toy) are confused with one another, but seen as different from the child's wishes. The child knows that punishment will follow antisocial acts. The Level 2 child begins to realize that moral conventions are less important and even arbitrary compared with morally based social regulations, but this distinction breaks down if children think they can get away with a forbidden behavior. At level 3, most conventions are distinguished from moral constraints: the latter are rule-governed, the former are not.

385. Turiel, E. (1983a). *The development of social knowledge: Morality and convention.* New York: Cambridge University Press.

Conceptions of morality are constructed out of the child's social interactions that involve intrinsic effects related to the well-being or rights of others. Actions within the moral domain are not arbitrary and social regulations are unnecessary. Even if a teacher said it was all right to pinch a child -- hurting another is wrong. The conceptual domain of morality is contrasted with that of social conventions which are contextual. Individuals construct social conventions out of experiences with social actions whose propriety is determined by social context; their meaning comes from within a given social system. The child's perception of this type of event as a social conventional transgression would be based on understanding whether or not there was a rule against the behavior.

386.Turiel, E. (1983b). Domains and categories in social-cognitive development. In W. Overton (Ed.), *The relationship between social and cognitive development* (pp. 53-89). Hillsdale, NJ: Lawrence Erlbaum.

Children's social world consists of persons and relations between persons in three general categories: psychological knowledge of persons, knowledge of systems of social relations, and moral. Children learn that conventions, such as modes of greeting and forms of address, serve to coordinate and keep stable social interactions between people. In contrast, moral prescriptions are not alterable. Two events illustrate these differences:

Event A: A number of nursery school children are playing outdoors. There are some swings in the yard, all of which are being used. One of the children decides that he now wants to use a swing. Seeing that they are all occupied, he goes to one of the swings, where he pushes the other child off, at the same time hitting him. The child who has been pushed is hurt and begins to cry. Event B: Children are greeting a teacher who has just come into the nursery school. A number of children go up to her and say "Good morning, Mrs. Jones." One of the children says "Good morning, Mary." (p. 78)

Both events are social in nature. But children at all grades and ages respond to moral transgressions as wrong. In preschools, 86% of children, and in grade schools, 87% of children stated that hurting another would not be right even if no rule existed in the school. They focused on the intrinsic consequences of actions, while for transgressions of social conventions, they focused on features of social organization. Moral interpretation means that children judge a hurting act as wrong even if there would be no rule against it. They regard moral acts as having intrinsic validity. Children very early come to realize the distinction between rules that people in power (such as teachers and parents) make and rules that reflect the need for all persons to act in prosocial and non-harming ways with each other.

387. Turiel, E., & Smetana, J. G. (1984). Social knowledge and action: The coordination of domains. In W. M. Kurtines & J. L. Gewirtz (Eds.), *Morality, moral behavior, and moral development.* New York: Wiley.

This chapter explores the complex relations between social judgments and actions. Moral decisions may involve moral judgments of harm, rights and justice, societal concepts, such as social conventions, etc. What might appear to be contradictory orientations are all part of a person's moral reasoning. The meaning and functions of moral prescriptions, such as not harming others, or helping someone in distress, are different from the meaning and functions of conventions in social organizations (such as children being required to wear a certain costume or say special politeness words). Children regard moral prescriptions as obligatory, universal, and generalizable. They regard conventions as simply conforming to authority. Thus, conventions can be evaded or ignored, whereas moral prescriptions, often involving prosocial actions, are incumbent upon a person no matter what social convention rules might be. When the domains are in conflict (e.g. a parent makes a prohibition, but a peer needs you to violate that rule in order to be helpful and kind), different children use different strategies to coordinate or resolve these conflicts between moral and conventional rules.

388.Turnure, C. (1975). Cognitive development and role-taking ability in boys and girls from 7 to 12. *Developmental Psychology, 11,* 202-209.

Ten boys and ten girls at three age levels (7, 9, and 12 years), matched on IQ, were given a social-role-taking task and two Piagetian tasks. Performance on all tasks generally increased with age, but correlations between performances on the two types of tasks were generally not significant. There were no significant sex differences. IQ was correlated with performance on the role-taking task but not with the Piagetian tasks, which were highly correlated with each other. The ability to "think about possibilities" did not differ significantly for the age or sex groups, but was significantly related to performance on the experimental task for the younger subjects.

389.Tyler, F. B., & Varma, M. (1988). Help-seeking and helping behavior in children as a function of psychosocial competence. *Journal of Applied Developmental Psychology, 9,* 219-231.

Indian children, eight to ten years old (N=112), completed the Psychosocial Competence Incomplete Stories Test. Scores were used in grouping the children into "high" and "low" psychosocial competence groups. Children were then randomly assigned to same-sex experimental pairs in the following combinations: high competence help-seeker and helper; high competence help-seeker and low competence helper; low competence help-seeker and high competence helper; and low competence help-seeker and helper. Help-seekers received block design sets with instructions to replicate designs portrayed on cards and were told they could ask their partners for help if the help-

seeker so desired. Helpers were told they could
choose to help. High competence help-seekers
made more constructive efforts to complete the
block task, sought help more readily when
needed, and used help more constructively than
those in the low competence group. Helping
attempts were also significantly more
constructive among high rather than low competence helpers.

390.Underwood, B., & Moore, B. (1982a). The
generality of altruism in children. In N.
Eisenberg (Ed.), *The development of prosocial
behavior*. New York: Academic Press.

Staub's definition of altruism is used:
"action that appears to have been intended to
benefit others rather than to gain material or
social rewards", in contradistinction to a
prosocial behavior like cooperation where there
could be rewards for both recipient and helper.
This review of altruism studies looks for
consistency across situations, behaviors, and
time. For younger children, research suggests
that situational factors and different
individual characteristics control sharing and
intervening behaviors. Thus, there may not be
a highly generalized prosocial syndrome. The
relationships among different kinds of prosocial
responding are not strong, nor are there
invariably high correlations with age. However,
there have been some researches suggesting
consistency *across* age. Nurturant interactions
with adults, and adult *permission* to engage in
prosocial action lead to more altruism. An
interactionist model seems most appropriate –
one that includes personality characteristics
and situational elements. The same children
may not show the same *forms* of prosocial
behaviors.

391. Underwood, B., & Moore, B. (1982b). Perspective-taking and altruism. *Psychological Bulletin, 91,* 143-173.

In general, older children are more likely to engage in helpful acts than are younger children. The developmental mechanism most frequently given to explain this age-related increase is the increasing ability of a child to take the point of view of another person. This perspective-taking ability includes: a) predicting the literal visual perspective of another; b) identifying another's thoughts, intentions, motives, or social behaviors; or c) inferring another's feelings, reactions, or concerns. Flavell has suggested that perceptual perspective-taking is a precursor to the development of social and affective perspective-taking. Moral judgment is based on this ability but children could be aware of the consequences of their actions on others and still not base their judgments on that information. Empathy too depends on vicariously experiencing affect of another. Meta-analyses of the relationship between these variables are provided in this paper. Underwood and colleagues gave elementary school children 25 pennies for helping. The children could then donate anonymously to peers unable to earn pennies. The children also took the Piaget 3 mountain task, as a measure of their perspective-taking, which turned out to be significantly correlated with grade level and with generosity. Krebs' work is cited as supporting a positive relationship between elementary school children's perspective-taking skills and both teacher-rated and observed altruism in classroom and on playground.

Meta-analyses of researches do not suggest that there is a strong relationship between empathy and altruism, but this may be due to poor measures. When multiple measures from videotaped behavior sequences (where the subject child can take some altruistic action to alleviate the distress of the videotape-pictured child) were used by Peraino & Sawin, then state empathy was found reliably related with altruism although trait empathy may not be.

392.Vikan, A. (1981). Taking the role of the other to self: A developmental study. *The Journal of Genetic Psychology, 139,* 285-294.

Children from seven to 11.5 years (N=30) participated in "the game of the castle". Some were observers. Others took the role of thief, guest, or postal worker and had to walk a 15 meters-long road ending at a point represented as a "castle" by the use of a pile of boxes. The postal worker was instructed to walk freely, while hiding a packet of envelopes inside his shirt. The guest was instructed that the road was very dirty and that he had to walk on road stones to keep shoes clean. The thief had to sneak and steal along. Role and behavior were specified. However, some children were instructed to behave incongruent with their role. There was a "house" along the road to the castle. The children were asked, "What did those persons in the house think you were when you passed on your way to the castle?" and "What person would the guard in the castle think that you were when s/he observed you approaching?" Children showed a growing awareness with age that the subject's role could not be accurately predicted if it was not role-played in character. Taking on the role of the other was rather difficult even for subjects 11.5 years old. Thus, some kinds of prosocial behaviors that might depend on sophistication on making predictions about others' viewpoints may be difficult for children until Piagetian decentration has advanced developmentally.

393.Vitz, P. C. (1990). The use of stories in moral development: New psychological reasons for an old education method. *American Psychologist, 45,* 709-720.

Narratives are urged as an important tool for the moral education of children, since they provide detailed and vivid descriptions of moral dilemmas that people actually experience, and since, except for occasional service projects for the school or community at large, children get relatively little practice in moral development in their school experiences.

394.Water, E., Hay, D., & Richters, J. (1986). Infant-parent attachment and the origins of prosocial and antisocial behavior. In D. Olweus, J. Block, & M. Radke-Yarrow (Eds.) (1986). *Development of antisocial and prosocial behavior: Research, theories, and issues* (pp. 97-126). New York: Academic Press.

This essay summarizes research evidence that links infant-parent attachment in a process-level mode to later prosocial outcomes. The model proposes that both the child's identification with the parent and the parent's expectations for the child are key processes that mediate the influence of an early secure attachment on later positive socialization outcomes.

395.Weissberg, R. P. (1985). Designing effective social problem-solving programs for the classroom. In B. Schneider, K. H. Rubin, & J. Ledingham (Eds.), *Peer relationships and social skills in childhood: Vol. 2. Issues in assessment and training* (pp. 225-242). New York: Springer-Verlag.

The SPS program for enhancing elementary school children's social skills is described.

396.Weissberg, R. P., Gesten, E. L., Rapkin, B. D., Cowen, E. L., Davidson, E., Flores De Apodaca, R., & McKim, B. J. (1981). The evaluation of a social problem-solving training program for suburban and inner-city third-grade children. *Journal of Consulting and Clinical Psychology, 49,* 251–261.

The Social Problem-Solving (SPS) program was effective in enhancing social skills in elementary classrooms.

397.Whiting, B. B. (1983). The genesis of prosocial behavior. In D. L. Bridgeman (Ed.) *The nature of prosocial development: Interdisciplinary theories and strategies* (pp. 221–242). New York: Academic Press.

Current theories of prosocial development focus on a biological model, a cognitive-developmental model, and a socialization model. From the records of boy and girl behaviors (ages 2–12 years) from six cultures, acts were coded as *nurturant* (helping and supporting others perceived to be in need) and *prosocial dominance* (acts required of a child to make positive expected contributions to community and family). In all samples, girls were observed caring for children more frequently than boys, and thus having more practice in prosocial behaviors. Nurturance increased with child age. Girls were more nurturant than boys in 64% of 73 comparisons and boys in 3% of dyadic interactions. Girls had more practice in prosocial dominance while they cared for toddlers. The researchers cannot untangle the influences of biology or social conventions on the sex differences found.

398.Whiting, B. B., & Whiting, J. W. (1975). *Children of six cultures: A psychocultural analysis.* Cambridge, MA: Harvard University Press.

Anthropologists studying six widely different cultures found that when children help care for younger siblings and interact with a cross-age variety of children in social groups in non-school settings, they are found to be more helpful toward other family members and with peers than are children in cultures where early caregiving responsibilities are not given.

399.Wilson, B., & Cantor, J. (1985). Developmental differences in empathy with a television protagonist's fear. *Journal of Experimental Child Psychology, 39,* 284-299.

This research was designed to test whether empathy depends on increasing cognitive role-taking skills or is a conditioned response resulting from pairing of an emotional situation with another's emotional expression. After viewing two experimental videotapes - 1) the back of a boy's head with bees swarming around, and 2) the boy's face shown sweating and frightened - then 125 3-5-year olds were asked how they felt while watching, and how they thought the boy felt. Younger children reported significantly fewer negative feelings and were less aroused in the character's fear condition than in the fear-provoking stimulus condition. The inability to take a role hampers empathic emotional sharing among younger children.

400. Windmiller, M., Lambert, N., & Turiel, E. (1980). *Moral development and socialization*. Boston: Allyn & Bacon.

This book examines theories of moral development including Damon's structural-developmental theory, Turiel's theory of social-conventional and moral concept development, Sieber on a social-learning theory approach to morality, and the psychoanalytic perspective as described by Tice. Sullivan's chapter addresses the question, "Can values be taught?"

Contains: Sieber, J. E. (1980)

401. Wispe, L. G. (1972). Positive forms of social behavior: An overview. *Journal of Social Issues, 28,* 1-19.

In this comprehensive review of the 1970's literature on positive social interactions, the author suggests that prosocial behaviors are acts with positive social consequences (e.g. empathy, sharing, cooperation, donating, and helping). Enhanced *self-esteem* of the prosocial child as well as enhancement of the welfare of others is hypothesized as an outcome of prosocial interactions. Thus, prosocial patterns of interaction are seen as a benefit to the giver as well as the recipient.

402. Wispe, L. (Ed.) (1978). Altruism, sympathy, and helping: *Psychological and sociological principles*. New York: Academic Press.

This edited volume contains chapters on: the biological bases of altruism and sympathy (by E. Wilson); the genetics of altruism (by D. Campbell); the logical, sociocultural, and cross-cultural aspects of altruism; the paradox of altruism, which seemingly involves no reward and yet has to be learned (by Rosenhan); psychoanalytic and Lewinian analyses of altruism; legal aspects of helping others; and professional helping roles.

Contains: Krebs, D. (1978)

403.Wodarski, J. S., Feldman, R. A., Ronald, A., & Pedi, S. J. (1976). Reduction of antisocial behavior in an open community setting through the use of behavior modification in groups. *Child Care Quarterly, 5* (3), 198–210.

Fifth- and sixth-graders with a high degree of antisocial behavior participated 2 hours per week in a physical activity and group discussion treatment program. A non-participant observer measured the frequency of prosocial, non-social, and antisocial behavior. Prosocial behavior increased significantly and antisocial behavior decreased significantly between the baseline and the reinforcement conditions as a function of the behavior modification program.

404.Wolfe, V. V. et al. (1983). Teaching cooperative play to behavior-problem preschool children. *Education and Treatment of Children, 6* (1), 1–9.

A token economy program was effective in increasing cooperative play of preschoolers who displayed inappropriate peer interactions.

405.Yarrow, M. R., Scott, P. M., & Waxler, C. Z. (1973). Learning concern for others. *Developmental Psychology, 8,* 240–260.

Two weeks following training, 84% of experimental children who had received prosocial training (with dioramas, plus pictorial materials plus real behavioral episodes from a nurturant caregiver); spontaneously gave help in one or both staged behavioral live distress episodes. Only 33% of the control children in that post-test offered help.

406.Yarrow, M. R., & Waxler, C.Z.(1976).Dimensions and correlates of prosocial behavior in young children. *Child Development, 47,* 118-125.

Three kinds of prosocial behavior (helping, sharing and comforting) were studied in experimental and naturalistic settings for 108 children ages 3 to 7 1/2 years. Helping was not related to and was more frequent than sharing or comforting (which did not vary with sex of child). For boys *below* the mean on peer aggression, there was a significant correlation between existing aggression and sharing-comforting in the natural setting. For the not-highly-aggressive children, *being the target of aggression was positively related to giving comfort and sharing.* In contrast, for boys high on aggression, there was a negative relation (r=.43) with prosocial actions.

407.Yarrow, M., Waxler, C., Barrett, D., Darby,J., King, R., Pickett, M., & Smith, J. (1976). Dimensions and correlates of prosocial behavior in young children. *Child Development, 47,* 118-125.

Three kinds of prosocial behavior – helping, sharing, and comforting – were studied in experimental and naturalistic settings for 55 boys and 53 girls, ages 3 to 7. Helping occurred more frequently in both settings.

In the tests of sharing, a young female adult helper was interested in the same material as the subject. The subject was enjoying something (e.g. a snack) and the helper was deprived. The helper complained and expressed disappointment. In a fishing game, the only available pole was given to the child, and the adult expressed a wish to try too, but she did not ask for sharing. In the tests of helping, the experimenter accidentally spilled a box of tennis balls or utensils, and acted busy, thus giving the child a chance to help. In the tests of comforting, an adult pinched her finger in a drawer and winced, or an adult started to sob softly, ostensibly over a sad story.

Prosocial acts occurred with low frequency in peer interactions, yet 52% of the children responded prosocially to at least one of the helping tasks, 33% responded to at least one of the sharing tasks, and 37% responded to at least one of the comforting tasks. During the 40-minute observations of behavior, prosocial acts were expressed by 87% of the children. No age or sex differences were found at all. For boys *below* the mean on aggression, there was a significant positive association ($r=.50$) between exhibited aggression and sharing-comforting in the natural settings. For boys above the mean, in contrast, the relation was negative ($r=-.43$). Helping seems unrelated to sharing and comforting. *Prosocial* needs to be defined with regard to the stimulus situation (how much fear, pain, inconvenience there is) and with regard to the different bases for responding. Such determinants are: expectations of approval, learned prohibitions, norms of responsibility, level of cognitive and social skills, anxiety caused by the distress, and the child's feelings of well-being or upset.

408.Zahn-Waxler, C., Chapman, M., & Radke-Yarrow, M. (Eds.) (1986). *Aggression and altruism: Biological and social origins.* Cambridge: Cambridge University Press.

Contains: Feshbach, S., & Feshbach, N. (1986)

409.Zahn-Waxler, C., Cummings, M., & Iannotti, R. (Eds.) (1986). *Altruism and aggression: Biological and social origins.* New York: Cambridge University Press.

Excellent articles in Part I include biological, sociobiological, and ethological approaches to the study of altruism and aggression. Part II includes: development, socialization, and mediators of altruism and aggression in children. An outcome of a conference held in 1982 at the National Institute of Mental Health, Bethesda, Maryland, this book focuses on the *etiology* of altruistic and aggressive behaviors and how children are socialized to become more altruistic. The significance of emotions (e.g. empathy, anger, and guilt) as mediators was a common theme that emerged. An attempt is made to foster an ecological approach throughout the book.

410. Zahn-Waxler, C., Radke-Yarrow, M., & Brady-Smith, J. (1977). Perspective-taking and prosocial behavior. *Developmental Psychology, 13,* (1), 87-88.

Girls and boys, aged 3 to 7, from white, middle-class families (N=108) were administered 10 perspective-taking tests and 6 prosocial tests in two 40 minute sessions embedded in play activities. The perspective-taking tasks include items such as setting the table for another person and choosing a birthday gift for a peer of the opposite sex.

In one perspective-taking task, in a 3-dimensional wood lot an angry-looking cat with bared teeth was visible in the bushes. The adult asked the child to pretend that they were two dolls (visible) walking down the path. They described the cat's feelings. Then the doll returned on the path to notice that the cat had its leg caught in a trap. The child was again asked what the doll thought about the cat's emotions.

Prosocial tasks focused on sharing, helping and comforting. Perspective-taking abilities were present in the preschoolers and prominent earlier in life than had been previously hypothesized. However, understanding of another's perspective did not predict prosocial behavior.

411. Zahn-Waxler, C., Radke-Yarrow, M., & Brady-Smith, J. (1988). Perspective-taking and prosocial behavior. *Developmental Psychology, 13,* 87-88.

Fifty-five girls and fifty-three boys (ages three to seven) responded to ten perspective-taking tasks and six tests of prosocial behavior within two 40-minute, naturalistic play sessions. Perspective-taking tasks were either perceptual or conceptual in nature (e.g., arranging objects to match a visual model, or assuming the role/perspective of another). Prosocial tasks involved sharing, helping, and comforting adults or "confederate" peers by sharing snack, picking up spilled materials, or soothing an adult who "pinched" her finger. Perspective-taking was scored as successful, "struggling toward perspective," or failure. Prosocial tasks were scored for intervention or non-intervention. Perspective-taking scores were positively correlated with age. Prosocial scores were significantly positively correlated with perspective-taking scores for three-year-olds only; correlations for the three older groups were all non-significant.

412. Zahn-Waxler, C., Radke-Yarrow, M., & King, R. A. (1979). Childrearing and children's prosocial initiations toward victims of distress. *Child Development, 50,* 319-330.

Mothers of children 1 1/2-to 2 1/2-years-old recorded their toddlers' reactions and their own behaviors in everyday encounters with expressions of distress, such as pain or sorrow, in others. Distress was also simulated by the mothers and the experimenters in staged episodes (such as the adult pretending to be hurt). Children were altruistic in about 34% of the distress situations where they were bystanders. Mothers who used physical restraint and physical punishment did not have altruistic toddlers. Empathic caregiving, where the mother was a model of tender concern if the child was distressed, was highly associated (46%) with child altruism compared with children of low-empathic mothers (24%). Mothers who communicated with high intensity and clarity focusing on the fact that hurting was unacceptable to them, had children who showed more altruism and reparations behaviors. Nurturance, high emotional investment, and inductive techniques promote altruism in toddlers.

413. Zarbatany, L. Hartmann, D., & Gelfand, D. (1985). Why does children's generosity increase with age: Susceptibility to experimenter influence or altruism? *Child*

Development, 56, 746-756.

First-, third-, and fifth-grade students voted on ways to spend money "donated" to their classrooms. Students volunteered their own ideas and teachers described additional options such as sharing the money among class members, buying things for the classroom/school, or donating to poor children. Children voted in one of five conditions. In the "no treatment condition," students cast a private vote in the voting booth. For the "peer knowledge" condition, children were told that each individual's vote would be posted for all class members to see. In the "experimenter" condition, the researcher confided that she was really doing a study on how children share. For "experimenter plus surveillance," the researcher confided the same information and said, "I'm going to watch you vote." Finally, in the "experimenter plus exhortation" condition, the researcher stated her interest in sharing and added, "It really *is* good to give to poor children." After voting was completed, one child from each condition was interviewed for information on their perceptions of the voting process.

Girls were more generous than boys in voting to share the donated money with poor children. Fifth-graders were more generous than first- or third-graders, particularly in the more intrusive conditions (e.g., experimenter plus surveillance, and experimenter plus exhortation). Only the fifth-graders' generosity was affected by condition. Interview information revealed norm-related motivations for giving to the poor (it's nice/kind to give), with empathy-related rationales rarely given (feeling badly for poor children).

414. Zarbatany, L., Hartmann, D., Gelfand, D., & Vinciguerra, P. (1985). Gender differences in altruistic reputation: Are they artifactual? *Developmental Psychology, 21,* 97-101.

In a middle class elementary school, 28 boys and 37 girls from three 5th-grade classes gave written descriptions of incidents in which they or some other child of their age (a) helped another child, (b) shared with another child, c) made another child feel better, (d) got another child out of a tough spot. After categorization of the stories, 13 items reflecting masculine, feminine and neutral items were selected and administered to a second group of 5th-graders.

Children were asked to nominate two classmates more likely to engage in each category of prosocial behavior or by indicating which sex was more likely to perform the behavior (gender rating). Overall, girls were judged to be more altruistic than boys. In general boys tended to endorse boys for helpful behaviors and girls tended to endorse girls. Inclusion of empirically derived, masculine-related items did not elicit endorsements of boys for prosocial behavior.

415. Ziegler, S. (1981). The effectiveness of cooperative learning teams for increasing cross-ethnic friendship: Additional evidence. *Human Organization, 40,* 264-268.

When children of different ethnic backgrounds were put into cooperative learning situations for 8 weeks, casual cross-ethnic friendships increased significantly.

Section 2

Practical Strategies, Ideas, and Games for Promoting Prosocial Behaviors

416. Adcock, D., & Segal, M. (1983a). *Making friends: Ways of encouraging social development in young children.* Englewood Cliffs, NJ: Prentice Hall.

After studying the play of preschoolers for years, the authors describe the importance of friends to children through examples of children's play scenes. Three types of play opportunities are discussed: playing in a twosome, interacting casually in a larger group, and participating in a joint venture with several other children. Children's exclusion of others occurs to strengthen friendships, sustain the play, and provide for privacy. The authors describe the play group as a medieval kingdom with children and teachers playing different roles. Lords, vassals, serfs, bishops, kings and queens are described. Each chapter concludes with ideas about how teachers can help each of these characters grow in the area of social development. Four goals of classroom management are: sharing toys, accepting peers, curtailing aggression, and maintaining order. The larger objective that teachers have for children is to help them put their feelings into words. Teachers are models who model language, generosity, kindness, and love. The kind of friendship and caring that teachers offer to children ultimately influences the kind of peer relations that will occur in the classroom.

Note: Cross-references are to works in both Section 1 and Section 2.

417. Adcock, D., & Segal, M. (1983b) *Play together, grow together.* Mt. Ranier, MD: Gryphon House. 20712.

This book describes cooperative activities that children cannot do alone. They require two or more children to work together. Sixty-seven activities, filling twelve major curriculum areas, help children learn to cooperate and work together. Preschool children learn to share, to play together in a group, and to make close friends. A special chapter is devoted to resolving conflict and helping both shy and aggressive children.

418. Aronson, E., Blaney, N., Stephan, C., Sikes, J., & Snapp, M. (1978). *The jigsaw classroom.* Beverly Hills, CA: Sage Publications.

Each child is provided with one piece of information about a lesson. Thus, children *must* work cooperatively in groups to learn all the materials in a given assignment.

419. Aronson, E., Stephan, C., Sikes, J., Blaney, N., & Snapp, M. (1978). *Cooperation in the classroom.* Beverly Hills, CA: Sage Publishing.

The "jigsaw techniques" incorporate beneficial features of cooperation and peer teaching into the highly structured atmosphere of the more traditional classroom. Students are required to utilize one another as resources rather than to depend on the teacher as the sole provider of information. Even students with low self-esteem should begin to realize that they too have special abilities and talents.

420. Asher, S. R., Williams, G. A., & Oden, S. (1987). *Children's social development: Information for teachers and parents.* Catalog #202. Urbana, IL: ERIC Clearinghouse on Elementary and Early Childhood Education.

Methods are discussed by which teachers and parents can help children without friends to develop friendships and peer interaction competencies. Children can be helped to become alert to relationship goals such as winning and maintaining a friendship and devising a strategy to meet their goals. Conflict situation and role-playing help in a situation where one child acts as guest, who gets up and changes the TV station. The host child in role-play needs to provide assertive but prosocial strategies that resolve the conflict while meeting *both* children's needs (for example, saying "Let's finish watching this show and then we will watch one that you want"). Coaching scripts are provided to help children think about ideas and actions that would maintain peer play, through cooperating and sharing.

421. Barton, E. (1986). Modification of children's prosocial behavior. In P. S. Strain, M. J. Guralnick, & H. M. Walker (Eds.), *Children's social behavior: Development, assessment, and modification* (pp. 331-372). New York: Academic Press.

Behavioral methods for facilitating children's prosocial behavior are discussed. Studies conducted in naturalistic or quasi-naturalistic settings are reviewed in the hope of providing information that has ecological validity and pragmatic value. Most of the behavioral attempts at facilitating prosocial behavior have concentrated on cooperation (52%) and/or sharing (48%). The techniques used by adults include: instruction, modeling, behavior rehearsal, positive reinforcement, prompting, positive practice, correspondence training (developing veracity between children's verbal report of their behavior and their actual behavior), strategic placement, picture-cue training, multi-method training packages, and major intervention programs. The author concludes that most of the techniques are potent enough to facilitate prosocial behavior. The sole use of instructions and/or modeling, however, does not appear to be effective. Multi-method training packages seem to be the optimal method for facilitating prosocial behavior. Barton includes information concerning activities and materials that promote prosocial behavior, how many children can be trained at once to be prosocial, how the presence of adults affect children's prosocial behavior, who the change agent should be, which prosocial behaviors should be taught, and how much prosocial behavior should be increased.

422.Battistich, V., Watson, M., Solomon, D., Schaps, E., & Solomon, J. (1989). The child development project: A comprehensive program for the development of prosocial character. In W. M. Kurtines, & J. Gewirtz (Eds.), *Moral behavior and development: Advances in theory, research, and application.* (Vol. 1). Hillsdale, NJ: Lawrence Erlbaum Associates.

Teachers, parents and school children together use in-classroom and community activities to promote prosocial development as an important curricular component of the entire elementary school.

423.Baumrind, D. (1977). Some thoughts about childrearing. In S. Cohen and T. J. Comiskey (Eds.) *Child Development: Contemporary Perspectives* (pp. 248-258). Itasca, IL: F. E. Peacock.

Authoritative (rather than authoritarian or permissive) parents are consistent and rational. They have firm rules, communicate clearly what is expected of the child, demand responsible high-level performance and offer warmth and unconditional commitment to the best interests of the child. They have children who behave more prosocially.

They set standards and enforce them, but do not regard themselves as infallible. They listen to the child but do not base decisions solely on the child's desires. They encourage verbal give-and-take and explain reasons behind their requests and demands. They focus on issues rather than personalities and value child compliance and obedience to adult requirements as well as independence.

424.Bettiner, B. L., & Lew, A. (1990). *Raising kids who can.* Newton Centre, MA: Connexions Press.

Using an Adlerian framework, as interpreted by Driekurs, the authors give parents ideas of the skills and abilities children need: to communicate, to use good judgment, to assume responsibility, to be self-disciplined, and to cooperate with others while maintaining respect for themselves and others. Guidelines are offered clearly and succinctly to help families attain these goals. For example, the guidelines for *Family Meetings* suggest: listening to others, recognizing all suggestions non-judgmentally, giving everyone an opportunity to speak, keeping attention focused on the problem to be resolved, and summarizing the cooperative solution that all members have agreed upon. *Logical Consequences* are taught as a kind, yet firm and respectful approach to discipline to be used instead of punishments and rewards. This technique provides choices for children to be kind and respectful in the family or face consequences, such as not having clothes washed that are not in a hamper, or not being driven to a sports event if one has been rude to a parent.

425.Birckmayer, J. (1984). *Discipline is not a dirty word.* Ithaca, NY: Cooperative Extension Distribution Center, Cornell University.

This workshop outline for parents, teachers, and caregivers of young children provides guidelines for discussion leaders on the topic of discipline. Discipline originates from the word "disciple". A disciplinarian can be thought of as a teacher or leader who helps children become self-disciplined and learn prosocial behavior. Seven principles of discipline are offered: focus on do's instead of don'ts; preserve children's feelings that they are lovable and capable; offer children choices only when you are willing to abide by their decisions; change the environment to enhance cooperation when possible; find mutually acceptable ways; give children safe, clear limits; maintain your authority; and set a good example.

426.Black, P. (1986). *Conflict Resolution.* PEACE LINKS, Jan Benham, 1329 Kansas, Normal, OK, 73069.

A bibliography is provided on PEACE LINKS (a national peace organization). This includes information on conflict resolution.

427.Bloch, J. S. (1987). *The five P's for children with special needs: Social development scales.* Syosset, NY: Variety Pre-Schooler's Workshop.

These scales are designed so that teachers can prepare individual IEP's to promote more appropriate positive social skills among special needs children. Some typical scale items are: "Negotiates compromises with significant adults", "Complies with directions given", "Begins to share toys with other children", and "Negotiates compromises with other children". Behaviors that interfere with the development of positive social skills, such as "Disrupts or destroys another child's play activities" are also on the checklists. These checklists assist a teacher in developing a social profile as a basis from which to work toward promoting more prosocial functioning.

A 26-minute video (VC#102) entitled "Teaching children self-control", is also available from this program. Practical management techniques are demonstrated to help severely impaired children cope with their hostile feelings and learn more appropriate prosocial interaction skills.

428.Borba, M., & Borba, C. (1985). *Self-esteem: A classroom affair* (Vol. 1) and (Vol. 2). Nashville, TN: School Age Notes.

Over 101 ways for children to help other children are provided. Activities focus on knowing oneself, being a member of the group, and on problem-solving skills to encourage healthy self-esteem.

429.Briggs, D. (1975). *Your child's self esteem*. New York: Doubleday.

In this for-parents, luminously written book, Briggs gives sensitive advice about how to bring up a kind, loving, cooperative child. Some of the vividly described secrets are:

Be a mirror that reflects the goodness and OKness of your child.
Enhance self-esteem.
Give your child "genuine focused attention".

Advice in this book could be useful for teachers who work with families whose denigrations or hurtful comments to children are interfering with that child's ability to build positive peer relationships in the classroom.

430.Brown, D., & Solomon, D. (1983). A model for prosocial learning: An in-progress field study. In D. L. Bridgeman (Ed.), *The nature of prosocial development: Interdisciplinary theories and strategies* (pp. 273-307). New York: Academic Press.

In the San Francisco Bay area, research knowledge about prosocial development has been translated over a 7 1/2 year period into ways parents, school teachers and children in 3 schools (with 3 control schools) collaborate on increasing prosocial attitudes and behaviors among the children. The components of the program include:

1. Involving children from about age 6 onward, with adult supervision, with responsibilities for caring for younger children.

2. Using "cooperative learning" that requires that children work with each other in order to master a lesson. Competitive learning in classes co-exists, but involves groups or teams of children.

3. Children are involved in structured programs of helpful activities that will be useful, such as visiting shut-ins, making toys for others, visiting the elderly, cleaning up or gardening in nearby parks and playgrounds.

4. Mixing children's ages in activities.

5. Having children regularly role-play situations where persons are in need of help in order that the children experience feelings of "victim" and "helper".

6. Children help with home chores on a regular basis with parent approval and cooperation.

7. The entire elementary school recognizes and rewards caring, helping, responsibility, and other prosocial behaviors whether they occur at school or at home.

8. Giving the children opportunities to learn about adult models who are prosocial in films, television, and media. Children watch for such models in the news and they clip newspaper articles; teachers invite such models to tell their stories to classes.

9. Adults provide empathy training so that children see examples of animals or children in distress, either in real life or in staged episodes so that they can hear adults comment on how to help someone in trouble;

and the children get to watch examples of helping behaviors.

10. Providing continuity and total saturation in a school program so that the climate in the demonstration schools and families communicates prosocial expectations and supports the learning and acting-out of prosocial behaviors.

431. Bullock, J. R. (1991). Supporting the development of socially rejected children. *Early Child Development and Care, 66,* 15- 23.

Children found to be socially incompetent with peers are at risk for a variety of mental health, social, emotional, and cognitive adjustments later in life. Techniques for identifying such children are peer nomination methods or observations of peer popularity in the laboratory as well as natural settings. Children are then classified as popular, liked, neglected, rejected, and mixed/controversial (engaging in both prosocial and antisocial ways). Techniques of teaching social skills, such as modeling, coaching, and happy, rough and tumble play, are discussed.

432. Caldwell, B. M. (1977). Aggression and hostility in young children. *Young Children, 32* (2), 4-14.

Caldwell offers sound advice for helping caregivers deal with aggressive behavior in young children: a. Physical punishment of aggression is not the answer. b. Ignoring aggression in children is not the answer. c. Permitting aggression or hostility to be expressed, and assuming that this will "discharge" the tension, will not work. d. In order to minimize aggression, we need parent cooperation. e. In order to control aggression, we must strengthen altruism. f. Non-permissiveness in our attitudes toward aggression may be as important as punishment for aggressiveness. g. We must help children de-escalate their aggressive behavior. h. Children need to learn different alternatives to problem situations. i. We need to be more willing to play with children and to help them learn how to play well together.

Caldwell states, "Our number one objective as teachers should be to facilitate the development of children's behavior that is cooperative and supportive of one another, altruistic and prosocial rather than aggressive" (p. 12).

433. Caldwell, B. M. (1986, Fall). Helping children "do unto others". *ECE Teacher, 5-6.* Instructor, PO 6099, Duluth, MN 55806.

Caldwell uses the word "prosocial" to describe positive social interactions between any two or more individuals--interactions that involve mutually supportive behavior likely to lead to gratification and pleasure for all concerned, not for just one person. She recommends that early childhood classroom teachers (1) not expect an instant response from children who are first experiencing group care, (2) recognize and reward prosocial behavior, and (3) consider using a formal program designed to strengthen prosocial behavior.

434. Callard, E. (1978). Can children learn to love? *Childhood Education, 55* (2), 68-75.

The author examines three childrearing conditions that have significance for developing prosocial behavior in young children. Gratification in the early years, modeling and reinforcement of prosocial behaviors, and developing children's sense of worth are experiences that children need in order to become a loved and loving person. Cross-cultural insights from Tokyo, Hong Kong, Asia are provided.

435.Camp, B., Blom, G., Herbert, F., & VanDoornick, W. (1977). Think aloud: A program for developing self-control in young aggressive boys. *Journal of Abnormal Child Psychology*, 5, 157-169.

Children are taught to use a thinking-out-loud strategy for themselves in struggling toward less aggressive and more socially positive ways of interacting. They are to say: "What is my problem?; What is my plan?; Am I using my plan?; How did I do?"

436.Carlson, H. (1991). Helping children resolve conflict peacefully: A professional development model. *Early Child Development and Care*, 68, 162-173.

Family day care providers (N=36) in heterogeneous groups met together for 10 weeks to share active learning experiences, observe actual samples of behavior, have reflective, non-judgmental discussions, and learn observational skills in order to become more sensitive toward positive discipline techniques, ways to encourage child initiations, ways to enhance positive conflict-resolution skills, and ways to encourage empathic understanding among preschoolers. Building mutual respect between caregiver and children in a just environment promotes more prosocial interactions between adults and children as well as peers. This model of training is recommended for professional development of prosocial skills for caregivers.

437.Carroll, J. A. (1988). *Let's learn about getting along with others*. Carthage, IL: Good Apple.

Each section in this volume for teachers provides activities that will help young children learn how to be fair, follow rules, give and share, help, use good manners, make friends, and get along with others. Specific techniques are illustrated. Teachers, for example, are taught to model phrases like, "Would you like some help?" or "I could certainly use some help with this". The author provides techniques such as providing a classroom helper chart with illustrations; using children's illustrated helper tickets to create gifts for their families; and even spaces in this workbook for children to write or dictate, "This is how I am a good friend." Teachers read books such as the Berenstein Bears books about how a family tries to help children discuss how they could get along better and solve social problems. Bibliotherapy can promote prosocial behaviors.

438.Cartledge, G., & Milburn, J. F. (Eds.) (1980). *Teaching social skills to children*. New York: Pergamon Press.

Diagnostic teaching techniques are suggested by the authors: define in specific behaviorally stated terms the social skills to be taught; assess student level of competence;

teach the behaviors lacking in the learner's repertoire; evaluate the results of teaching; and provide opportunities for practice and generalization of transfer of new positive social skills to new situations.

439.Child Development Project (1985). *Working together.* 130 Ryan Court, Suite 210, San Ramon, CA.

This newsletter provides ongoing information on the techniques and findings of the 5-year Child Development project (see Battistich, V., Watson, M., Solomon, D., Schaps, E., & Solomon, J., 1989). Data from classroom observation, small group activity sessions, and interviews show that in three CDP program schools, compared with three contrast schools, children are more likely to be spontaneously helpful, demonstrate concern for others, take turns and support each other and behave positively toward each other and their teachers.

440.Cohen, E. G., & Benton, J. (1988, Fall). Making groupwork work: The potential benefits of groupwork are enormous, but they can't be reaped without careful planning. *American Educator,* 10-17.

For conceptual learning, students will assimilate new concepts and learn more effectively by using each other as resources in order to understand the task. Disagreement and intellectual conflict are a desirable part of the interaction in a problem-solving group. The teacher gives each student a special, specific role to play in the group. This will reduce problems of one or more members making no contribution. Cooperative classrooms help

the children develop positive social skills as
well as intellectual mastery.

441. Condon, C., & McGinnis, J. (1988). *Helping kids
care: Harmony building activities for home,
church, and school*. Bloomington, IN: Meyer-
Stone Books.

This how-to book provides activities for
peacemaking and increasing children's awareness
of others including those of other nations, the
aged, other children's needs and ideas. Some of
the activities are Peace Soup, Try on My Shoe,
Sticks and Stones, and Friends and Enemies.
There are discussion questions. Teachers are
given clear directions for carrying out each
activity with pairs or groups of children in
order to promote skill sharing, conflict
management, and learning from differences.

442. *Cooperating*. Good Apple, Box 299, Carthage,
IL 62321.

This activity book for children in
intermediate grades encourages cooperation
rather than competition among students. Over
60 activities encourage a win-win rather than
a win-lose atmosphere in the home or
classroom.

443. Copple, C., Siegel, I. E., & Saunders, R.
(1979). *Educating the young thinker*. New York:
Van Nostrand.

Chapter seven, "The Social Domain," outlines
the cognitive processes necessary for the
acquisition of social knowledge and also
suggests classroom activities to enhance
development of these processes. For example,

role-playing and perspective-taking games are suggested to handle disagreements so that preschoolers can come to more cooperative resolution of conflicts.

444. Crary, E. (1984). *Kids can cooperate. A practical guide to teaching problem solving.* Seattle, WA: Parenting Press, Inc.

Crary provides helpful suggestions illustrated by examples of how children can be helped to cooperate with adults and with each other. Suggestions include:

Give age-appropriate affirmations.
Encourage negotiation where children can win.
Set age-appropriate limits.
Structure the environment to reduce conflict.
Model problem-solving.
Teach children to ask for attention constructively.
Recognize the child as a competent individual.
Develop plans and evaluate them with children.

445. Crary, E. (1990). *Pick up your socks and other skills growing children need!* Seattle, WA: Parenting Press.

The idea of this how-to book is that children and parents form a responsible *team*. Families learn how to implement plans to encourage children, to motivate their helpfulness, to make effective contracts, set possible consequences, give reminders, and use responsive language and humor to encourage child responsibility and helpfulness at home and in school.

446.Damon, W. (1988). *The moral child: Nurturing children's natural moral growth.* New York: The Free Press.

This book, written by an expert researcher, helps teachers and parents who want to make moral education part of the curriculum of the home and school. The author writes fairly, clearly and reasonably. "There are no simple answers to the question of whether moral ideas lead to moral actions" (p. 46). Moral judgments operate in conjunction with social-contextual factors. For example, children's sharing behavior is linked to trends in their understanding of fairness concepts, but may be weakened by particular circumstances. Thus, children who do empathically understand other people's points of view, such as that of a poor child who would not have any candy if the target child did not share, will still donate candy far more when an adult is present to *monitor* the sharing.

Another example is when children are given a story problem and have to think up a fair distribution of money or goods for a bunch of kids who have worked on a project. They can come up with merit-based solutions. But in real life situations, they will do this far more if they themselves have the strongest claim to preferred treatment; otherwise, they tend to favor more equal solutions. Self-interest is a mitigating factor.

Children's sharing arises as a natural response to common social experiences. The sources are children's initial tendency to approach peers through common interests in play; the pleasure derived through the symmetrical rhythm of turn-taking with toys; the insistence of peers and parents that objects be divided and shared when possible; the child's natural empathic response to another with a strong desire to have a turn, bolstered by a reasoned adult message that the peer will be unhappy if the child does not share; and the child's pragmatic wish to keep the playmate happy because of expectations of future reciprocal sharing. As more abstract notions such as "equality, merit, benevolence, and compromise" are grasped, children's sharing becomes more consistent and generous. Self-interest never disappears, but it takes its place in the perspective of others' needs and claims to justice.

If parents and teachers are to contribute positively to children's moral growth, then they must become aware of children's developmental needs, especially for full and active participation in the kinds of social experiences that will build upon the child's growing moral sensibilities. "Respectful engagement" with the child is urged. "Moral education" must be a cooperative enterprise between adult and child.

Damon makes a strong plea for teaching values in schools so that children can detect moral issues in complex social situations. He suggests that community people who have distinguished themselves through prosocial and moral actions should be introduced to classroom situations as "moral mentors". He urges that *all children spend some free time in real helping, charitable activities.*

447. Damon, W., & Colby, A. (1987). Social influence and moral change. In W. M. Kurtines & J. Gewirtz (Eds.), *Moral development through social interaction.* New York: Wiley.

"Moral exemplars" need to be available for students. A moral exemplar is a person who shows a sustained commitment to and acts in accordance with moral principles, including a willingness to risk personal well-being for the sake of principles. Dedication to and responsiveness to the needs of others exists along with talent for inspiring others to such actions. This person also has a sense of humility rather than egotism about moral actions.

448.Davis, D. E. (1977). *My friends and me.* Circle Pines, MN: American Guidance Service.

This curriculum package contains 190 items divided into 2 major aspects: personal identity, and social skills and understanding. This program was used successfully by the Frank Porter Graham Child Development Center (see Finkelstein, 1982).

449.Dil, N. (1983 January). Affective curricula: Theory, models, and implementation. *Topics In Early Childhood Special Education, 2,* (4), 25-33.

Prosocial curricula for preschool children with special needs are reviewed.

450.Dinkmeyer, D., & Dinkmeyer, D., Jr. (1982). *Developing understanding of self and others (Rev. DUSO-R).* Circle Pines, MN: American Guidance Service.

DUSO the dolphin, other puppets, audio-cassettes, activity cards, and charts are provided so that teachers can guide children toward learning social skills and awareness of feelings, priorities, and choices. Children also learn appreciation of individual strengths and acceptance of limitations from the kit materials.

451. Dixon, D. (1981). *Teaching Children to Care.* Twenty-third Publications, Box 180, Mystic, Ct. 06355.

This program is designed for use in early childhood classrooms to promote prosocial behaviors. It includes 80 "Caring Circle" activities with descriptors and lesson extenders.

452. Doescher, S., & Sugawara, A. (Summer 1989). Encouraging prosocial behavior in young children. *Childhood Education, 65* (4), 213-216.

The authors provide a review of the prosocial literature examining differences in prosocial behavior among boys as compared to girls, children from different social classes, and children of different ages. Three general strategies for promoting prosocial behavior include:

I. Teachers become aware of children's prosocial developmental levels and abilities. Preschool children are primarily egocentric, but they are beginning to recognize that others have feelings too. It is helpful, then to provide young children with descriptions of the thoughts of others. Teachers can talk about one's own feelings, as well as listening to others describe their feelings. Believing that young children can demonstrate prosocial behavior is important.

II. Examine teacher techniques for the classroom. Teachers are powerful models who can be influential in encouraging prosocial behavior among children.

III. Evaluate the classroom *environment* and curriculum to create a more prosocial environment.

453.Dreikurs, F., & Cassel, C. K. (1970). *Discipline without teachers: What to do with children who misbehave.* New York: Hawthorne Books.

Children's annoying, destructive, hostile behavior shows that they are trying to fill inner needs or subconscious goals of attention seeking, power and control, revenge, or helplessness. The teacher should determine the child's goal or goals through observation and questioning and then emphasize improvement, and refrain from placing students in competition against one another. *Encouragement* rather than praise is promoted. The teacher arranges logical consequences for the offending student to experience.

454.Drew, N. (1987). *Learning the skills of peacemaking. An activity guide for elementary-age children on communicating, cooperating, resolving conflict.* Rolling Hills Estates, CA: Jalmar Press.

This guide for teachers, parents, and other caregivers who wish to bring the skills of peacemaking to life for children focuses on four major concepts:

a. Accepting self and others
b. Communicating effectively
c. Resolving conflicts
d. Understanding intercultural differences

Peacemaking skills are presented in fifty-six lessons. The class or family meeting is recommended to help adults set the context for cooperation. Ideas for disciplining with love are included. The win/win guidelines (whereby both parties are satisfied) for conflict resolution are promoted as critical to the skills of peacemaking.

455.Edwards, C. P. (1986). *Promoting social and moral development in young children*. New York: Teachers College Press.

Edwards suggests thinking games, activities, and discussions to help children become aware of social knowledge, racial and cultural categories, gender identity and sex roles, friendship and kinship concepts, and economic and occupational concepts. Photographs, puppets, skits, dialogues, and lists of helpful books are recommended. Guidelines for positive resolutions of social conflicts are concrete.

Some classroom activities to promote understanding of causality in social interactions and representational competence in interpreting social behaviors are:

Sociodramatic play
Cross-age child caring with older children responding to the needs of younger ones
Circle and group games
Use of collage and paper plate faces to reflect different feelings, along with discussions of why particular faces look sad, etc.
Feeling-face masks
Teacher photos of children acting out emotions
Acting out sensory awareness games, such as pretending (with the use of ear covers) to be a child who cannot hear at all
Pretend games such as a birthday party for a specific child where you have to think of

a gift that the particular child would really like

Thinking games on moral intentionality and moral responsibility (modeled after Piaget's problems)

In intervening in conflicts, the teacher needs to provide children with opportunities to express and work through their conflicting emotions within a climate of support and encouragement. Teachers can:

1. Support children's initiatives and self-determination.

2. Encourage negotiation at the highest interpersonal level of the children's repertoire.

3. Help children become aware of each others' feelings.

4. Point out the results of the children's actions upon each other.

5. Respect the children's own standards of what constitutes a fair or acceptable solution to their social problem.

6. Help children understand the difference between interpersonal moral rules to behave fairly and kindly, and social rules, such as combing your hair and putting on fancier clothes for a party.

Many good discussions are provided which teachers can use to spark prosocial learning, on topics such as how to share toys. Children can discuss solutions with teachers to enhance awareness and skills in considerate ways of interacting with each other.

456.Edwards, C., Logue, M., & Russell, A. (Nov. 1983). Talking with young children about social ideas. *Young Children, 39,* (1), 12-21.

To implement their program goals for facilitating children's understanding of social behavior, the authors focus on three different kinds of learning encounters: the *dramatic skit*; the *thinking game*; and the *spontaneous discussion*.

457.Eggeman, K. W. (1982). Magic circle for the family: A bonding formula. In N. Stinnett, J. DeFrain, K. King, H. Lingren, G. Rowe, S. Van Zandt, & R. Williams (Eds.), *Family strengths 4: Positive support systems* (pp. 141-151). Lincoln, NE: University of Nebraska Press.

The author suggests incorporating a *family circle* into family life, in order to solve family issues more positively. The "Circle" experience reenacts the function of positive ritual in the family, provides sanction and structure for family affirmation, permission for positive feelings and positive sharing. The "Circle" serves as a celebration of family joy in sharing, in becoming close and yet respecting each others' space. Everyone gets a turn to share and listen equally. Children learn the ground rules of prosocial interactions in the safe ritual of the regularly scheduled family "Circle" time.

458.Elardo, P.T., & Cooper, M. (1977). *AWARE: Activities for social development.* Menlo Park, CA: Addison Wesley.

This activity manual contains classroom program ideas specifying lesson objectives, overview, activity and discussion in dozens of social situations which may begin with episodes of jealousy, jeering, fear, conflicts, cheating, snubbing, loss of belongings, etc. The teacher is encouraged to use *story episodes* to help children think of prosocial ways to understand, empathize, and resolve different types of social difficulties.

459.Elardo, P. T., & Elardo, R. (1976). A critical analysis of social development programs in elementary education. *Journal of School Psychology, 14,* (2), 118-130.

Several programmatic approaches are described to facilitate the prosocial development of children, such as:

1. *A "causal" approach. Ojemann's program.* This program teaches children that there are causes for behavior. Teachers help children (a) take account of reasons in dealing with peers and (b) become more sensitive to the reasons behind peers' behaviors, and (c) become more adept at learning to identify and consider alternative solutions and their consequences for dealing with problems. But there is little attempt to deal with developmental differences in children's ability to think causally. (Ojemann's work is not referenced in this bibliography because it is dated in the 1950's and 1960's.)

2. *Bessell & Palomares' Human Development Program* (published in 1969). The premise of this program is that personal growth is related to the ability to gain approval in social relationships. In the classroom, teachers hold 20-minute Magic Circle meetings daily. They facilitate, review and summarize what social learning has gone on in each daily circle discussion on topics

such as how a child was made to feel bad or good by another and how the participating child made another feel good or bad. (See Palomares and Ball, 1974.)

3. *Developing Understanding of Self and Others (DUSO)*. Dinkmeyer's program goals are to provide experiences through which children can learn more words for feelings which are dynamically related to goals and behaviors. The kit for teachers has colorful pictures, charming stories and puppet characters that children enjoy. (See Dinkmeyer & Dinkmeyer, 1982.)

460. Elardo, R. (Winter, 1977). Facilitating prosocial behavior. *Day Care and Early Education, 4,* 24-25.

Helping, cooperating, empathizing, displaying friendly behavior in group situations, and behaving morally are all examples of prosocial behavior. Adults can foster positive social behavior by setting up situations to encourage constructive social behavior, giving reinforcement (your attention) to specific instances of cooperation, helping, and sharing, avoiding lecturing when children are not sharing, being a good model, and looking for situations to develop empathy. Additional ways to increase the amount of positive social play among preschoolers are discussed.

461. Elias, M. J., & Clabby, J. F. (1991). *School-based enhancement of children's and adolescents' social problem solving skills.* San Francisco, CA: Jossey-Bass.

Teachers in schools are taught how to implement a program to build positive social coping skills and prevent mental health problems in children. The Improving Social

Awareness-Social Problem Solving Project (ISA-SPS) tries to promote social competence by focusing on critical social decision-making, self-control, group participation, and social awareness skills.

462.Enright, R. (1981). A classroom discipline model for promoting social cognitive development in early childhood. *Journal of Moral Education, 11,* 47-60.

Specific positive teacher discipline techniques promote social and cognitive development in the early childhood classroom.

463.Eyre, L., & Eyre, R. (1984). *Teaching children responsibility.* New York: Ballantine.

Chapter 12 of this book gives parents ideas to help their children understand the concept of service and to feel satisfaction in helping others, particularly children who are less fortunate than they are. Ideas presented are:

1. Hold a neighborhood charity concert with children performing and proceeds donated to a needy child.
2. Help a needy family.
3. Start a family tradition of service to others.

464.Faber, A., & Mazlish, E. (1987). *Siblings without rivalry. How to help your children live together so you can live too.* New York: W. W. Norton.

Parents are given many practical ways to create peace among siblings. Some of the ideas are:

1. "Strength bombardment": each child has to write down three things he or she likes about the other child.

2. Acknowledge the children's anger to each other; listen to each child's side with respect; and show appreciation for the difficulty of a situation for the child.

3. Express faith in the children's ability to work out a mutually agreeable solution, but do offer some suggestions to get them started.

4. If two children are aggressing, describe what is happening and say "This is a very dangerous situation and we must have a cooling-off period. Quick you go to your room and you to your own room. No hurting will be allowed in our home."

5. Let no one lock a child into a mean or victim role. Free a bully child to be compassionate. Encourage that child firmly: "You have a superior capacity to be nice. Use it."

6. Give direct verbal assists: "Try asking your brother (sister) differently. You may be surprised how generous he (she) can be". Then express appreciation for more pro-social interactions that the child has accomplished.

465.Factor, D. C., & Schilmoeller, G. L. (1983). Social skill training of preschool children. *Child Study Journal, 13* (1), 41–56.

Of 36 half-day preschool children (mean age 50.9 months), 20 were chosen as an experimental group in which the children were encouraged to play together according to Oden & Asher's Social Skill Training Procedures. These include: *communication* (including politeness words and listening to another who is talking); *participation* (getting involved with peer in an activity); *cooperation* (sharing, asking turns); *validation/support* (helping another have fun together). Ten 8-minute sessions with four children per group consisted of verbal instruction, explanations, discussion, questions and answers, modeling, and opportunity for practicing prosocial skills in playing together. Sociability was defined as Group Positive Behavior in contrast to Group Negative Behavior. Children who received the social skills training were significantly more sociable in the special training classroom than during the training. At follow-up, their negative behavior was less than the control group's, but these gains were not evident during the follow-up week in the *regular* preschool classroom. Teachers may need to use sustained as well as specialized training procedures in order to obtain generalization from special procedures to enhance prosocial skills.

466.*Feelings: Friends and foes.* The Center for Applied Psychology, Inc., 441 N. 5th Street, 3rd floor, Philadelphia, PA 19123.

"Transforming" beautifully colored hand puppets show children that negative emotions can be turned into more positive functional ones.

467.Finkelstein, N. (Sept. 1982). Aggression: Is it stimulated by day care? *Young Children, 37* (6), 3-13.

After finding that the Frank Porter Graham Child Development Day Care Center children were more aggressive and hostile than the control group children who did not attend the program, the staff worked together to plan a program, including the "My friends and me" package, to enhance the social skills of the program children. Staff development and activities for the children are described.

468.Fox, L. (1980). *Communicating to make friends*. Rolling Hills Estates, CA: B.L. Winch.

This program for the classroom teacher helps change the attitudes of the "established" student toward the "isolated" student. "Making friends" provides the regular classroom teacher with an easy, specific, step-by-step program to help students get along together by first learning about each other. The program also helps students who are simply not as good at making friends as their classmates are. The specific objectives include:

a. helping students understand emotions.
b. helping students be more understanding and accepting of individual differences.
c. helping every student see similarities between themselves and their peers.
d. helping every student learn to solve interpersonal problems.
e. helping every student learn to share common interests and feelings.
f. helping every student increase communication skills.

Students are assigned a partner of the same sex, with whom they will work for the duration of the program. Students follow the activities in the program and interview each other to make a book about their partner. Accepted students are paired with isolated students. Each lesson requires approximately one hour to complete.

469.Fry-Miller, K., & Myers-Walls, J. (1988). *Young peacemakers project book.* St. Paul, MN: Toys 'n Things Press.

Imaginative learning activities introduce young children to fundamental concepts of peacemaking and the core values of peace education.

470.Fugitt, E. (1983). *"He hit me back first!" Creative visualization activities for parenting and teaching.* Rolling Hills Estates, CA: Jalmar Press.

This book presents activities for home and school that will help youngsters become aware of choice and of their own inner authority. *Creative visualization exercises* help children imagine the natural and logical consequences of their choices *before* they've acted.

471. Giveans, D. L. (1991). Gentle connections "fosters" positive intergenerational sharing. *Day Care and Early Education, 18* (3), 42-45.

The 20-minute video described here fosters caring relationships between preschoolers interacting caringly with senior citizens. An extensive "hands-on-hands" guide gives suggestions for teachers to initiate a preschool visitation program with senior citizens to enhance children's compassion and empathy. Other prosocial videos promoting intergenerational kindness are described.

472. Goffin, S. G. (1987). Cooperative behaviors: They need our support. *Young Children, 42* (2), 75-81.

Teachers can learn to arrange interdependent behaviors between and among children. These cooperative behaviors are recognized in the classroom when children share mutual goals, ideas, and materials, as well as when they negotiate and bargain in decision-making and accomplishing goals.

473. Goldstein, A. (1989). *The PREPARE curriculum. Teaching prosocial competencies.* Champaign, IL: Research Press.

This prosocial curriculum for adolescents and young children (who are aggressive, antisocial, withdrawn, or socially isolated) stresses teaching interpersonal skills, anger control, moral reasoning, cooperation, problem solving, empathy, stress management, group dynamics, and "recruiting supportive models." There are 50 *specific skills* (e.g. starting a conversation, apologizing) that constitute successful adolescent functioning at home or with peers. Goldstein provides a description of the behavior that constitutes each skill, trainer notes, and suggested content for effective modeling.

474. Goldstein, A., Sherman, N., Sprafkin, R. P., Gershaw, N. J., & Glick, B. (1978). Training aggressive adolescents in prosocial behavior. *Journal of Youth and Adolescence, 7,* (1), 73-92.

Aggressive adolescents can be taught prosocial skills (negotiation, self-relaxation, and anger control) through structured learning therapy (SLT) which involves modeling, role-playing, social reinforcement, and transfer of training. Ideas for enhancing transfer of training to real-life situations are given.

475.Goldstein, A. P., Glick, B., Irwin, M. J., Pask-McCartney, C., & Rubama, I. (1989). *Reducing delinquency: Intervention in the community.* Elmsford, NY: Pergamon Press.

This how-to, practical guide teaches ART (aggression replacement training). Differential, tailored, individualized interventions teach delinquents a) structured learning of prosocial alternatives to aggression; b) training in control of anger arousal; and c) moral education to instill a sense of fairness, justice, and empathy. Descriptions reveal how these three approaches are carried out in a community-based project. An evaluation of ART after two years with post-release youth who had met twice a week for 1 1/2 to 2 hours weekly for 3 months showed self-reported interpersonal skill levels improved for youths trained alone or with family training also, in comparison with control youth. Recidivism following release was 15% for the two ART groups and 43% for the control group. Anger control did not change for the children if there was strong provocation, such as physical abuse.

476.Gordon, T. (1970). *Parent effectiveness training.* New York: Wyden.

Gordon's PET (Parent Effectiveness Training) methods are among the most-widely used techniques to help children develop with good self-esteem and prosocial, empathic skills in interacting with peers and adults. The main messages are: Figure out who owns the social problem. Use *I messages* (to express your feelings and concerns) if you, the adult own the problem. Use *active listening* to reflect the child's feelings, frustrations, angers and upsetments if the problem belongs to the child. Hold meetings to discuss social problems with your children and use the no-lose method of resolving problems. All involved must be able to think up reasonable solutions that they are willing to abide by, so that no one person feels like a loser or a total winner in resolving conflicts.

Active listening (AL) is a technique that fosters catharsis, so that children can find out exactly what they are feeling and become less afraid of negative feelings. AL promotes warmth between caregiver and child. Empathy for the child involves the adult in deep caring and love as the adult joins with the child to help him or her solve a social difficulty. AL helps children start thinking for themselves, conveys trust, and helps the child feel more kindly and more generous toward caregivers and teachers.

477.Gordon, T. (1974). *Teacher effectiveness training for the classroom: How teachers can bring out the best in their students*. New York: Peter Wyden.

Children and teachers in classroom conflicts that involve non-cooperation, or put-downs, will profit from Gordon's TET principles. He suggests the use of communication facilitators (door openers; passive listening; acknowledgement of responses) and *active* listening with feedback reflecting the child's feelings. When teachers or parents own the problem, they can use *I-messages* effectively. As well, they can modify the class *environment* to arrange for more cooperative and positive social relationships in the classroom. Gordon explains the *win-win* method of problem-solving when social conflicts occur.

478.Gottman, J., Gonzo, J., & Schuler, P. (1976). Teaching social skills to isolated children. *Journal of Abnormal Child Psychology, 4,* 179-197.

Techniques were developed for teachers to coach social skills to assist children of low social status. In coaching, the teacher gives direct instructions and suggests strategies to use to achieve more positive peer interactions. Children get opportunities to practice more cooperative skills and are encouraged to think about how they can use these new skills in their play with other children.

479.Graves, N. B., & Graves, T. D. (1983). The cultural context of prosocial development: An ecological model. In D. L. Bridgeman (Ed.), *The nature of prosocial development: Interdisciplinary theories and strategies* (pp. 243-272). New York: Academic Press.

Orientations to prosocial development emphasize either *enculturation* or *individual development.* In a Polynesian island society, the authors found that children very early on learned a high degree of group participation, identification, and helpfulness. Five- and six-year-old boys and girls (N=49) were observed in the home by native teachers. Modern conditions (with electricity and freezers) are resulting in fewer social relationships for children in more exclusive family groups, compared with rural extended families. Girls had far more practice in meeting the needs of adults. Being given responsible tasks promoted altruistic acts.

Fully half the acts by town children were non-social, compared with less than a third for rural children, who cooperated often in joint tasks.

In a second study, the longer that the Polynesian children were in school, the closer their non-prosocial behaviors approximated those of New Zealand children. Boys and girls who lived in nuclear families were far more likely to be rivalrous (67%) than those from traditional families (34%). Prosocial behaviors may change as schools prepare children for work toward personal aspirations. Using the Madsen Cooperation Board, 45% of the island children achieved cooperation compared with 12% of New Zealand children. Thus, *ecological context* is very important in the emergence of prosocial behavior among children.

Implications for teachers are given in order to foster cooperation:

1. Create a common bond within the classroom by creating a class identity. Give each child a role, functions, and a sense of belonging, and occasions for unity experiences with the group.

2. Incorporate a variety of persons within the classroom, and include professionals, relatives, and lay persons.

3. Change the classroom style of social interaction by providing students with opportunities to direct others, to be directed, to receive group as well as individual rewards, and to move toward a mixture of cooperative, competitive, and individualistic activities.

4. Plan concrete and tangible tasks so that children can realize their contribution to group goals within the classroom and the

wider community.

480.Gresham, F. M. (1981). Social skills training with handicapped children: A review. *Review of Educational Research*, *51* (1), 139-176.

Behavioral techniques are recommended for promoting prosocial behaviors among handicapped children, so that they will be better accepted by peers in an integrated setting. Research has shown that handicapped children are not very well accepted by their non-handicapped peers and that there are typically low rates of social interaction between mainstreamed handicapped children and their non-handicapped peers. Techniques reviewed include:

(1) *Manipulation of antecedents*: Teachers can set the occasion for social interaction. A non-handicapped peer confederate is taught to initiate social interaction with a handicapped child to get the handicapped child to play with him or her in a free-play environment. Sociodramatic activities in which handicapped children assume the role of characters in familiar children's stories are effective in increasing rates of social interaction between children. Prompts, modeling of responses, and social praise are used to facilitate participation. Five investigations have demonstrated that the arrangement of cooperative game-playing activities or providing information on a child's competence in game playing can facilitate social interaction or peer acceptance of handicapped children.

(2) *Manipulation of consequences*: Teachers are advised to use contingent social reinforcement, token reinforcement programs, primary reinforcement, group contingencies, home-based contingencies,

and differential reinforcement.

(3) *Modeling*: The use of live modeling in which the target child observes the social behaviors of models in the classroom and playground and symbolic modeling in which a target child observes the social behaviors of a model via videotape/film format are recommended.

(4) *Cognitive* behavioral techniques: Coaching is a direct verbal instruction technique which has been successfully used to help non-handicapped children learn social skills. Children are verbally instructed in social skills and these skills are rehearsed or role-played in non-threatening situations. Self-control techniques teach children to evaluate and control their own behavior.

Social skills training with handicapped children has the potential of facilitating mainstreaming efforts.

481. Grineski, S. (1989). Children, games and prosocial behavior--insights and connections. *Journal of Physical Education, Recreation & Dance, 60* (8), 20.

The author points out the importance of thinking about the outcome of physical education on young children's social and affective skills. He provides a review of the research concerning the importance of providing opportunities for children to develop prosocial behaviors and *methods* for facilitating prosocial behavior. The goal structure of group games can be divided into two categories, competitive and cooperative, with cooperative goal structures designed to promote mutual interdependence between players in order to achieve the desired goal.

Given the lack of materials that describe cooperatively structured games, the author recommends that teachers modify existing games, create games, or use student-designed games if they are to teach games that promote prosocial behaviors. After one young child was interviewed concerning a competitive game he said, "Out, take chairs out; sit down; wait; lose." Following the cooperatively structured game, the same child said, "Be with people; fun; laugh; everybody; one chair; together; fun." Children exposed to both cooperative games and competitive games reported that the cooperatively structured game was their favorite game because, "You help people" and "It's fun." Specific games designed to be played cooperatively are shared, such as: musical chairs, partner hoop, hoop ball, long long jump, jump along, fish gobbler, and others.

482.Grusec, J. E., & Arnason, L. (1982). Consideration for others: Approaches to enhancing altruism. In S. G. Moore & C. R. Cooper (Eds.), *The young child. Reviews of research. Vol. 3.* (pp. 159-174). Washington, DC: National Association for the Education of Young Children.

This short, clear review of research on prosocial development and what adults can do to promote it could be useful for brief training of caregivers. Succinctly presented are the major points about the effectiveness of: modeling over preaching; teaching role-taking skills; orienting children to think about the effects of their misdemeanors on others; the use of other-oriented discipline rather than power assertive discipline; and character attribution techniques where children are told they are kind, neat, and considerate.

483.Han, E. P. (1991, Winter). You be the baby bear. *Dimensions, 192,* 14-17.

Teachers who help children enact dramas through story dramatization are promoting creativity, oral communication, and self-confidence, symbolic play and sequencing abilities. In selecting the story, teachers should make sure there is plenty of interesting action, as in "Caps for Sale", and they may need to eliminate too much narrative or change it to dialogue and change too-difficult vocabulary words. Children often feel better about themselves because of a special role they have played, such as the brave goat in "The Three Billy Goats Gruff". In fairy tales there are characters (witches, trolls and wolves) who do "bad" things people are not supposed to do. The children learn vicariously the results of such negative social actions and thereby learn what society values: kindness, unselfishness, forgiving and thoughtful actions. Before dramatization, read the story and encourage children to join in with repetitive chants (as in "The Three Bears"), so children understand the mood of the story and remember some of the dialogue. Next, organize the materials: set the stage, organize scenes spatially, bring in classroom materials as props, and encourage timid children to be part of the setting. As well, teachers in casting the story need to cast the most competent students for the first dramatization. Avoid sex-role stereotyping, and provide reminders about the limits and rules for story role-playing.

484.Hazen, N. L., Black, B., & Fleming-Johnson, F. (1984). Social acceptance: Strategies children use and how teachers can help children learn them. *Young Children, 39* (6), 26-36.

A peer choice technique (present photos and say "Show me which child you like to play with the most") revealed four groups: popular, rejected, controversial (high social acceptance and high social rejection), and neglected (low acceptance and low rejection). Peer interaction skills were filmed. The popular children were most efficient in directing their social communications to others. They established eye contact, touched the other child, addressed the child by name, and were fair to all other peers when playing in a group of several others. They had a wide range of social initiation strategies (rather than stereotyped, rigid and self-focused routines) and were able to adapt these to the individual interests and needs of different playmates.

Teachers can help promote some of these positive skills. "Help an entering child focus on the interests and ongoing activities of the play group they wish to enter, rather than on their own need to become involved" (p. 34). Provide on-the-spot guidance to facilitate more positive, clear communication patterns that would contribute to the maintenance of cohesive play. For example, say "I don't think Jack knows you are talking to him. How can you let him know?" Or, "Mark pushed you because he wants to play with you. That's his way of trying to be your friend. Maybe you can let him know how you would like him to play here. What could he do?" Teachers can help a child figure out the group's play theme, and think of a role she or he could play. Teachers may need to orient an inappropriate child specifically: "Look at Jim's face. Do you think he likes it when you kick at his block tower? If you want to build with him, how can you let him know? How can you help each other play together?"

Teachers may also have to facilitate the group in prosocial responses to an unpopular child. For example, the teacher could point out apparent intentions: "Jane is trying to figure out how to be in your game and play with you. If you don't need another mommy, can you figure out who she could be instead?"

485.Higgins, A. (1989). The just community approach to moral education: Evolution of the idea and recent findings. In W. M. Kurtines & J. Gewirtz (Eds.), *Moral behavior and development: Advances in theory, research, and application.* Vol. 1. Hillsdale, NJ: Lawrence Erlbaum.

Kohlberg's cognitive development paradigm for the development of advanced moral thinking is carried out in a public school. Through the active participation of students and staff in democratic dialogues, problem-solving interactions in a "just community", forums for student participation in school governance, and weekly community meetings to discuss school policies and rules, children learn to understand and help formulate moral rules and are most willing to enforce them.

486.Hill, T., & Reed, K. (1990). Promoting social competence at preschool: The implementation of a co-operative games programme. *Early Child Development and Care, 59,* 11-20.

An intensive cooperative games program was instituted in four kindergarten sessions over a 12- week period with Australian children. Half of the children were chosen to provide a model of social competence. The others were chosen because of social isolation or aggressiveness. The games were called: "Sharing", "Helping", "Listening", and "Talking positively to others". Teacher observations showed that the children enjoyed the games and learned more positive social interactions. Teacher enthusiasm, skill and interest were crucial for the program to succeed.

487.Hillard, S. W., & Hill, M. P. (1979). Fostering prosocial behaviors in children: What is the adult role? *Dimensions, 7* (3), 77-80.

The authors provide specific techniques for teachers to foster prosocial interactions:

1. Control antisocial behaviors by defining children's limits.

2. Make non-verbal and verbal messages congruent. Be firm, for example, in telling
a child "I do not like to be kicked".

3. Help children use words instead of physical hurting.

4. Verbalize feelings and encourage children to do so to release tensions and to clarify a situation.

5. Problem-solve with a child.

6. Develop and reinforce altruism. Urge a child to look at another's face and think about how the other child is feeling.

7. Value and model altruistic behavior.

488.Hoffman, S., & Wundram, B. (1984, March/April). Sharing is... *Childhood Education, 4*, 261-265.

Parents of three-year-olds in a nursery school program were asked how they taught their children to share. In the school, a situation was staged in which children (individually) had an opportunity to demonstrate their sharing techniques without the intrusion or benefit of an adult. For example: Chip entered the screened-off area of the playroom where peanut butter, bread, and juice for one person were placed on the table. A peer came in, and the friend asked for some, and was ignored. The friend asked again to be given some upon his return and he left briefly. On his return Chip had stuffed the sandwich entirely into his mouth but solved the sharing problem by pouring juice into a glass and offering that to the friend. Teachers need to create caring environments in which children are provided with opportunities for helping others and where helping and sharing are valued.

489.Hollifield, J. (1989). *Children learning in groups and other trends in elementary and early childhood education.* Catalog #204. Urbana, IL: ERIC Clearinghouse on Elementary and Early Childhood Education.

Cooperative learning strategies are explained in several articles in this book. Cooperative learning is a classroom instructional process in which students work together in 4-5 member heterogeneous teams to accomplish an academic task. The teacher may designate a broad topic that the students then break down into subtopics to investigate. Students seek information from many sources in and outside of school. The essential elements of Group Investigation include: cooperative planning, the teacher serving as a resource person and facilitator, and a series of six consecutive states of implementation: "identifying the topic and organizing pupils into groups, planning the learning task, carrying out the investigation, preparing a final report, presenting the final report, and evaluating the process" (p. 3). Other chapters include: "Cooperative learning strategies in children" and "Cooperative problem-solving".

490. Hollinger, J. D. (1988). Social skills for behaviorally disordered children as preparation for mainstreaming: Theory, practice, and new directions. *Perceptions, 23* (2), 19-27.

Major approaches to social skills training are provided for teachers of emotionally disturbed children. Teachers need to work on specific behaviors rather than on cognitive strategies. They identify upset feelings associated with interpersonal problems and try to help a child find and use another more effective solution. Teachers also teach peers to ignore inappropriate initiations of a behaviorally disturbed child or to offer suggestions on how the child could best meet his or her goals (group entry for play, for example). Teachers can enlist peers as behavior change agents. Teachers can stage role-playing of an ambiguous provocation. Then all children are given the opportunity to rehearse the social skills they have been taught and practice appropriate responses to inappropriate behavior.

491. Holloway, S. D., & Reichhart-Erickson, M. (1988). The relationship of day care quality to children's free-play behavior and social problem-solving skills. *Early Childhood Research Quarterly, 3*, 39-53.

The subjects were 45 children attending 15 day care centers and nursery schools. When age- appropriate materials were available and where space was arranged to accommodate groups of varying sizes, children gave more prosocial responses and fewer antisocial responses. In the classroom, the teacher facilitates or inhibits prosocial behavior through arrangement of space, routines for moving between activities, and provision of varied and age-appropriate materials.

492.Honig, A. S. (1985). Research in review. Compliance, control and discipline. *Young Children, Part 1, 40* (2), 50-58; *Part 2, 40* (3), 47-52.

Compliance refers to a child's immediate and appropriate response to an adult's request. A control technique refers to attempts to change the course of a child's activity. Teachers need skills to enhance compliance. Social cooperation is a joint enterprise of adult and child. This review of researches reveals that secure early attachments predict increased compliance. Mothers who use more non-directive speech, and are less critical/ suppressive/ interfering, have more compliant babies. Positive parenting techniques, such as attracting the child's attention *prior* to using a control technique also work well. They ensure that a child is focused on the caregiver making the request. Physical and negative controls are particularly likely to result in child defiance rather than compliance. Self-regulation is the goal of adult techniques. Suggestions are culled from research to enhance this goal:

1. Be contingent and positive in response to child compliance.

2. Use your presence to enhance a child's sense of security in the classroom.

3. Play sociodramatic games to give children success in role-playing appropriate interactions.

4. Refocus children from inappropriate to appropriate interpersonal behaviors.

5. Provide sufficient rich materials to increase chances of positive social peer play.

6. Model considerateness, courtesy, and helpfulness. Pair a shy, fearful child with a gregarious, kindly peer.

7. Encourage children to think of positive alternatives to solving their social problems.

493.Honig, A. (1986). Stress and coping in children. Research in Review. *Young Children, Part 1, 41* (4), 50-63; and *Part 2, 41* (5), 47-59.

This thorough review of causes and aspects of stress in children's lives includes discussion of researches on the effects of age, sex, ecological stressors such as dangerous neighborhoods, hospitalization, terrorism and war, birth of siblings, bereavement, psychiatric symptoms in parents, marital problems and divorce factors, negative caregiver discipline strategies, and child abuse on children's stress levels and social actions. Caregiver techniques that can buffer children and support resiliency and positive coping skills are suggested:

1. Model self-control and coping skills with voice tones and calmness in handling problems.

2. Encourage children to develop special skills to enhance self-worth and self-esteem.

3. Help children understand the consequences of inappropriate or antisocial actions in response to stressors.

4. Acknowledge children's feelings and encourage verbal mediation rather than impulsive antisocial actions.

5. Use gentle humor.

6. Structure classroom materials and activities so that cooperation rather than competition is stressed.

7. Make clear choices and rules so that children understand the positive interactive rules of the classroom.

8. Find individual talk time with children having social difficulties.

9. Mobilize other children to help an unhappy, stressed peer.

10. Use bibliotherapy materials: read books to help children identify with characters who found more positive social solutions to their problems.

11. Use art and music so that children can express deep feelings that may be interfering with their ability to respond more prosocially.

12. Encourage children to act out prosocial roles and more positive coping skills with dolls, puppets and in dramatic play.

13. Provide verbal stems so that children can get used to thinking about how they feel and how they could cope (e.g. "One way I can

act if another kid is looking upset is to...).

14. Use *proactive* interventions, so that you head off stress troubles or non-prosocial responses before they occur.

15. Help children think out the consequences of different ways they can react with peers. Play "What will happen then" games, to help them think up more positive resolutions.

494.Honig, A., & DiPerna, C. (1983). Peer relations of infants and toddlers. *Day Care and Early Education, 10* (3), 36-39.

This summary of research written in an easy-to-read style provides information on the effects on peer behavior of parent-child interactions, individual differences, and quality of child care. Ideas for child care providers to promote prosocial behavior include: careful arrangements of activity areas and placement of toys; promotion of dyadic as well as group interactions; being nurturing models; judicious use of time-out; and nurturing of male toddlers' neediness to support their comfort and promote cross-sex and same-sex harmony in play; as well as adult active suggestions and cues to enhance positive peer play.

495.Horwarth, M. (1989). Rediscovering the power of fairy tales: They help children understand their lives. *Young Children, 45* (1), 58-65.

Teachers are urged to use fairy tales to promote prosocial values: to be kind, unselfish, forgiving, and thoughtful of others. Teachers need to choose well and help the children *talk* about the fairy tales to learn what society values.

496.Huybrechts, K., & Huybrechts, F. (1988). *The Watchkins adventures: Teachers guide. Kindergarten and primary edition and The Watchkins adventures teaching kit.* New York: UMA Entertainment Productions and Scholastic Press.

This program, "Watchkins adventures", consists of a series of videos with original music, and animated characters, to instill values of cooperation, self-worth, politeness, self-control, dependability, loyalty, and perseverance. There are editions for preschool through third grade. The featured characters are Winnie and Wally Watchkins, round, fuzzy-looking animated creatures who live inside a book. Also included are sunflower puppets named Sol and Flora and child actors. A typical episode might have Leon the Frog singing the blues about a naughty, impolite little frog and the importance of respecting the rights and feelings of others.

A teacher's guide discusses how to create a cooperative classroom through:

1. Offering children choices
2. Talking about feelings
3. Encouraging problem-solving
4. Acknowledging cooperative behaviors
5. Having children role-play and act out pictures they draw and scenes they have seen

497.Jampolsky, G. G. (Ed.) (1982). *Children as teachers of peace.* Berkeley, CA: Celestial Arts.

Young children's essays, drawings, poems, short sayings and letters to the President form this book's collection and give poignant testimony to the ability of young children to be aware of how precious and important gentle, kindly and considerate relations are for nations as well as individuals.

498.Johnson, D. W., & Johnson, R. T. (1975). *Learning together and alone: Cooperation, competition, and individualization.* Englewood Cliffs, NJ: Prentice-Hall.

A theory of cooperative classroom learning is offered with suggestions for application. The use of cooperative goal structures are recommended. These exist when students perceive that they can obtain their goal if, and only if, the other students with whom they are linked can also obtain their goal. A competitive goal structure exists when students perceive that they can obtain their goal if, and only if, the other students with whom they are linked fail to obtain their goal. Individualistic goal structure exists when the achievement of the goal by one student is unrelated to the achievement of the goal by other students; whether or not a student achieves her goal has no bearing upon whether other students achieve their goals. Schools should encourage students to function as problem-solvers. The authors stress that the continual use of competitive goal structures is that intrinsic motivation for learning and thinking becomes subverted, because a highly competitive person does not learn for intrinsic reasons; learning is a means to an end – winning. Myths supporting the use of competition are examined and the authors give concrete suggestions for implementing cooperative goal structures.

499. Johnson, D. W., & Johnson, R. T. (1984). *Circles of Learning*. Alexandria, VA: Association for Supervision and Curriculum Development.

This small book is packed with information about why cooperative learning is important in the elementary school classroom, how to implement cooperative learning, how to teach students cooperative skills, how to supervise and support a teacher's use of cooperative learning, and how teachers and districts have successfully used cooperative learning for more than 10 years.

500. Jones, L. (Ed.) (1983). *Keeping the peace*. Philadelphia, PA: New Society Publisher.

Contains: Wichert, S. (1983)

501. Kamii, C., & DeVries, R. (1980). *Group games in early education: Implications of Piaget's theory*. Washington, DC: National Association for the Education of Young Children.

Research within a Piagetian framework supports the use of cooperative rather than competitive games. Ideas for group games that encourage prosocial interactions are offered.

502. Katz, L. G., & McClellan, D. E. (1991). *The teacher's role in the social development of young children*. ERIC Cat. #207. Urbana, IL: ERIC/EECE.

Teachers are offered practical strategies they can use to help children develop positive social skills. The authors emphasize establishing authentic communication and credibility with children, to motivate them without denigration, to appeal to their good sense, and to use social troubles as *opportunities* to teach and develop respect for the feelings of children. A balance of individual and group activities is suggested as best in a curriculum to foster positive social growth.

503.Kemple, K. M. (1991). Research in review. Preschool children's peer acceptance and social interaction. *Young Children, 46*(5), 47-54.

Research shows that the early use of aggression or prosocial behaviors, such as cooperation, predicts children's social acceptance later in preschool and kindergarten. Well-liked children use more clearly directed communications to maintain smooth discourse in social play situations. They respond to peers in a more relevant manner, are more likely to offer a reason for rejection of a peer-proferred play theme, and suggest possible alternatives that a peer can agree to. Even when teachers try to identify the prosocial skills children need and help them learn to use them, social reputation (for being aggressive) may make it difficult for children to be welcomed into play. Teachers may have to point out to the other children how the child's behavior is changing and guide the others to respond in more prosocial ways to the excluded child.

Teachers need to be judicious in pairing a child lacking in social skills with a peer more effective in social skills or with a younger peer. Sometimes a child has effective skills, but lack of confidence. Pairing such a child with a younger child may boost social confidence and allow opportunities to show more positive skills. Thus, cross-age play opportunities may promote more positive sharing in play for such children.

In order to behave prosocially, a child must first recognize that help or cooperation would be appropriate in a particular situation, then decide to behave prosocially, and next figure out what specific behavior would be called for and how to carry it out. Adults need to guide young children through the steps of this reasoning out process.

504.*KidSkills.* (1985). Family Skills, Inc., One Galleria Tower, #1940, Dallas, TX.

KidSkills is a curriculum package that promotes children learning interpersonal skills. The package includes story books, parent guides, activity guides, and audio cassettes. A learning package has been designed for children from 6-10 years and one for children 2-5 years.

505.Killoran, J., Rule, S., Stowitscheck, J. J., & Innocenti, M. (1982). *Let's be social.* Logan, UT: Outreach Division, Developmental Center for Handicapped Persons, UMC 6805, Utah State University.

Materials include a teacher's guide, audio-cassettes, and 26 lesson units for teachers to use to promote friendliness and positive social interactions among preschool children, with a more specific goal of enhancing the social integration of handicapped youngsters. Black and white drawings enhance the lesson goals. Units include: let's help our friends; let's share; let's join in; let's play another way if our friend says "No"; and let's work it out.

506. Kobak, D. (1979). Teaching children to care. *Children Today, 8,* 6-7, 34-35.

In a special school setting for socially maladjusted and disturbed children, the author, a psychiatric school social worker, created a curriculum for a Caring Classroom, where the CQ (Caring Quotient) of the children was as important as IQ. A daily class dialogue period is described. The teacher asks empathy questions such as "What are some of the hardships of your parents?" The children discuss philosophical questions such as "Who is your enemy". Children are helped to dialogue about how caring can change enemies to friends, and decrease parent worries. The class is enlisted to help a child (who beats up other children) to avoid fights. Lists of cruel names are drawn up, and the class solves problems, for example, when a child feels bad because a borrowed item has not been returned, or a schoolmate has been truant from school. In *anger* and *justice* dialogues, children discuss value systems, choices and decision-making.

Homework may involve keeping a log of all caring situations experienced in a 24-hour period. Art and poetry are used to stimulate discussions on sadness or on the internalization of positive socialization skills. Enactments of children role-playing instances of caring are videotaped and then shown to the children. Action projects involve the children in projects such as saving pennies for hungry children, or practicing showing thankfulness to another person. At semester end, an award for Excellence in Caring is given out along with other scholastic awards.

507. Kohlberg, L. (1985). The just community in theory and practice. In M. Berkowitz & F. Oser (Eds.), *Moral education* (pp. 27-88).

Hillsdale, NJ: Erlbaum.

Kohlberg views traditional schools as places where part of a teacher's role is to be a policeman. Yet the *Just community* approach requires transforming the school into a shared decision-making democracy. In a democratic school Kohlberg argues that friends don't play policemen, but should feel a mutual concern for fairness and loyalty to each other within the larger moral community of the school.

508.Kohn, A. (1988). Beyond selfishness. *Psychology Today, 22,* 34-42.

In order to raise a helping child, this review article in a popular style suggests that caregivers focus on the positive, explain the reasons why altruism is desirable, set an example, let children help, promote a prosocial self-image, and be a warm and empathic model of caring.

509.Kreidler, W. (1984). *Creative conflict resolution.* Evanston, IL: Scott, Foresman.

The author provides many excellent examples that caregivers can use to promote cooperative games and activities for children.

510. Krogh, S., & Lamme, L. (1985). "But what about sharing?" Children's literature and moral development. *Young Children, 40*(4), 48-51.

Children's literature facilitates young children's thinking about topics such as distributive justice - fairness in sharing situations. Very clear ideas are presented

concerning how teachers can select good stories and lead group discussions. Table 1 details
stages of children's moral development and
Table 2 lists books and questions to stimulate
discussion of sharing.

511. Kuhmerker, L. (1990). *The Kohlberg legacy
for the helping professions.* Birmingham, AL:
Religious Education Press.

Educational practitioners are provided with
a comprehensive overview of Kohlberg's theory
and research. Applications to educational
practice are discussed, such as how to set up
and lead moral dilemma discussions.
Applications of Kohlberg's moral development
work to faith development and counseling are
suggested.

512. Ladd, G. W. (1984, July). Promoting children's
prosocial behavior and peer relations in
early childhood classrooms. A look at four
teacher roles. *Dimensions, 12*(4), 6–11.

There is a relationship between the *quality*
of young children's peer relationships and their
social and academic adjustment. Thus, teacher
roles in the classroom are important to
promote prosocial skills. By arranging for
children to observe and learn specific positive
skills by watching peers perform them, or
watching short videotapes, teachers can serve
as highly influential prosocial models
themselves, and also encourage the children to
model. Teacher praise and attention shape
more helpful behaviors. Teachers can "teach".
By direct instruction, they may suggest
specific prosocial skills, such as sharing,
taking turns, initiating and joining play as
strategies for achieving social goals, such as
making a friend or resolving a conflict

peacefully. Teachers provide *rules* that emphasize the functions and consequences of particular social modes. Teachers as planners can arrange opportunities for children to interact with peers who are more skilled in positive social interactions. Arrangements of physical resources with varieties of materials can encourage more flexible, more socially positive play. Cooperative rather than competitive games help. Unstructured play materials, such as blocks, puppets, and play costumes, enhance fantasy and sociodramatic play and increase the likelihood of more advanced social interaction coordinations. With videos and books, teachers help children learn about how to make and keep friends, and skills to get along positively and helpfully with each other. After the use of bibliotherapy and video materials, teachers need to provide opportunities to *apply* this knowledge in actual games and prosocial scenarios.

513. Lapinski, S. (April, 1988). Raising kids who care. *American Baby, 82,* 69–71.

Not all parents believe that the best for their kids means the most expensive things they can buy. Some parents want to give their children gifts of the spirit, ones they can use over a lifetime. Helping children feel helpful is a wonderful way of empowering them. A child can develop a sense of mastery when that child has *direct* experiences with helping. Research studies completed by Zahn–Waxler & Radke–Yarrow and researches on attachment are summarized in an easy–to–read manner for parents of young children.

514. Levine, M., & McColoum, J. (July 1983). Peer play and toys: Key factors in mainstreaming

Infants. *Young Children, 38*(5), 22-26.

Ideas are offered for increasing social interaction between handicapped children and typical children in a mainstreaming classroom. The role of toys is discussed as playing a special role in enhancing the interactions between handicapped and non-handicapped infant peers.

515. Lickona, T. (1985). Parents as moral educators. In M. Berkowitz & F. Oser (Eds.), *Moral education: Theory and application* (pp. 127-146). Hillsdale, NJ: Erlbaum.

Parents are identified as primary moral educators of their children. The author suggests specific behaviors that can further young children's moral development.

The nine ideas Lickona presents for raising children are:

1. Morality is respect.
2. A morality of respect develops slowly through stages.
3. Foster mutual respect.
4. Set a good example.
5. Teach by telling.
6. Help children learn to think for themselves.
7. Help children take on real responsibilities.
8. Balance independence and control.
9. Love children.

516. Lickona, T. (1989). Moral development in the elementary school classrooms. In W. M. Kurtines & Gewirtz (Eds.) ,*Moral behavior and development: Advances in theory, research, and application* (Vol. 1). Hillsdale, NJ: Lawrence Erlbaum.

Applications of Kohlberg's constructivist perspective as well as his socialization ideas are provided to enhance teachers' ability to promote prosocial behavior in classrooms.

517. Lillie, D. L. (1982). *Carolina Developmental Curriculum (Book 3): Activities in social-emotional development.* New York: Walker Educational Book Corporation.

Eighty activities are provided to help children develop social skills, learn to share, wait for turns, work in groups, and show respect for others. Head Start teachers have reported fewer discipline problems after several years of use.

518. Linn, R. (1984). Practising moral judgment within the day care center: A look at the educator's moral decision under stress. *Early Child Development and Care, 15* (Nos. 2 & 3), 117-132.

Each of 38 experienced early childhood educators (who work with preschoolers) was tested on Kohlberg's Standard Moral Judgment Interview on a Moral Action Dilemma. The Kohlberg ratings go from Level 1 pre-conventional thinking (obedience for its own sake and for avoidance of punishment), through Level 2 conventional thinking (fulfilling others' expectations, maintaining rules of good behavior at stage 3 and fulfilling social duties in stage 4) to level 3 post-conventional principled thinking (life and liberty and equality of human rights are prime). The educators' moral stage, as a group, was about stage 4, but their reasoning about a real life dilemma concerning children in day care was at a *lower* stage. Thus, moral and prosocial behaviors under stress may not be congruent with the highest levels of moral reasoning that persons attain cognitively. Training for ECE teachers needs to address threats and anxieties occasioned by real-life classroom dilemmas.

519. Lipman, M., & Smith, T. L. (Eds). (1981). *PIXIE*. New York: Rockefeller Foundation.

Early elementary grade stories about PIXIE, a precocious character who is impatient, a tease, and a mimic, help children become more aware of relationship difficulties and resolutions.

520. Luvmour, S., & J. (1988). *Everyone wins: Cooperative games and activities.* Philadelphia, PA: New Society.

Activities and games (150) color-coded by age and activity level, group size, and location, are offered to enhance communication, inspire creativity and resolve conflicts for children.

521. Marantz, M. (1988). Fostering prosocial behaviour in the early childhood classroom: Review of the research. *Journal of Moral Education, 17* (1), 27-39.

Seven approaches for the classroom (positive reinforcement, discipline, modeling, verbal instruction and exhortation, cooperative exercises, role-playing, and emotional self reflection) are conceptualized as congruent with four categories of learning: (1) learning through behavioral consequences, (2) learning by observation, (3) learning through verbal prescription, and (4) learning through personal experience. Real-life modeling, emotionally delivered verbal prescriptions from a nurturant, caring teacher, emotionally intense inductive discipline, classroom role-playing and classroom cooperative experiences hold the most promise for effective prosocial education with the very young child.

522.Marcus, R. F., & Leiserson, M. (1978). Encouraging helping behavior. *Young Children, 33*(6), 24-34.

Helping behavior includes any behavior which is an attempt to ameliorate distress in another (e.g. rescuing, removing cause of distress, defending) or which facilitates another's work or play activity (e.g. sharing materials, giving information). Potential advantages for children learning helping behaviors include: a sense of competence in assisting others, an increase in their sense of friendship, improved sensitivity to another's "need" for help, and learning how to receive help from others. Encouragement of helping behaviors may also mean gains for the classroom and the world as a whole. Practical suggestions are provided for encouraging helping behavior through classroom climate and modeling, classroom structure, activities, and materials.

523.Marion, M. (1991). *Guidance of young children*. New York: Macmillan.

Chapter 11 of this applied text for teachers is entitled "Nurturing the roots of prosocial behavior". The author gives definitions and specific techniques for teachers to promote prosocial behaviors. These include: model; state expectations to the child; use positive discipline; verbally label and discuss altruistic actions; give practice opportunities; reinforce prosocial interactions.

The teacher can keep track of kindnesses and helpful acts and then sing a short song at the end of the day to tell about how all the children helped each other. To the tune of "Mary had a little lamb", she can sing:

Bill and Jim cleaned up the paints,
Cleaned up the paints, cleaned up the paints.
Bill and Jim cleaned up the paints
When they came to school.
Anne Marie put away her trike
Put away her trike, put away her trike.
Anne Marie put away her trike,
When she came to school.

524.Maxwell, M., & Hamilton, C. (1980). *Feelings and friends*. Washington, D.C.: National Endowment for the Humanities.

Lessons to enhance self-concept and non-verbal communication skills are provided.

525.McGinnis, E., & Goldstein, A. (1990). *Skillstreaming in early childhood*. Champaign, IL: Research Press.

This prosocial skills training program for children ages 3 through 6 stresses the importance of teaching prosocial skills to children at an early age, especially for those children who exhibit withdrawal, aggression, behavioral problems, or learning disabilities.

The curriculum includes six skill groups:

1.   Beginning social skills

2. School-related skills
3. Friendship-making skills
4. Dealing with feelings
5. Alternatives to aggression
6. Dealing with stress

Teaching techniques include modeling and role-playing exercises. This skill-streaming program includes assessment measures and forms to identify children most in need of training, assess their strengths and weaknesses, assign them to groups, and evaluate progress. Teachers are offered a variety of management techniques to deal with problem behaviors encountered during group sessions.

526. McGinnis, E., Goldstein, A. F., Sprafkin, R. P., & Gershaw, J. (1984). *Skill-streaming the elementary school child: A guide for teaching prosocial skills.* Champaign, IL: Research Press.

Teachers are given concrete techniques for group instruction in prosocial skills for mainstream and special education classes. The authors advocate teaching prosocial skills using planned and systematic applied psychoeducational techniques such as teachers do with academic skills. In the skillstreaming approach, first, teachers show youngsters desirable prosocial constructive behaviors which they may have seen. Sixty specific prosocial skills (e.g. joining a game, responding to teasing) are identified and the behavioral steps to enacting that skill are presented. Each child in the group gets up and rehearses or role-plays the steps of that behavior. The group then gives feedback, and via homework assignments and other techniques, the leaders encourage children to use the new prosocial skills out in the real world, such as the street

343

or playground.

Examples of a group structured learning session are provided to facilitate teachers' use of the program. The curriculum is divided into the following content areas: (1) dealing with feelings, (2) classroom survival skills, (3) alternatives to aggression, (4) friendship making skills, and (5) dealing with stress. A student skill checklist, completed by the student, assesses the student's perception of the skills he or she needs to learn. A teacher skill checklist, completed by the teacher or other professional, provides a picture of the student's behavior in a variety of settings and evaluates each student's progress.

527.McGinnis, E., Goldstein, A., Sprafkin, R. P., & Gershaw, J. (1984). *Skillstreaming the elementary school child. Program forms booklet.* Champaign, Illinois: Research Press

Designed to be used in conjunction with *Skill-streaming the elementary school child: A guide for teaching prosocial skills,* 28 different forms are provided. These forms include: student self-assessment forms, homework report forms, contracts, self-monitoring forms, and award certificates. All of the forms may be photocopied for classroom use.

528.McMath, J. S. (1989, Fall). Promoting prosocial behaviors through literature. *Day Care and Early Education, 17*(1), 25-27.

Picture books with stories for preschoolers are described and care ivers are given ideas about how to use open-ended questions to help children think about and understand the motives and actions of the story characters. Adults can help children relate their learning to help or care for others to the prosocial actions of the storybook children or creatures. Examples of such books are: "It's Your Turn, Roger", "The Animal Cafe", or "Angel Child, Dragon Child", (which portrays sharing, cooperation, and sympathizing with a child who has just come to America from Vietnam without her mother), helping, protecting animals, and coming to the aid of others who are less fortunate. Strategies are suggested for facilitating children's thinking about the story ideas.

529.Meadow, K., & Larabee, G. (1982). The feeling wheel: A sharing activity. *Teaching Exceptional Children, 15,* 18-21.

Eight to nine-year-old hearing-impaired children and their teachers used a "feeling wheel" to discuss their feelings. The wheel, divided into 16 segments labeled with feelings, not only helped students discuss how and why they felt a particular way, but also helped them understand other peoples' emotions.

530.Melson, G., & Fogel, A. (1988). Research in review. The development of nurturance in young children. *Young Children, 43*(3), 57-65.

This review of research provides information about how young children can become tuned in to cherish and be altruistic with young infants. Research by Weinstock (1979) found that five-year-olds, when given a dish of candy and shown a picture of a "poor" one-year-old baby, shared candy. Boys donated more. Young children show most interest in babies of the same sex. When asked to take care of a baby, 5-year-old girls act like little mothers, although they may act domineering, while older boys ignore or avoid a baby. Child care workers need to expose young children to live babies to help them learn about appropriate tender responsiveness. Adult guidance is needed to encourage the children. Male models are urgent, as boys need more male nurturing role models. Taking care of pets or hosting elderly or handicapped visitors may enhance early nurturing.

531. Mitchell, G. (1982). *A very practical guide to discipline with young children.* Marshfield, MA: Telshare Publishing.

Very down-to-earth, specific scripts help a parent or teacher increase children's positive social interactions. Techniques include: the use of puppets, quiet places, reading stories (as bibliotherapy), setting limits, teaching social skills as curriculum, having rules, using water play to resolve tension, easing transition times, using a tape-recorder to vent negative feelings, and having a talk-it-over chair.

532. Mize, J., & Ladd, G. W. (1991). Toward the development of successful social skills training of preschool children. In S. R. Asher & J. D. Coie (Eds.), *Peer rejection in childhood.* New York: Cambridge University Press.

Trained caregivers encourage social skills, using specific, effective strategies, and the preschool years are the best time for this work. This model advocates: 1. teaching social concepts to children who lack this knowledge; 2. helping children to *use* this knowledge in modifying their behaviors; and 3. encouraging children to *monitor* their own social behaviors. Children who receive coaching and support from nurturant caregiver trainers show gains in peer acceptance.

533.Mulles, R. L. (1983). Prosocial behavior in young children and parental guidance. *Child Study Journal, 13*, 13-21.

Parents need to take a more concerted and active role in helping young children develop prosocial awareness and abilities.

534.Necco, E. (1983). Affective learning through drama. *Teaching Exceptional Children,* 15 (1), 18-21.

Structured dramatic activities such as role reversal and situational tests are given to foster personal and social growth.

535.Orlick, T. (1982). *Winning through cooperation: Competitive Insanity- cooperative alternatives.* Washington,DC: Acropolis Books.

The spirit of excessive competition can cause harm to children. Cooperative sports and games provide five freedoms: freedom from competition, freedom to work out problems, freedom from exclusion if less skilled, freedom from hitting (aggression), and freedom to be responsible for self.

536.Orlick, T. (1985). *The second cooperative sports and games book.* New York: Pantheon Press.

Challenge without competition and non-competitive, indoor and outdoor games for players of all ages, sizes, and abilities are highlighted. There are separate chapters on cooperative games for preschoolers, three to seven-year-olds, and eight to twelve-year-olds.

537.Palomares, U. H., & Ball, G. (1974). *Human development program: Magic Circle – an overview of the Human Development Program.* La Mesa, CA: Human Development Training Institute.

The Magic Circle program allows teachers to become leaders in helping children develop awareness, self-mastery, and positive social interaction skills. The children sit around in groups to share socioemotional experiences. The teacher does not evaluate these feelings, whether angry, ashamed, funny or sad. Non-judgmental listening teachers let children know that it is safe to explore feelings. Strategies using single circles are described for use with preschoolers through grade six. The youngest children can begin coping with mixed feelings, self-awareness, and increased understanding of how trusting relationships are developed. Topics for Positive Behavior Circles include: "How I made someone feel happy", "We did something for each other", "A good friend", and "How I show someone that they can trust me". Many other feeling lessons are suggested and open-ended questions for the teacher group leader are provided.

538. Pines, M. (1979). Good samaritans at age two? *Psychology Today, 13,* 66-74.

Research by Yarrow and Zahn-Waxler reveals that, as early as one year, some babies are capable of comforting others who are crying or in pain. Before age two, some children displayed even more sophisticated altruistic behavior. Clearly, children have a capacity for compassion and for various kinds of prosocial behavior from at least the age of one, though it may coexist with the capacity for aggression and rage. Babies ranging in age from nine months to twenty-one months were observed for nine months (they were then between 19 months and two-and-a-half years old). Enormous individual differences in altruism were found among the children—differences that became increasingly clear in the period between 18 and 24 months, and these differences were related to different styles of child-rearing. Mothers who: (1) expressed firm disapproval in not accepting aggression as a means for their infant to resolve social conflicts, (2) were empathic and tender when the child was distressed, and (3) modeled loving care to the child and others, had toddlers who were much more empathic and cooperative with peers and others in distress. These behaviors were stable as indicated by teacher ratings five years later. This review is delightfully written and would make a good reading to assign in training infant caregivers.

539. Pines, M. (1984, December). Children's winning ways: Some children are naturally skilled at silent persuasion. Their reward: affection and power. *Psychology Today, 18* (12), 58-69.

The work of the French ethologist Hubert Montagner, based on behavioral observations of young children classifies actions as:

1. Actions that pacify others or produce attachment, such as offering another child a toy

2. Threatening gestures that scare others and make them fight or flee

3. Gestures of fear or retreat

4. Actions that isolate a child, such as crying alone or sucking thumb in a corner

Teachers need to note the body language of toddlers and preschoolers to help them learn how to get the things they want. For example, a two-year-old girl in his films approached two boys, tilted her head sideways and smiled at one. He smiled back at her, while the second boy reached for his toy car and gave it to her. Teachers who become good observers of toddler body language can shape more successful social functioning.

540. Price, R., Cowan, E., Lorion, R., Ramos-McKay, J. (Eds.) (1988). *14 ounces of prevention: A casebook for practitioners.* Washington, DC: American Psychological Association.

Contains: Shure, M., & Spivack, G. (1988)

541. Prutzman, P., Sgern, L., Burger, M. L., & Bodenhamer, G. (1988). *The friendly classroom for a small planet: Children's creative response to conflict program.* Philadelphia, PA: New Society.

Classroom games, specifically explained, will enable children to learn cooperation. Use of comic strips, songs (such as "The More We Get Together"), sharing feelings and a host of other activities are provided. *Musical laps* is a good example of a game that is modified from a familiar game, *musical chairs*, to promote inclusion of others. Instead of one child being out when the music stops, a child must find a lap to sit on or provide a lap for another. Loosening-up body games and mirror exercises, where children try to imitate each other's actions at the same time, alternate with more sedentary games such as discussion of wishes, feelings, and the use of a rock as a "magic microphone" that gives you a turn to talk as it is passed around and comes into your hand. Extended role-playing is encouraged to help children think about and feel other children's ideas and feelings.

542. Putallaz, M., & Gottman, J. M. (1981). An introductional model of children's entry into peer groups. *Child Development, 52*(3), 986-994.

In order to promote children's ability to join in groups of others who are playing, the authors suggest teaching children to ask questions as they approach a group at play in order to determine the interests and goals of the players. Some questions might be: "What are you building?" or "What are you playing?" or "Who are you pretending to be?" Children who are familiar with the intentions of the players and the direction of their play will be better able to judge how to integrate their play desires into the perspective of the group.

543. Rasmussen, B. I. (1980). *Character craft: A source book in moral education.* Redlands, CA: Parent Scene, Box 2222.

Small illustrative stories, talk-it-over exercises, poems, quizzes, multiple choice questions for class discussions and other modes are offered. Each chapter is designed to help a teacher enhance children's awareness of moral issues and their willingness to behave in more generous, kind, and prosocial ways. The variety of techniques includes small homilies and individual parables, as well as biographical examples and sayings. This adds interest and gives choices to the teacher who wishes to include moral education in the curriculum.

544. Rogers, D. (1987). Fostering social development through block play. *Day Care and Early Education, 14* (3), 26-29.

The author highlights the value of blocks in the early childhood classroom for the development of young children's positive social interaction. Research suggests that block play has the potential to foster prosocial behaviors between young children. Children have opportunities to engage in "social problem solving" when playing with blocks. For example, they must make decisions about who gets the last block or who will build which part of a structure. Children can cooperate and share the blocks and work together to build a large structure that one child alone could not build. Many positive suggestions are made for teachers to use to help children learn prosocial behaviors. Grouping the less socially developed children with the more socially competent children may help the socially inept.

545.Rogers, D., & Ross, D. (1986). Encouraging positive social interaction among young children. *Young Children, 41* (3), 12-17.

Peer interactions provide children with real social problems to solve, and children who play with altruistic peers show significantly more altruism than those who do not have such models. Other children's positive responses to children's prosocial behaviors reinforce the behaviors. Teachers need to circulate among groups engaged in spontaneous dramatic play or playing with blocks, sand, or water. First observe and identify the social skills, roles, and difficulties of the children. The authors found that the most socially competent children are able to select a strategy to meet both their needs and the needs of other children at the same time. Teachers can use *indirect strategies* such as asking a child playing alone with a car, "Does your car need gas?" thus suggesting that the child approach others who are acting a game of gas station attendants. Sometimes the teacher must use more direct encouragement and clarify the prosocial interactions expected, by direct modeling of appropriate comments.

Teachers can ask questions to help children think about their feelings and the feelings and intentions of others. For example, after a hitting episode, the adult can ask: "How do you think Benjy felt when you hit him? What words can you say to get him to give back your toy truck?" The authors provide many effective techniques for enhancing positive peer interactions.

546.Roopnarine, J., & Honig, A. (1985). Research in review: The unpopular child. *Young Children, 40* (6), 59-64.

This review of research addresses the following questions regarding unpopular children:

a. What constitutes unpopularity in the peer group?
b. What types of interaction patterns do unpopular children engage in with peers compared to their more popular counterparts?
c. What types of parent-child interaction patterns tend to result in popular or unpopular children?
d. What can researchers, parents, and teachers do to help the unpopular child?

Suggestions given for parents and teachers include:

1. Identify socially withdrawn or inept children and encourage them to participate comfortably in *smaller* groups.
2. Use puppets, reverse-role-play (taking one character's part and then another), and bibliotherapy - story books that can enhance the positive social repertoire of the children.
3. Emphasize a clear prosocial curriculum as an integral component of the home and/or child care facility.

547.Rosen, H. (1980). *The development of sociomoral knowledge: A cognitive-structural approach.* New York: Columbia University Press.

This volume carefully covers Piaget's, Kohlberg's, and Selman's theories of the development of moral knowledge. There is a section on therapeutic intervention with children who have not yet learned to distinguish own wishes from the wants of others. If a child needs therapy to enhance social skills, parents are encouraged to assist the therapists by helping a child understand and articulate the viewpoints of others, so that the ineffective child can learn prosocial interactions with peers.

548.Rowen, L. (1988). *Beyond winning: Sports and games all kids want to play.* St. Paul, MN: Toys 'n Things Press.

For school-age children, 42 games (such as Do-si-do tag, Rhino ball, and Nose bozos) help emphasize teamwork rather than winning and athletic prowess. Suggestions are given for dealing with overly timid or aggressive children as well as how to pick teams and how to do post-game evaluations.

549.Samuels, S. C. (1977). *Enhancing self- concept in early childhood.* New York: Human Sciences Press.

The author offers curricular ideas to enhance the child's self-concept and social self-concept, as well as ideas to enhance non-sexist and multi-cultural acceptance. Some curricular ideas for teachers to promote positive feelings about the family are:

1. Have children bring in family photos and draw family members.
2. Discuss ways family members can help one another.
3. Encourage children to talk openly and acceptingly about all kinds of families.
4. Invite family members to share their skills, customs, and foods.
5. Use books to introduce ideas about friends who enjoy sharing experiences and care for

each other.

550.Sapon-Shevin, M. (1986). Teaching cooperation in early childhood settings. In G. Cartledge & J. F. Milburn (Eds.), *Teaching social skills to children: Innovative approaches* (pp. 229-248). Elmsford, NY: Pergamon Press.

Cooperative games are classified according to four key social competencies: sharing and taking turns; including other children who have been left out; helping others and touching others gently; talking nicely to others, being positive and emphasizing others' strengths. Cooperative games can be arranged to vary in complexity. Teachers form heterogeneous groups so that socially competent children can become models for those who need to learn such skills. Children's literature is suggested as another way to teach alternatives to fighting or helplessness. For example, in the book "Two good friends", Bear, an excellent cook but sloppy housekeeper, and Duck, who is neat, team up to cooperate so that both their lives are happier.

551. Schmitz, D. (Undated). *The design and implementation of 40 manipulative tasks to develop cooperation in a kindergarten class at Palmer School.* ERIC Document Reproduction Service (No. 226-845). Urbana, IL: ERIC Clearinghouse.

Small-muscle as well as gross motor activities can be used to promote cooperation between children.

552.Scott, M., & Saunders, K. (1989). On target for friendships. *Teaching Exceptional Children, 21,* 54-57.

Sample lessons help behavior-disordered children learn how to make friends. The lessons incorporate "arrow language", which has been successful in presenting relations in mathematics education. Increased understanding of friendship skills is promoted.

553.Shaffer, D. R. (1988). Altruism and prosocial development. In *Social and personality development,* Chapter 10 (pp. 274-311). (2nd edition). Pacific Grove, CA: Brooks-Cole.

This chapter is an excellent textbook overview of researches and practical implications of research in prosocial development. A useful section provides teachers with methods to promote childrens' altruism. Prosocial effects of commercially broadcast programs suggest that programs like Lassie, The Waltons, Fat Albert, and the Cosby Kids help children to verbalize prosocial themes and to deal more prosocially with a host of social problems in their lives.

554.Sheppard, W. C., Shank, S. B., & Wilson, D. (1977). *Teaching social behavior to young children.* Champaign, IL: Research Press.

This behaviorist work helps a caregiver identify a child's behavior to be changed, cues to present, and the immediate consequences, whether to accelerate (or increase the rate of a behavior, such as sharing) or to decelerate (unwanted behaviors). Caregivers are taught, for example, how to hug, praise, to offer non-verbal approval (smile, grin, interested look) immediately after a prosocial activity the adult wants to increase. Adults are taught to observe children, create objectives, and evaluate the effectiveness of the techniques used on the child's rate of learning new social behavior, such as cooperating. Record charts are provided so that an adult can monitor the learner's progress.

555. Shure, M. B., & Spivak, G. (1979). *Problem solving techniques in child rearing.* San Francisco, CA: Jossey-Bass.

Shure and Spivak's interpersonal cognitive problem solving (ICPS) program helps children cope better with social frustrations and conflicts. The techniques that work best are: *ability to foresee the consequences of an action* and *ability to generate alternative ways to handle conflict.* Sequential daily lesson plans are specified for preschooler teachers to help children learn ICPS concepts and ideas. Assessment tools are provided to help measure changes in the ability to generate alternative solutions to social conflicts and to think of the consequences of each alternative behavior.

556. Shure, M. B., & Spivack, G. (1980). Interpersonal problem solving as a mediator of personal adjustment in preschool and kindergarten children. *Journal of Applied Developmental Psychology, 1,* 29-44.

The goal of this preventive program for elementary school children rated as aggressive, over-emotional and inattentive by teachers was to help children on their own to think of ways to solve their social problems and increase their ability to take the roles of others. The training program lasted 12 weeks. Children were taught how to use words such as "same" and "different" and "not" that help them think about when their wishes and feelings are/aren't different from their playmates. Children were shown pictures of children in distress, (for example, falling off a bike), and were asked to identify the consequences of these unhappy events and how the children might feel, and what they could think of to make such children feel happier. Children were asked to act out dialogues (sometimes with puppets) of problem situations. For example, if a classmate is not allowed a turn, act out how he might feel and what he could say or do. Impulsive preschoolers who participated in the program were then better able to take turns and share with others.

557. Shure, M., & Spivack, G. (1988). Interpersonal problem solving. In R. Price, E. Cowan, R. Lorion, & Ramos-McKay, J. (Eds.), *14 ounces of prevention: A casebook for practitioners* (pp. 69-82). Washington, DC: American Psychological Association.

The authors describe their ICPS (Interpersonal Cognitive Problem Solving) program, which has proved effective in enhancing positive social interaction patterns whereby children can resolve social conflicts.

The format of this program is a script in the form of a carefully sequenced series of lesson-games the teacher conducts for 30-40 minutes, 3-4 times per week over a period of 4 1/2 months. Concepts focus on sensitivity to one's own and other's feelings, on the perspective of all involved as to the nature of the problem and on the importance of listening to others. The Interpersonal Cognitive Problem Solving Skills sessions focus on promoting children's ability to generate multiple solutions, to anticipate consequences of options, and to plan step-by step how to reach stated interpersonal goals.

Based on stories of over 1000 children and teachers, as early as age four, children who learn to use ICPS skills become less overemotional, less aggressive, and better liked as well as more concerned about peers in distress. Overly inhibited youngsters become more outgoing, better able to express their feelings, and more likely to enter into activities with others.

558.Sieber, J. E. (1980). A social learning theory approach to morality. In M. Windmiller, N. Lambert, & E. Turiel, *Moral development and socialization* (pp. 129–160). Boston, MA: Allyn & Bacon.

Social learning theory takes the position that a strong nurturant emotional attachment between parent and child is crucial for moral development. The adult model of care and consideration permits the child to *internalize* social rules and anxiety about transgressions that lead to withdrawal of love. Internalization permits self-criticism, confession, and reparation.

The Sears, Maccoby, and Levin researches in the 1960's are reviewed. Parents who were firmly intolerant of child aggression and low on severe punishment had the least aggressive children. Sieber advocates moral reasoning and education whereby parents and teachers help children 1) examine the consequences of interpersonal actions, 2) think about how people with different information reach different conclusions on moral questions, and 3) examine instances of problematic issues, where moral and non-moral norms are confused. Adults need to encourage role-playing, simulated political decision-making activities, and honest inquiries into other peoples' life-styles (e.g. visit a jail, a home for the aged, etc.) with subsequent discussions.

559.Slavin, R., Sharon, S., Kagan, J., Lazarowitz, R., Webb, C., & Schmuck, R. (Eds.) (1985). *Learning to cooperate, cooperating to learn.* New York: Plenum Publishers.

The reports in this collection evaluate new small-group cooperative learning techniques and extend existing methods to new situations to improve student achievement, peer relations, self-esteem, and attitudes towards school.

Contains: Solomon, D., Watson, M., Battistich, V., Schaps, E., Tuck, P., Solomon, J., Cooper, C., & Ritchey, W. (1985)

560.Smith, C. (1982). *Promoting the social development of young children: Strategies and activities.* Palo Alto, Mayfield.

Many games and specific group activities are provided to enhance positive classroom behaviors.

Activities to promote body awareness include: Space person; Frankenclass; I like me; and Wow! This is me. Activities to help children discover emotions and empathy include working with children to develop lists of things that bring real happiness, joy, and a sense of fulfillment to a child's life. Teachers ask children to talk about what sadness means, what anger , love, and fear mean in real-life situations for them. Children are asked to

describe their rules for games and the teacher
discusses whether another child would really
understand the rules the way they are
expressed. Does the child take another's
perspective into account? Irrational beliefs
about emotions are discussed in class: for
example, there may be an irrational belief that
only sissies and babies cry; big boys don't cry.
The teacher discusses with the children the
rational belief that "crying sometimes helps
when people feel sad, tears are like words our
heart uses to tell others how sad we feel" (p.
195). Emotion pictures and action cards can be
found and described from magazines.

In discussions, the teacher introduces
concepts of affiliation and how to develop
significant, emotionally satisfying relationships
with peers. Many group activities, such as
Classy Tree, Classmobile, and Win In are
described. These can help increase group
sensitivities and cohesion. A chapter on
cooperative resolutions to conflicts also
provides discussion ideas and specific
activities (e.g. Card Partners and Group Pass
Pictures). Smith advises that adult comments
about children can influence how the children
work together on a task. For example, in a
research by Jensen & Moore, children worked
more supportively in pairs with a partner when
told: "You really get along with others. You
play fair. You are willing to share" (p. 171).

Chapter 7, entitled: "Kindness: The child's
expression of care and affection" may depend on
how dependent or active the recipient is and on
the physical or psychological actions required
of the helper. Teachers can discuss varieties
of situations where kindness will help. Praise
the children for their good ideas. This book is
crammed with excellent suggestions for teachers
to use in promoting a compassionate, nurturing
climate in the classroom.

561. Smith, C. (1986). Nurturing kindness through storytelling. *Young Children, 41* (6), 46-54.

Children view life as a story, and find themselves starring in particular adventures or events. Stories teach by metaphors – powerful images that provide children with insight into themselves and others. The Brave Tin Soldier in Hans Christian Anderson, for example, serves as a metaphor for affection, devotion, and perseverance. The Little Red Hen teaches that in order to share in the benefits of work (such as fresh baked bread), each has to make an effort to contribute to the work. The Little Engine That Could evokes admiration and desire to emulate the caring little train that tried to make children happy by bringing toys over the steep mountain. Storytelling can nurture compassion, when children respond to another's distress with emotions similar to what the other is feeling. In Doctor Rabbit's Foundling, a kindly rabbit adopts an abandoned infant toad who matures quickly and goes away. Children can sympathize with his sadness as he sees someone he loves leave him. Children between 2- and 6-years begin to realize that others have inner states of their own. "Compassionate stories have an important role to play during this period by providing a glimpse into the minds and motives of story characters" (p. 50).

562. Smith, E. (1989, May). The new moral classroom. *Psychology Today, 23,* 32-36.

Educators in schools from inner-city Chicago to upper-class Massachusetts are developing programs to foster "prosocial values", "character development" and "democratic virtues" in school children. Those who oppose such approaches argue that children come from so many different cultural, ethnic and religious backgrounds that it is difficult to agree on which values to teach. Others say that even if they could agree on values to teach, they don't know how to teach ethics outside of a framework provided by religion. Lickona, a developmental psychologist, believes that we can: "Teach people the distinction between private morality (religion) and public morality -those kinds of things that are universal values to which we are all obligated, like it or not" (p. 34).

To solve the problem that community options vary on the topic, schools have invited members of their communities to come together to work out acceptable approaches. Maryland's Baltimore county community members decided to base the list of values to be taught on the Constitution. The group came up with 24 "core" values including compassion, courtesy, freedom of thought and action, honesty, human worth and dignity, respect for other's rights, responsible citizenship, rule of law, and tolerance.

Cooperative learning, involving small groups of children working on a common, usually academic task, is now widely used for the purpose of promoting cooperation, problem-solving skills, and the ability for children to see other points of view.

Are these programs successful? While conclusions vary, a support for moral education grows. Lickona believes that people really do want to create a society where they can count on their neighbors to be decent human beings. The schools can't ignore them and the families know they can't do it alone.

563.Sobell, J. (1988). *Everybody wins*. St. Paul, MN: Toys 'n Things Press.

Almost 400 non-competitive games, easily
adaptable to a variety of classroom situations
with children ages 3-10, emphasize sharing and
cooperation.

564.Solomon, D., Watson, M., Battistich,
V.,Schaps, E., Tuck, P., Solomon, J., Cooper,
C., & Ritchey, W. (1985).

A program to promote interpersonal
consideration and cooperation in children. In R.
Slavin, S. Sharon, S. Kagan, R. Lazarowitz, C.
Webb, & R. Schmuck, (Eds.), *Learning to cooperate.*
Cooperating to learn. New York: Plenum
Publishers.

This chapter describes the Child
Development Project whose purpose is to
develop and evaluate the effectiveness of a
comprehensive school- and home-based program
in California to enhance prosocial tendencies in
young children. A figure of the "hypothesized
determinants of prosocial behavior" is included
that will be very helpful to those interested in
prosocial development. The figure includes a
list of prosocial behaviors; a summary of the
cognitive, affective/ motivational, behavioral,
and personality factors that help determine
whether or not a person will behave prosocially; and a list of the external /
environmental determinants of prosocial
behavior (such as opportunities to learn and
approval or reward for prosocial behavior).

The intervention program developed consists
of five major components:

(I) cooperative activities, in which students
work on learning tasks in cooperative
groups and play cooperative games

(2) regular participation in helping and sharing activities
(3) opportunities for children to experience others (adults as well as children) setting positive examples (i.e. being considerate, cooperating, taking responsibility, helping, and sharing)
(4) role-playing and other activities designed to enhance children's understanding of other people's needs, intentions, and perspectives;
(5) positive discipline, which includes the development and the clear communication of rules and norms that emphasize the individual's rights and responsibilities with respect to others as well as discipline techniques that both use the minimal force necessary to obtain compliance and explain the reasons for rules; emphasize the potential effect of one's behavior on others; provide firm, fair, and consistent guidance; foster nurturant adult-child relationships; and offer age-appropriate decision-making opportunities to children.

Each of these program components is described in detail. A summary of the first year of program implementation includes initial approaches to participating schools and the surrounding community, program planning and refinement, program training and the start of implementation, school-wide activities in the first program year, and evaluation of the program. Summaries are provided of the assessment procedures and the variables assessed.

565.Spivack, G., & Shure, M. B. (1974). *Social adjustment of young children.* San Francisco: Jossey-Bass.

Children are taught by a teacher in small groups for about 20 minutes per day for 45 sessions. The group is presented with a social dilemma such as getting a peer to let you have a turn with a toy that the friend has played with for a long time or asking someone to move over to make room for you at a table. The teacher uses pictures, miniature figures, puppets, toys, and story props to help children consider the causes of behaviors, as many alternative solutions to the social problems as they can, and the possible consequences of each social solution. The Socratic instructional style that teachers use leads children to generate social rules that can enhance own positive social functioning.

566.Stinnett, N., DeFrain, J., King, K., Lingren, H., Rowe, G., Van Zandt, S., & Williams, R. Eds.) (1982). *Family strengths 4: Positive support systems.* Lincoln, NE: University of Nebraska Press.

Contains: Eggeman, K. (1982)

567.Trepanier, M. L., & Romatowski, J. A. (Undated). *Classroom use of selected children's books to facilitate prosocial development in young children.* Dearborn, MI: Michigan University. (ERIC Document Reproduction Service No. ED 208 967). Urbana, IL: ERIC Clearinghouse.

Children in kindergarten and first-grade classes (N=99) were given a pretest and asked to answer questions about pictures and stories depicting conflict. In the experimental condition, children who did not initially give sharing responses to the pretest tasks were read three stories per week for three weeks.Teachers focused on the feelings of story characters and the solutions to the conflict situation the story. They emphasized the role that sharing played in resolving the conflicts. Nine books not focused on sharing were similarly read to the control subjects. From pre- to post-test, experimental children showed a 21% increase in sharing responses compared to a 13% increase for the control children. Bibliotherapy materials, if used frequently and judiciously, can enhance prosocial interactions.

568.Trovato, C. (1987a). *Teaching kids to care: 156 activities to help young children cooperate, share, and learn together.* Cleveland, OH: Instructor Books.

This workbook begins with a quiz to help teachers gauge their current level of knowledge about prosocial development. The sections of the book are: "Getting ready to teach prosocial behavior", "Prosocial fun for everyone", "Parents as partners in prosocial development", "Friends with special needs" and "Friends around the world." Activities presented range from how to make pinatas and puppets to stories to read to children to help them learn about comforting, sharing, cooperation, helping, and making friends.

569.Trovato, C. (1987b). Teaching today's kids to get along. *Early Childhood Teacher, 34,* 43-45.

Puppets are recommended to enhance prosocial behaviors in young children. The cardboard puppets, Hattie Helper, Carl Cooperator, Robert Rescuer, Debra Defender, Kevin Comforter, and Sharon Sharer, are included along with many detailed ideas for how to use the puppets with children to act out prosocial behaviors in the classroom. For example, the teacher holds up a puppet and says "This is a new friend who is going to join our group. Her name is Sharon Sharer. She wants all of her new friends to learn how to share all the wonderful toys, games and puzzles in our room. Can anyone tell us what a sharer does? That's right! A sharer lets other children play with her toys and use her paints" (p. 44). Then the teacher draws attention to the puppet's eyes and face. She explains that the eyes are sparkling and the puppet is happy because when she shares with others, they are happy too, and they share back toys for her to play with. A bibliography of children's books which have prosocial themes is included.

570. Vorrath, H. (1985). *Positive peer culture.* New York: Aldine.

In residential placement centers, youngsters interact with one another, explore, and solve moral and cottage issues and conflicts with adult supervision. Terms like "inconsiderate to others" and "aggravating others" are used to label inconsiderate behaviors. Terms like "considerate toward peers" and "positive leadership" are used for prosocial behaviors. Thus, group leaders foster dialogue and role-taking through these verbal modalities.

571. Watson, M., Hildebrandt, C., & Solomon, D. (1988). Cooperative learning as a means of promoting prosocial development among kindergarten and early primary grade children. *International Journal of Social Education, 3(2), 34-47.*

Work in small groups where each child in the group is an important contributor to the project can facilitate a more prosocial classroom climate.

572.Weissberg, R. P., Caplan, M., Bennetto, L., & Jackson, A. S. (1990). *New Haven social development program: Sixth-grade social problem-solving module.* New Haven, CT: Yale University, Department of Psychology.

This curriculum grows out of 12 years of experience developing social problem-solving programs. The goal is to teach students a 6-step problem-solving process that is illustrated by a traffic light poster. The guide contains 27 lessons divided into 8 units (beginning with an introduction and ending with an application unit) that are structured around the six problem-solving steps of: 1) Stop, calm down and think before you act, 2) Say the problem and how you feel, 3) Set a positive goal, 4) Think of lots of solutions, 5) Think ahead to the consequences, and 6) Go ahead and try the best plan. The activities are designed to take place in a 45-minute class period. The lesson plans are scripted for teachers to use direct instruction, class discussions of real-life problems, role-plays, cooperative and competitive games, viewing and discussion of videotapes, as well as extensive visual aids and visual material (30 student work sheets). Each unit has introductory material intended to help organize and orient the teacher including a *Unit at a Glance, Purpose of the Unit, Student Objectives, and Background Information.* A section called *Promoting a Problem-Solving Climate* helps teachers understand how to manage the classroom climate to encourage and foster problem-solving.

573.Weissberg, R. P., Gesten, E. L., Caplan, M., & Jackson, A. S. (1990). *Social problem-solving training for fourth graders*. New Haven, CT: Yale University.

This manual is an abridged revision of the Rochester Social Problem-Solving Program. It has 21 lessons that follow the *Stop...Think...and Go!* problem-solving steps introduced on "traffic light" poster. The steps taught in this manual are: 1) Stop and think before you act, 2) Think about the Problem, 3) Think of lots of ways to solve the problem, 4) Think ahead to the consequences, and 5) Go ahead and try the best plan. Nine student handouts, eight student work sheets, and twenty mini-posters are included to provide visual materials for students.

574.Weissberg, R. P., Gesten, E. L., Liebenstein, N. L., Doherty-Schmid, K., & Hutton, H. (1980). *The Rochester social problem-solving (SPS) program: A training manual for teachers of 2nd-4th grade children*. Rochester, NY: University of Rochester.

This training manual has 34 lessons divided into five units: Unit 1 - Feelings in ourselves and others; Unit 2 - Problem sensing and identification; Unit 3 - Generation of alternative solutions; Unit 4 - Consideration of consequences; and Unit 5 - Integration of problem-solving behaviors.

The steps taught are 1) Stop and think before you act, 2) Think about the problem, 3) Think of lots of ways to solve the problem, 4) Think of the consequences of what you do, and 5) Go ahead and try the best plan. Thus, this is a Stop, Think, and Go program.

575.Wichert, S. (1983). Keeping the peace: Practicing cooperation and conflict resolution with preschoolers. In L. Jones (Ed.), *Keeping the peace*. Philadelphia, PA: New Society Publishers.

Adults are helped with practical suggestions to foster children's conflict resolution through teaching techniques of careful listening, clear communication, empathy, understanding consequences, cooperation, and negotiation.

576.Wilson, J. (1990). *A new introduction to moral education*. Rutherford, NJ: Cassell.

The author offers a list of moral components for teachers and researchers as well as practical methods for teaching moral education in classrooms and schools.

577.Wittmer, D. (Fall, 1985). The biting child. *Caring*. A quarterly newsletter for caregivers of infants and toddlers. Resources for Child Care Management. Available from Donna Wittmer, University of Colorado-Denver, School of Education, Box 173364, Campus Box 106, Denver, CO, 80217.

Ten possible reasons why young children bite are given and program solutions are suggested for helping caregivers handle the "biting child" sensitively and responsively.

578.Wittmer, D. (Spring 1986). Getting along with others: The development of social skills. *Caring* 3-8, a quarterly newsletter for caregivers of infants and toddlers, originally published by Resources for Child Care Management. (Available from Donna Wittmer, University of Colorado-Denver, School of Education, Box 173364, Campus Box 106, Denver, CO, 80217.)

Children who feel loved and secure give back love to others. Social development begins with strong bonds to adults and from that foundation grows to include relationships with other children. As caregivers nourish the "roots" of social development, the child's branches will be strong and reach out to care for and nourish others. The development of children's social skills with adults is charted for the first three years of life, and activities are suggested for encouraging social development with caregivers.

579. Wolf, D. (Ed.) (1986). *Connecting: Friendship in the lives of young children and their teachers.* Redmond, Washington: Exchange Press Inc., PO Box 2890.

Articles are included on the nature and stages of children's friendships, coping with difficulties and stresses in children's peer relations, facilitating friendships, and reflecting on friendship.

580. Wolfgang, C. (1977). *Helping passive and aggressive preschoolers through play.* Columbus, OH: Charles E. Merrill.

Wolfgang provides principles and goals of intervention to move children into more socially positive and appropriate modes of play. Teachers need to establish a body level of trust by being *available* in the classroom and they need to use materials carefully. *Fluid*

materials may cause disorganization in an
aggressive preschooler, but *structured*
materials, such as blocks, may promote more
organized and appropriate peer play. Teachers
can move from giving physical help and modeling
toward more verbal directives and then toward
a more non-directive stance as a participant
observer presence when play becomes more
positive socially. Symbolic role-play is an
important skill that children can learn in
special isolated play areas with the teacher.
Chants and rhyme games and body awareness
games, such as tracing the child's body or using
a flashlight to cast shadows to increase body
awareness are suggested. When children can
act out symbolically with toys to create make-
believe stories and also can play symbolically
with toys with peers (e.g. in the dress-up
corner) then they are on the way toward
becoming "productive players". Pretend games
help. For example, pretend you are a tree
heavy with snow, or rocking birds to sleep.
Books are listed for teachers to help children
move to become "star players" who are
positively and productively engaged with peers.

581.Yarrow, M. R., & Waxler, C. Z. (1977). The
emergence and functions of prosocial
behaviors in young children. In C. Russell,
C. Smart, & M. S. Smart (Eds.), *Readings in
child development and relationships*, (2nd
edition) (pp. 244-247). New York: Macmillan.

This is a very brief condensation of some
of the prosocial researches of Yarrow and
Zahn-Waxler. They describe their prosocial
researches clearly and explain the significance
of the findings for enhancing and understanding
of prosocial development and peer interactions.
Thus, this synopsis would be useful for training
caregivers to enhance their awareness of
findings about prosocial responding from

infancy through the preschool years.

582.Yawkey, T. D., & Jones, K. C. (1982). *Caring: Activities to teach the young child to care for others.* Englewood Cliffs, N.J.: Prentice-Hall.

Specific teacher and parent activities are designed to help children become more altruistic. Creating a happy atmosphere and building confidence are inherent in the games. A sample activity is: watch a contact sport and talk about how it feels to be hit or to do angry actions. A variety of daily routines, such as toileting or clean-ups are used as the settings for many of the caring games. Activities include: share stories of your friend via felt board figures; be a friend to a pet; find caring actions done by comic cartoon strip characters; talk about how it felt when you were victim of another's aggression; carry out tasks, such as carrying a heavy object or washing a car, that two children can do together; encourage children to talk about feelings -- even conflicting feelings.

583.Zahavi, S. L., & Asher, S. R. (1978). The effect of verbal instructions on preschool children's aggressive behavior. *Journal of School Psychology, 16,* 146-153.

Children who participated in a brief discussion with their teacher about the effects of positive and negative behaviors on peers, tended to become more prosocial and less aggressive toward classmates. Direct instruction techniques can work in classrooms.

584.Zenner, S., Boxx, D., & Makovec, M. C. (1990). *The cooperative learning activities handbook.* Minneapolis, MN: T. S. Denison & Co.

Teachers are given specific curricular ideas for arranging children into small heterogeneous groups to carry out learning activities in a wide variety of learning domains, including science, creative writing, and social studies. The rules for cooperative learning groups are: everyone helps; everyone gets a turn; everyone listens; and use quiet "inside voices" while working.

SUBJECT INDEX